Frommer's®

Vancouver
& Whistler
dayBY**day**™

1st Edition

by Matt Hannafin

WILEY

Wiley Publishing, Inc.

Contents

Published by:

Wiley Publishing, Inc.

111 River St.
Hoboken, NJ 07030-5774

ISBN 978-0-470-39322-2 (USOC Edition)
        978-0-470-53802-9
Editor: Naomi P. Kraus
Special thanks to Linda Barth
Production Editor: Heather Wilcox
Photo Editor: Richard Fox
Cartographer: Andrew Dolan
Production by Wiley Indianapolis Composition Services

For information on our other products and services or to obtain technical support, please contact our Customer Care Department within the U.S. at 877/762-2974, outside the U.S. at 317/572-3993 or fax 317/572-4002.

Wiley also publishes its books in a variety of electronic formats. Some content that appears in print may not be available in electronic formats.

Manufactured in China

5 4 3 2 1

A Note from the Editorial Director

Organizing your time. That's what this guide is all about.

Other guides give you long lists of things to see and do and then expect you to fit the pieces together. The Day by Day guides are different. These guides tell you the best of everything, and then they show you how to see it *in the smartest, most time-efficient way*. Our authors have designed detailed itineraries organized by time, neighborhood, or special interest. And each tour comes with a bulleted map that takes you from stop to stop.

Hoping to explore Vancouver's plethora of first-rate art galleries, dine in its many cafes and restaurants, or shop your way down Robson Street? Planning to drive the scenic Sea to Sky Highway or take in the flowers at Victoria's Butchart Gardens? Want to ski the slopes or hike the trails at Whistler? Whatever your interest or schedule, the Day by Days give you the smartest routes to follow. Not only do we take you to the top attractions, hotels, and restaurants, but we also help you access those special moments that locals get to experience—those "finds" that turn tourists into travelers.

The Day by Days are also your top choice if you're looking for one complete guide for all your travel needs. The best hotels and restaurants for every budget, the greatest shopping values, the wildest nightlife—it's all here.

Why should you trust our judgment? Because our authors personally visit each place they write about. They're an independent lot who say what they think and would never include places they wouldn't recommend to their best friends. They're also open to suggestions from readers. If you'd like to contact them, please send your comments our way at feedback@frommers.com, and we'll pass them on.

Enjoy your Day by Day guide—the most helpful travel companion you can buy. And have the trip of a lifetime.

Warm regards,

Kelly Regan

Kelly Regan, Editorial Director
Frommer's Travel Guides

About the Author

Matt Hannafin is a freelance writer, editor, and musician based physically in Portland, Oregon and spiritually in his hometown of New York, NY. Coauthor of *Frommer's Cruises* and *Frommer's European Cruises,* he also writes a daily blog and biweekly column for Frommers.com and contributes to numerous newspapers, magazines, websites, and books, including the bestseller *1,000 Places to See in the USA and Canada Before You Die* and *National Geographic Traveler New York*. His editing clients include major consulting firms, UN agencies, and book publishers, and his musical activities range from Persian classical music to contemporary free improvisation and sound sculpture.

Acknowledgments

Giant thanks to my editor, Naomi Kraus, and Frommer's Editorial Director Kelly Regan, who both should have chopped my head off when I was late with the manuscript, but didn't. Thanks also to all the folks who helped me on the ground in BC, and to my wife, Rebecca, who held down the fort while I was traveling, walked the dog in the rain, and dealt with my usual finishing-the-book angst.

An Additional Note

Please be advised that travel information is subject to change at any time—and this is especially true of prices. We therefore suggest that you write or call ahead for confirmation when making your travel plans. The authors, editors, and publisher cannot be held responsible for the experiences of readers while traveling. Your safety is important to us, however, so we encourage you to stay alert and be aware of your surroundings.

Star Ratings, Icons & Abbreviations

Every hotel, restaurant, and attraction listing in this guide has been ranked for quality, value, service, amenities, and special features using a **star-rating system.** Hotels, restaurants, attractions, shopping, and nightlife are rated on a scale of zero stars (recommended) to three stars (exceptional). In addition to the star-rating system, we also use a **kids** icon to point out the best bets for families. Within each tour, we recommend cafes, bars, or restaurants where you can take a break. Each of these stops appears in a shaded box marked with a coffee-cup-shaped bullet ☕.

The following **abbreviations** are used for credit cards:

AE	American Express	DISC	Discover	V	Visa
DC	Diners Club	MC	MasterCard		

Frommers.com

Now that you have this guidebook to help you plan a great trip, visit our web-site at **www.frommers.com** for additional travel information on more than 4,000 destinations. We update features regularly to give you instant access to the most current trip-planning information available. At Frommers.com, you'll find scoops on the best airfares, lodging rates, and car rental bargains. You can even book your travel online through our reliable travel booking partners. Other popular features include:

- Online updates of our most popular guidebooks
- Vacation sweepstakes and contest giveaways
- Newsletters highlighting the hottest travel trends
- Podcasts, interactive maps, and up-to-the-minute events listings
- Opinionated blog entries by Arthur Frommer himself
- Online travel message boards with featured travel discussions

A Note on Prices

In the "Take a Break" and "Best Bets" sections of this book, we have used a system of dollar signs to show a range of costs for 1 night in a hotel (the price of a double-occupancy room) or the cost of an entree at a restaurant. Use the following table to decipher the dollar signs:

Cost	Hotels	Restaurants
$	under $150	under $15
$$	$150–$225	$15–$30
$$$	$225–$400	$30–$40
$$$$	over $400	over $40

An Invitation to the Reader

In researching this book, we discovered many wonderful places—hotels, restaurants, shops, and more. We're sure you'll find others. Please tell us about them, so we can share the information with your fellow travelers in upcoming editions. If you were disappointed with a recommendation, we'd love to know that, too. Please write to:

Frommer's Vancouver & Whistler Day by Day, 1st Edition
Wiley Publishing, Inc. • 111 River St. • Hoboken, NJ 07030-5774

13 Favorite
Moments

13 Favorite **Moments**

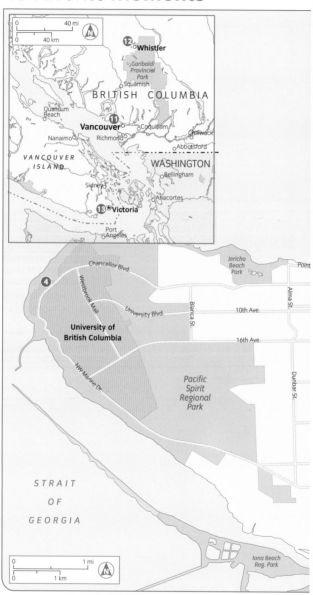

Previous page: Sunrise at Green Lake in Whistler, British Columbia.

1 Stanley Park Seawall
2 Granville Island Public Market
3 English Bay Beach
4 UBC Museum of Anthropology
5 Raincity Grill
6 Dr. Sun Yat-sen Garden
7 False Creek ferries
8 Vanier Park
9 South Granville Galleries
10 Vancouver Aquarium
11 Lighthouse Park
12 Whistler-Blackcomb
13 Victoria

People love Vancouver. Maybe it's the location, ringed by water and snow-capped peaks. Maybe it's the international vibe, fed by huge Asian and European communities. Maybe it's the restaurants, with their seafood-and-fresh-produce menus. Or maybe credit goes to the city's planners, who made it dense, vibrant, walkable, and green—both literally and environmentally. Add in the city's Hollywood rep (it's a major film and TV center), its fit and healthy population, and its thriving businesses and arts scene, and you start to see why it's among the world's most livable—and visitor-friendly—cities.

1 Walk or ride the Stanley Park Seawall. Stanley Park is the jewel of Vancouver. Located at the western end of the city's downtown peninsula, its 404 hectares (1,000 acres) are completely encircled by an 11km (6.5-mile) walking and biking trail that offers views of the city, sea, and mountains and gives access to beaches, a totem pole park, a host of sculptures and other public art, and sites such as the Vancouver Aquarium. *See p 85,* **1**.

2 Browse the Granville Island Public Market. A year-round feast of fresh local produce, seafood, artisanal cheeses, fresh bread, baked goods, spices, sweets, cookbooks, and all things culinary, all under one roof, just minutes from the city center. Foodies should plan on spending the day. *See p 33,* **1**.

One of English Bay Beach's magnificent sunsets.

3 Watch the sun set over English Bay. Along the south edge of Vancouver's downtown peninsula,

A ride on one of the False Creek ferries is a Vancouver must-do activity.

Colorful kites soar over Vanier Park every summer at the Pacific Rim Kite Festival.

centered on Denman Street, English Bay Beach is one of those spots that utterly transforms at sunset. By day the place is busy with runners, walkers, and bikers, but as the sun goes down so does everyone's blood pressure, and as the golden rays do their thing over English Bay, the beach takes on the aura of an outdoor wine-and-cheese party. Find a perch on one of the many logs that acts as bleachers in the sand, or visit the cocktail bar at the Sylvia Hotel, whose windows provide a perfect frame. *See p 12,* 12.

4 View First Nations art at the UBC Museum of Anthropology. Perched on a cliff above the Strait of Georgia, 20 to 30 minutes outside Vancouver's downtown, the Museum of Anthropology highlights the artistic traditions of British Columbia's First Nations peoples. Totem poles, feast dishes, canoes, blankets, jewelry, and monumental carvings—including many by Haida master Bill Reid—are all displayed in an incredible building by B.C.'s most influential architect, Arthur Erickson. *See p 16,* 6.

5 Dine on fresh regional food. Over the past decade-plus, many Vancouver restaurants have built a reputation not only for the tastiness of their cuisine, but for their efforts

to promote local organic farming and sustainable fishing practices. Raincity Grill set the bar with its "100-Mile Tasting Menu," but it's only one of many standouts. *See p 97.*

6 Spend a rainy day at the Dr. Sun Yat-Sen Garden (or even a sunny one). Nestled behind high white walls in the heart of Vancouver's old Chinatown, this is one of the most authentic Chinese gardens outside of China, offering a peaceful lesson in yin-yang harmony. Everything is perfectly balanced, and it even seems to account for weather: On Vancouver's frequent rainy days, its central koi pond reflects the lowering skies while raindrops drip meditatively around its covered walkways. *See p 16,* 4.

7 Ride the False Creek ferries. Vancouver is defined by its relation to the bays, straits, rivers, and inlets that surround it, so getting out on the water during your visit is a real must. The easiest way, and one of the most fun, is via the cute car-size ferries that crisscross False Creek, shuttling passengers between downtown, Yaletown, Vanier Park, and Granville Island. *See p 13,* 13.

8 Fly a kite in Vanier Park. Between Granville Island and Kitsilano

Feeding the adorable sea otters at the Vancouver Aquarium is a fun way to get up close with the city's marine life.

Beach, just across False Creek from downtown, Vanier Park is the place people go in Vancouver to fly kites, both the dime-store variety and the kind that participate in the annual Pacific Rim Kite Festival here every June. On any given day, you're likely to see dozens in the sky overhead. *See p 19,* ❸.

⑨ **Gallery hop on South Granville Street (and beyond).** Vancouver's "Gallery Row" boasts eight outstanding contemporary art galleries within a few blocks, while other parts of downtown and the West Side are dotted with their own international-quality venues. *See p 31,* ㉔.

⑩ **Feed the sea otters at the Vancouver Aquarium.** Sure, the Vancouver Aquarium has beluga whales, sea lions, and Pacific white-sided dolphins, but is anything cuter than a sea otter? Every morning (by reservation only), you can take part in a "Sea Otter Encounter" that includes time helping the animals' trainers at a feeding session. *See p 37,* ❶.

⑪ **Picnic at Lighthouse Park.** About a half-hour from downtown, in West Vancouver, Lighthouse Park gives you a good introduction to British Columbia's natural beauty, with some of the largest and oldest trees on the Lower Mainland, 10km (6.2 miles) of groomed hiking trails, and amazing views of the Point Atkinson lighthouse, Burrard Inlet, Vancouver Island, and the distant city. Bring a picnic lunch. *See p 88.*

⑫ **Ski, mountain bike, or hike the slopes at Whistler-Blackcomb.** Two hours' drive north of Vancouver, the Whistler-Blackcomb resort has been called the best ski resort in the world, and now it's claiming title to "world's best mountain bike resort" too. Whatever season you visit and whatever sport you choose, the mountains offer gorgeous panoramas—even if you just take the gondola and chairlift up to the mountaintop hiking trails. *See chapter 13.*

⑬ **Take the ferry to Victoria.** A 4-hour trip gets you to British Columbia's provincial capital, with its mix of 19th-century British architecture and traditions and 21st-century Pacific Rim culture. *See p 138.* ●

Victoria's scenic Inner Harbor is as beautiful at night as it is by day.

1

The Best **Full-Day Tours**

8

The Best in **One Day**

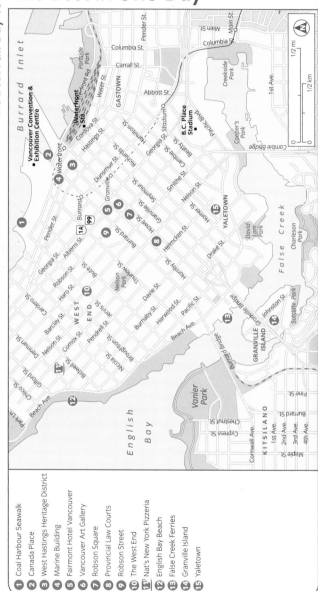

1 Coal Harbour Seawalk
2 Canada Place
3 West Hastings Heritage District
4 Marine Building
5 Fairmont Hotel Vancouver
6 Vancouver Art Gallery
7 Robson Square
8 Provincial Law Courts
9 Robson Street
10 The West End
11 Nat's New York Pizzeria
12 English Bay Beach
13 False Creek Ferries
14 Granville Island
15 Yaletown

Previous page: Centennial Totem Pole of Haida-Tlingit design in Vanier Park.

Thank Mother Nature, loggers, and the Canadian Pacific Railway for the fact that Vancouver began where it did— on a small, idyllic peninsula surrounded by water and mountains, and thus not predisposed to easy sprawl. Today the city does cover some 114 sq. km (44 sq. miles), but its urban core remains centered on the original settlements. The tour below will guide you from downtown's north shore to its south, through its vibrant business district and most beautiful residential areas, and introduce you to some of its best culture. START: **Begin at Coal Harbour Park, at the corner of Jervis St. and W. Hastings St. Take in the view of Coal Harbour and Burrard Inlet, then walk down the stairway to your left and head east.**

① ★★★ **Coal Harbour Seawalk.** Vancouver is all about coastal paths, of which the lovely 1,600m (mile-long) promenade along Coal Harbour is the newest. To the west, you can see the beginnings of Stanley Park, the city's largest, which boasts its own, much longer seawalk (p 85, ①). In Coal Harbour, look for funky houseboats moored among hundreds of luxury yachts and sailboats. Across Burrard Inlet, Cypress Mountain, Grouse Mountain, and Mt. Seymour loom above the homes of North Vancouver. The seawalk itself is bordered by luxury condominiums, marine outfitters, several cafes and restaurants, and lovely Harbour Green Park, dotted along its length with public art (p 45, ②). 🕑 *30 min. The seawall* *stretches from Stanley Park in the west to the Convention Centre in the east. Bus: 19.*

② ★★ **Canada Place.** Jutting out into the waters of Burrard Inlet, Canada Place is a combo convention center, cruise ship terminal, and hotel and office complex. What's remarkable about it is its design. Its Convention Centre extension is topped by a 2.4-hectare (6-acre) living roof—one of North America's largest—planted with indigenous plants and grasses that capture usable rainwater, reduce building heat, and clean the downtown air by trapping dust and creating oxygen. Next door, the cruise terminal is itself shaped like a ship, with five

The five "sails" atop Canada Place's cruise terminal make it easy to identify from afar.

The Marine Building, reflected in the glass of one of Downtown's many skyscrapers.

Teflon "sails" forming its roof. Both buildings are encircled by seaside promenades, letting you walk all the way around them for wonderful views. ⏱ *30 min.–1 hr. At the northern end of Burrard & Hornby sts. SkyTrain: Millennium, Expo, or Canada lines to Waterfront Station. Bus: 4, 7.*

❸ ★ **West Hastings Heritage District.** West Hastings Street was the city's main banking and commercial street in the early 1900s, and today the distinguished century-old buildings between Richards and Burrard streets house high-end luxury shops: Birk's jewelers in the Romanesque former CIBC headquarters (698 W. Hastings St.), Montecristo jewelers at the former Credit Foncier Franco-Canadien building (850 W. Hastings St.), and a number of high-end shops at the Sinclair Centre (757 W. Hastings St.), a complex of four former government and commercial buildings dating back to 1910. ⏱ *15 min. www.sinclaircentre.com. Bus: 10, 44. SkyTrain: Millennium, Expo, or Canada lines to Waterfront Station.*

❹ ★★★ **The Marine Building.** The 21-story Marine Building (opened in 1930) is one of downtown's most beautiful landmarks.

Designed in the art deco style, it's decorated inside and out with the kind of exuberance typical of the period. Check out its facade and cathedral-like entranceway, adorned with stylized sea horses, crabs, and other sea creatures, then duck into the vaulted lobby, an ornate masterpiece full of stained glass, gorgeous tilework, gleaming brass, and lighting sconces shaped like the prows of ships. ⏱ *10 min. 355 Burrard St. Bus: 10, 44. SkyTrain: Millennium, Expo, or Canada lines to Waterfront Station.*

❺ ★★ **Fairmont Hotel Vancouver.** Going south on Burrard Street, you'll pass several distinctive modern buildings (see "Art & Architecture" tour, p 24) before arriving at the chateau-style Fairmont Hotel Vancouver (p 126), the grand dame of the city's hotels. Opened in May 1939 for a visit by King George VI and Queen Elizabeth, the 17-story hotel was Vancouver's tallest building until 1972, and even today its steep green-copper roof is a fixture on the Vancouver skyline. On the outside, you can see a wealth of

The classically designed Vancouver Art Gallery is home to a surprisingly modern collection.

Robson Street is Vancouver's prime spot for shopping and socializing.

gargoyles and Renaissance detailing, while the lobby offers shopping, a lovely bar, and dogs whose job it is to greet guests. ⏱ *10 min. 900 W. Georgia St. www.fairmont.com/hotel vancouver. Bus: 2, 22, 44. SkyTrain: Millennium or Expo lines to Burrard Station.*

6 ★★ Vancouver Art Gallery. On first glance you think, "Staid old traditions," because the Gallery's 1912 building was originally a courthouse, designed in a classical Greco-Roman style by noted architect Francis Rattenbury (1867–1935). Then you spot the colorful boats up on the roof—a harbinger of the collection inside, which includes works from throughout the 20th century, paintings by regional modernist Emily Carr, and rotating temporary exhibits that range from early photography to contemporary video art. The building's glass-topped dome floods the central rotunda with light, while ornate plasterwork and marble put a classical frame on many thoroughly modern pieces. In 2014, the museum is expected to move to a much larger new home on the shore of False Creek. ⏱ *1½ hr. 750 Hornby St. (btw. Robson & Georgia sts.).* ☎ *604/662-4719. www.vanartgallery. bc.ca. Admission C$20 adults, C$15 seniors, C$6.50 kids 5–12, free 4 and*

under. *Prices about C$4 less Jan–May. Daily 10am–5:30pm (Tues & Thurs until 9pm). Bus: 5. SkyTrain: Millennium or Expo lines to Burrard Station.*

7 ★ Robson Square. Facing the Art Gallery, Vancouver icon Arthur Erickson's modernist, concrete complex (built in 1980) is essentially a park built atop ground-hugging offices, with hundreds of trees and other plants surrounding a block-long reflecting pool and three waterfalls that flow from the Provincial Law Courts (below). Take a walk among its pathways, ziggurat stairs, and verdant greenery, or rent some skates at the domed ice rink near the Art Gallery. ⏱ *20 min. At Robson St., between Hornby and Howe sts.*

8 ★★ The Provincial Law Courts. The high point of Robson Square, the Law Courts offer one of Vancouver's most stunning interiors: a tree- and greenery-filled public atrium the size of a football field, with tiered terrace gardens rising five stories beneath an enormous, sloping glass roof. ⏱ *15 min. Enter at the corner of Hornby and Nelson sts. Free admission. Mon–Fri 9am–4pm.*

9 ★★★ Robson Street. The section of Robson Street between Burrard and Bute streets is one of the busiest shopping stretches in

English Bay Beach is the best place to sunbathe in Vancouver.

Canada, lined with big-name shops such as Salvatore Ferragamo, Armani Exchange, Tommy Hilfiger, HMV, Aveda, and Canada's own Roots. Farther west, the street becomes a hot social scene for young Asians, full of restaurants, cafes, coffee shops, and bubble-tea houses. On weekend evenings, the entire stretch west of Burrard turns into one giant party. ⏱ *30 min., more if you shop or people-watch. Bus: 5.*

🔟 ★★ **The West End.** Turn left off Robson Street at Bute Street and within a block you'll be in another world, where modern high-rises,

Victorian and Edwardian houses, early 20th-century apartment buildings, and restful pocket parks mix along tree-lined residential streets. To get a real sense of the neighborhood, follow the "Coal Harbour, Downtown & the West End" walking tour (p 44) from here to English Bay. ⏱ *45 min. Bus: 5.*

In the West End, Denman Street is to eating and snacking what Robson Street is to clothes shopping. You can choose from more than a dozen cafes and restaurants within a few blocks, including **11** **Nat's New York Pizzeria,** which totally lives up to its name. *1080 Denman St.* ☎ *604/642-0700. www.natspizza.com. $.*

⓬ ★★★ **English Bay Beach.** English Bay is where Vancouverites come to stroll, picnic, take in views of distant Vancouver Island, and watch the sunset from dozens of huge logs scattered across the mile-long beach. On warm days there's no place finer, with sunbathers on the sand, sailboats tacking offshore, and runners and bikers doing their thing. ⏱ *30 min., or as long as you'd like to linger. Along Beach Ave., between Burnaby & Bidwell sts. Bus: C21, 5.*

Arthur Erickson

Born in June 1924, native son Arthur Erickson is Vancouver's most famous and influential architect. After studying at the University of British Columbia (UBC) and Montreal's McGill University, he traveled extensively in Europe and the Far East before returning to establish his Vancouver practice in 1953. From the mid-'60s up until today, he's redefined Vancouver's cityscape with buildings and public spaces such as **Robson Square** and the **Provincial Law Courts** (p 11, ➐ and ➑), the **MacMillan-Bloedel Building** (p 26, ➋), the new **Ritz-Carlton,** and UBC's **Museum of Anthropology** (p 16, ➏), the latter considered among the definitive buildings of modern Canadian architecture.

⓫ ★★★ False Creek Ferries.

Vancouver is defined by its relationship to the inlets, bays, and rivers that hem it in on three sides. The easiest way to get out on the water, and one of the most pleasurable, is via the cute car-size ferries that crisscross False Creek, shuttling passengers from various downtown and Yaletown docks to Granville Island (p 13, ⓮), Vanier Park (p 19, ❸), and the Telus World of Science (p 39, ❽). ⏱ *15 min. Aquabus runs to Granville Island from the foot of Hornby St.* ☎ *604/ 689-5858. www.theaquabus.com. False Creek ferries run to Granville Island and Vanier Park from the Aquatic Centre, 1050 Beach Ave., at Thurlow.* ☎ *604/684-7781. www. granvilleislandferries.bc.ca. Fares to Granville island C$2.50 adults, C$1.25 seniors & kids 4–12; service runs every 15 min.*

⓮ ★★★ Granville Island.

Granville Island began as an industrial park built on reclaimed land in 1915, but in the late 1970s its industries had fallen on hard times and the city began encouraging people-friendly redevelopment. Today, the 15-hectare (37-acre) pseudo-island (it's actually more of a peninsula, jutting out into False

Creek under the Granville Bridge) is a playground for Vancouverites and visitors, its old warehouses and factories housing restaurants, theaters, shops, artists' workshops and galleries, museums, an art school, two small breweries, and a few remaining heavy industries to keep things real. Near the ferry docks, the Public Market (p 33, ❶) is a mecca for Vancouver's foodies. ⏱ *2 hr. www. granvilleisland.com. Bus: 50. Ferries: Aquabus or False Creek (p 13, ⓫).*

⓯ ★★ Yaletown.

Across False Creek, the former warehouse district of Yaletown was rediscovered during the late 1990s, when its large industrial spaces were transformed into dot-com offices. Today it's Vancouver's trendiest neighborhood, full of excellent restaurants, nightlife, shopping, and attractive young couples pushing baby carriages. The area is centered on Hamilton, Mainline, and Davie streets. For a detailed tour of the neighborhood, see p 52. ⏱ *1 hr., or more if you stop for dinner (p 89) or drinks (p 99)—which you should. Ferries from Granville Island (see above) run to the Yaletown marina every 15 min. Fare C$3.50 adults, C$2 seniors & kids 4–12. Bus: 6.*

The charming restaurants, art galleries, and shops of Granville Island make it a favorite of locals and visitors alike.

The Best in **Two Days**

1 Stanley Park
2 Gastown
3 Irish Heather
4 Dr. Sun Yat-sen Chinese Garden
5 Chinatown
6 UBC Museum of Anthropology
7 Nitobe Memorial Garden

Y ou spent your first day in Vancouver seeing the city's most vital organs: its coast, its hippest neighborhoods, and its beating cultural heart. Now it's time to get out into its parks, explore the neighborhood where the city began, and get an introduction to two of its most important peoples. START: **Stanley Park entrance, west end of Georgia St.**

1 ★★★ kids **Stanley Park.** First opened in 1888, Stanley Park is a 404-hectare (1,000-acre) peninsular oasis located at the west end of the West End and surrounded by English Bay and Burrard Inlet. It's almost as large as downtown and the West End put together, and is packed with opportunities for outdoor recreation (p 84) and family fun (p 36). At a minimum, rent a bike and circumnavigate the park's seawall, an 11km (6.5-mile) biking and walking trail that circles the park's perimeter; it has amazing views of the sea, the city skyline, and the North Shore Mountains, and accesses some of the park's best sights, including the eight totem poles near Brockton

A totem pole at Brockton Point in Stanley Park.

Point and the lookout under the Lions Gate Bridge at Prospect Point. ⏱ *1½ hr. or more, depending on how many of the park's attractions you check out. Main entrances are via W. Georgia St. & Beach Ave.* ☎ *604/257-8400. www.city.vancouver.bc.ca/parks/ parks/stanley/index.htm. Bike rentals available from C$9.50/ hour. (C$26 half-day) at Spokes, 1798 W. Georgia St., at Denman St.* ☎ *604/688-5141. www. vancouverbikerental.com. Bus: 19.*

2 ★★ **Gastown.** Vancouver's oldest neighborhood, Gastown grew up around a saloon opened by former river pilot Gassy Jack Deighton in 1867 to serve the nearby logging

Victorian-flavored Gastown is known for its nightlife, boutiques, and dining options.

The entrance to a Buddhist temple in Chinatown.

camp. Today the neighborhood retains a Victorian flavor, full of low, shoulder-to-shoulder brick buildings, ornate streetlights, and cobbled squares—all of it leavened by expensive condos, restaurants, high-end design stores, bars of all stripes, and a lot of souvenir shops along Water Street. For a comprehensive look at the neighborhood, follow the walking tour on p 52. ⏱ *1–2 hr. Between the waterfront and Hastings St., from Cambie to Main sts. Bus: 4, 7. SkyTrain: Millennium, Expo, or Canada lines to Waterfront Station.*

In Gastown's Maple Tree Square, the **3** **Irish Heather** is one of the most authentic Irish bars in town, with a nook-filled interior and a glass-enclosed sunroom in the back, overlooking charming, brick-lined Gaoler's Mews. There's a good pub menu, and, of course, beer. *210 Carrall St. ☎ 604/688-9779. www.irishheather.com. $.*

4 ★★★ **Dr. Sun Yat-Sen Chinese Garden.** Opened in 1981 and named for Dr. Sun Yat-Sen (first president of the Republic of China, in 1912), this is one of only a few classical Chinese gardens in North America, and was created by master artisans from Suzhou, the garden city of China. Its architecture is based on the yin-yang principle, in which harmony is achieved by placing contrasting elements in juxtaposition: soft water against solid stone, smooth swaying bamboo around gnarled immovable rocks, dark pebbles against light pebbles, and so on. Immediately next door, separated from the garden by only a classical footbridge and koi pond, the public Dr. Sun Yat-Sen Park is less meditative but beautiful in its own right, with walking paths winding among Chinese trees and foliage. ⏱ *1 hr. 578 Carrall St., between Pender and Keefer sts. ☎ 604/689-7133. www.vancouverchinesegarden.com. Admission to garden C$10 adults, C$9 seniors, C$8 students with ID, kids under 5 free; families (2 adults with up to 2 kids) C$24. Free admission to park. Daily 10am–6pm (9:30am–7pm summer, 10am–4pm winter). Closed Mon, Nov 1–Apr 30. Bus: 22, 19. SkyTrain: Millennium or Expo lines to Stadium-Chinatown.*

5 **Chinatown.** Surrounding Dr. Sun Yat-Sen Garden, the Chinatown neighborhood is a throwback to the days when Vancouver's Asian population could all squeeze into a tiny ghetto. Today, about 45% of all Vancouverites are Asian. See p 52 for a walking tour that takes you through Chinatown's highlights. ⏱ *1 hr. Chinatown is bounded by E. Hastings St. & Union St. to the north & south, Gore & Taylor sts. to the east & west. Bus: 22, 19. SkyTrain: Millennium or Expo lines to Stadium-Chinatown.*

6 ★★★ **University of British Columbia Museum of Anthropology.** Vancouver's finest museum opened at its current location in 1976, highlighting the artistic traditions of British Columbia's Haida, Kwakwaka'wakw, Gitxsan, Nisga'a, Haisla, Oweekeno, and other First Nations peoples. Enter its glass-walled Great Hall to view an incredible collection of totem poles, carved boxes, canoes, blankets, and carvings, including works by famous Haida artist Bill Reid. His iconic cedar sculpture *The Raven and the First Men* is the museum's best-known work. The museum's building is an attraction all by itself, a modernist interpretation of First Nations post-and-beam architecture by Vancouver's most influential architect, Arthur Erickson (b. 1924), who also created downtown's amazing Law Courts building (p 11, ⑧). Outside, among the clifftop views of sea and mountain, are a Haida clan house and a number of totems and other structures that would have been present in a 19th-century Haida village. ⏱ *1½–2 hr. 6393 NW Marine Dr.* ☎ *604/822-5087. www.moa.ubc.ca. Admission C$9 adults, C$7 seniors, free kids 6 and under. Mid-May to early Oct daily 10am–5pm (until 9pm Tues), early Oct to mid-May Tues–Sun 11am–5pm (until 9pm Tues). Bus: 4, 17 to the UBS transit center, then walk northwest (see www.maps.ubc.ca for campus maps & directions).*

⑦ ★★★ **Nitobe Memorial Garden.** Named for scholar and statesman Inazo Nitobe (1862–1933), the 1-hectare (2½-acre) garden is considered one of the finest traditional Japanese stroll gardens in North America. It was created in 1960 by Kannosuke Mori, Professor of Traditional Landscape Architecture at Japan's Chiba University, who carefully chose and placed every stone, tree, and shrub to reflect an idealized version of nature in perfect harmony. Pathways are arranged around a central pond and island, with stone lanterns placed at the crossroads to symbolize choices in life and encourage meditation. Benches are positioned to frame different garden views, which offer different highlights in every season: cherry blossoms in April and May, blooming irises in June, and colorful maple leaves in October. ⏱ *45 min. 1895 Lower Mall (at NW Marine Dr.), UBC Point Grey Campus.* ☎ *604/822-9666 or 604/822-6038. www.nitobe. org. Admission C$6 adults, C$5 seniors, C$2 teens (13–17), kids 12 and under free, families C$9. Daily 9am–5pm, but check in winter for shorter hours. Bus: 4, 17.*

The very peaceful grounds of the Dr. Sun Yat-Sen Chinese Gardens make for wonderful strolling.

The Best in **Three Days**

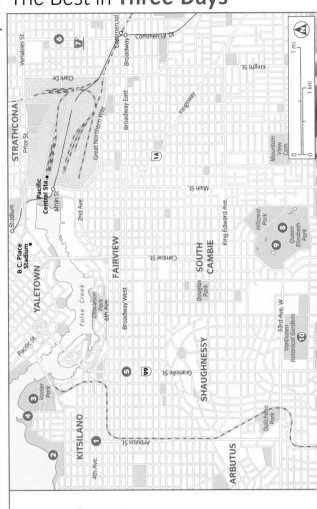

1 Kitsilano
2 Kitsilano Beach
3 Vanier Park
4 Vancouver Maritime Museum
5 South Granville Rise & Gallery Row
6 Commercial Drive
7 Caffe Calabria
8 Queen Elizabeth Park
9 The Bloedel Floral Conservatory
10 VanDusen Botanical Gardens

On your third day in town you can begin to work the city's periphery, getting out to one of Vancouver's best beaches; checking out the parks, shopping, and galleries across False Creek; warming up in a domed nature conservatory; and heading east for a cappuccino in the Italian cafes of Commercial Drive. START: **Take Bus 4, 7, or 44 to Vine St.**

1 ★ Kitsilano. Across English Bay from downtown, Kitsilano was one of the first Vancouver neighborhoods to be established off the downtown peninsula. In the '60s it was a counterculture haven, a distinction that persisted into the '70s and '80s when both Greenpeace and the BC Green Party were founded here. Today, Kits (as it's known to locals) is a much more gentrified place, but in that liberal, eco-conscious, organic, multicultural way that keeps neighborhoods interesting. Its side streets are a mix of small homes and apartment complexes, while 4th Avenue—Vancouver's answer to San Francisco's Haight-Ashbury in the '60s—is a major destination for restaurants and shopping, full of independent boutiques, coffee shops, bookstores, and more. For more details, follow the "Kitsilano & Granville Island" walking tour on p 60. ◷ *1½ hr. Kitsilano is bordered by English Bay to the north, 16th Ave. to the south, Burrard St. to the east & Alma St. to the west. Bus: 4, 7, 44.*

2 ★★ Kitsilano Beach. At the north edge of Kitsilano, along the shore of English Bay, Kitsilano ("Kits") Beach is one of the city's most popular. In warm weather, it's full of Vancouverites swimming and playing volleyball in the sand, with views of North Vancouver's snowcapped mountains in the distance. Facilities include washrooms, water fountains, concession stands, and tennis and basketball courts. At the beach's western end, the 137m, saltwater Kitsilano Pool is the largest in Canada, providing a safe "beach" swim for kids. ◷ *1 hr. The beach runs roughly from Yew St. to Maple St. Kits Pool is at 2305 Cornwall Ave. ☎ 604/731-0011. Open mid-May to mid-Sept. Hours vary. Pool C$5 adults, C$3.45 seniors, C$3.70 teens 13–18, C$2.50 kids 6–12. Bus: 4, 7, 44.*

A walking path from Kits Beach heads east toward your next two stops.

3 ★★ kids Vanier Park. Located just east of Kits Beach, Vanier Park

Sun-worshippers flock to Kitsilano Beach in summer.

feels miles removed from busy downtown, even though it's just a quick ferry ride across English Bay. It's popular with kite flyers for its constant breezes; with dogs and their owners, who flock to the popular dog beach at its western edge; to theater-goers, who come for summer's Bard on the Beach performances (p 113); and with city visitors for its amazing views of downtown and the North Vancouver mountains, and for its museums: the Vancouver Maritime Museum (see below), the Vancouver Museum (p 62, **⑧**), and the über-kid-friendly H.R. MacMillan Space Centre (p 38, **⑥**). ⏱ *45 min. 1000 Chestnut St. at Whyte Ave.* ☎ *604/257-8400. Bus: 2, 22. Also accessible from downtown via False Creek ferries from the Aquatic Centre, 1050 Beach Ave., at Thurlow.*

④ ★ kids Vancouver Maritime Museum. This little museum is centered on the Royal Canadian Mounted Police ship *St. Roch,* which patrolled the Canadian Arctic from 1928 to 1954 and was the first ship to ever sail the Northwest Passage from both east and west. You can climb aboard, and also view exhibits of shipping artifacts, Arctic artwork, and model ships created in the museum's open-view workshop. A children's discovery center has displays on why ships float, as well as a model bridge where kids can act like captains. Down by the ferry dock, the museum's Heritage Harbour holds a floating collection of vintage and replica vessels, including (in summer), the *Munin,* a half-scale Viking longboat. ⏱ *1¼ hr. 1905 Ogden Ave.* ☎ *604/257-8300. www.vancouvermaritimemuseum. com. Admission C$10 adults, C$7.50 seniors & kids 6–19. Tues–Sat 10am–5pm, Sun noon–5pm. Bus: 2, 22.*

⑤ ★★ South Granville Rise & Gallery Row. South Granville Rise is a stretch of upscale shopping running along Granville Street, beginning at 6th Avenue and extending south to 16th Avenue. It's full of men's' and ladies' fashions, Oriental rug merchants, bistros and coffee houses, and other retailers. The blocks between 5th Avenue and Broadway are known as Vancouver's "Gallery Row," with a number of significant galleries displaying contemporary works. For more on the galleries, see p 31, **㉔**. ⏱ *1½ hr. www.southgranville.org. Bus: 10, 98.*

Colorful fall foliage abounds in Vanier Park.

Interactive exhibits and vintage ships make a visit to the Vancouver Maritime Museum a rewarding one.

6 ★ **Commercial Drive.** Lest you leave Vancouver thinking the whole city is high-rise condos and expensive seaside property, take the SkyTrain out to Commercial Drive, whose 12-block stretch between E. 6th Avenue and Venables Street is a mix of 21st-century youth culture, holdover '60s culture, old immigrants, new immigrants, neo hippies, artists, and lefty families. You'll find cuisine from across the globe, record stores, bookstores (including the inimitable People's Co-op Bookstore, p 72), coffee bars, and, most alluringly of all, classic Italian cafes, bakeries, restaurants, and delis—thriving holdovers from the wave of Italian immigrants who settled here in the 1940s and '50s. ⏱ *1–2 hr.* www.thedrive.ca. SkyTrain: Millennium or Expo lines to Commercial Dr./Broadway Station.

Don't miss **7** **Caffè Calabria,** whose decor is pure over-the-top Italia: faux Roman statues and columns, marble cafe tables, chrome chairs, and a ceiling that's a take-off on the Sistine Chapel. Try a cappuccino, sandwich, gelato, or pastry while chatting with the super-friendly staff. *1745 Commercial Dr.* ☎ *604/253-7017. $.*

8 ★★ **Queen Elizabeth Park.** If you're more trees-and-flowers than counterculture-and-cappuccino, skip Commercial Drive in favor of a visit to Vancouver's second most popular park, located on the West Side atop a 150m (492-ft.) extinct volcano, on land that was once a basalt quarry. Highlights include the main and north Quarry Gardens, which transformed the old excavations pits into vibrant buckets of flowers, shrubs, and trees, all fed (in the main garden) by a tumbling waterfall. On the slopes around the gardens, the Arboretum displays a collection of trees native to nearly

For old-time Italian cafes and coffee bars, your best bet is Commercial Drive.

The quarry gardens at Queen Elizabeth Park.

every part of Canada. 🕐 *1–2 hr. Main entrance at 33rd Ave. & Cambie St.* ☎ *604/257-8400. www.city. vancouver.bc.ca/parks/parks/queen elizabeth. Free admission.*

⑨ ★ The Bloedel Floral Conservatory. Opened in 1969 and perched at the highest point of Queen Elizabeth Park, this huge, humid geodesic dome is made of triangular plexiglass bubbles and is filled with more than 500 varieties of tropical flowers and exotic plants, over 100 birds, and swimming koi—*très Silent Running,* minus the robots. Behind the conservatory, a large plaza is highlighted by a beautiful dancing fountain. 🕐 *30–45 min. Main park entrance at 33rd Ave. & Cambie St.* ☎ *604/257-8584. www.city. vancouver.bc.ca/parks/parks/bloedel. Admission C$4.60 adults, C$3.20 seniors, C$3.45 teens 13–18, C$2.30 kids 6–12, free 5 and under. Daily 10am–5pm. Bus: 15.*

⑩ ★★★ VanDusen Botanical Gardens. Just 3 blocks from Queen Elizabeth Park, this 22-hectare (54-acre) botanical garden is home to some 7,500 plant types from around the world, arranged to illustrate different botanical relationships—from plant groupings such as the Labernum Walk to geographic arrangements such as the Sino Himalayan Garden and historical gardens such as the VanDusen maze, an Elizabethan hedgerow maze made from 3,000 pyramidal cedars. All are interspersed with reflecting ponds and lawns, as well as a great collection of stone sculpture, much of it created on the grounds during 1975's Vancouver International Stone Sculpture Symposium. 🕐 *1–2 hr. 5251 Oak St. (at 37th).* ☎ *604/878-9274. http:// vancouver.ca/parks/parks/vandusen/ website/index.htm. Open daily at 10am. Closing time varies from 4pm Nov–Feb to 9pm June–Aug. Admission C$8.50 adults, C$6.25 seniors, C$6.50 teens, C$4.25 kids 6–12. Prices lower Oct–Mar. Bus: 15.* ●

Star Gazer lilies are just one of many floral species that can be found in The Bloedel Floral Conservatory.

Vancouver Art & Architecture

1. The Shangri-La
2. MacMillan Bloedel Building
3. Burrard Street's Architectural Landmarks
4. Marine Building
5. Bill Reid Gallery of Northwest Coast Art
6. Pendulum Gallery
7. Caffè Artigiano
8. Vancouver Art Gallery
9. Robson Square
10. The Provincial Law Courts
11. *Clouds*
12. Vancouver Contemporary Art Gallery
13. Beatty Walk
14. Cambie Bridge Ring Gear Monument
15. Cooper Mews
16. *Welcome to the Land of Light*
17. *Footnotes & Password*
18. Collection
19. *Terra Nova* & the Roundhouse
20. Granville Island Public Market
21. Emily Carr University of Art + Design
22. Railspur Alley Artist Studios/Galleries
23. Eagle Spirit Gallery
24. South Granville's Gallery Row

Previous page: A storefront on Commercial Drive, one of Vancouver's hippest shopping stretches.

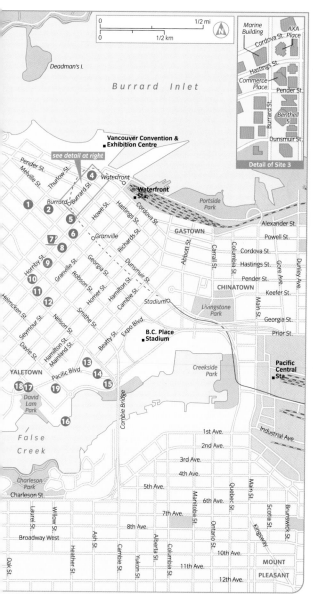

Deadman's I.

Burrard Inlet

Vancouver Convention &
Exhibition Centre

see detail at right

Waterfront

Waterfront Sta.

Portside Park

Pender St.
Melville St.
Thurlow St.
Burrard St.
Howe St.
Hastings St.
Cordova St.

GASTOWN

Granville
Richards St.
Georgia St.
Robson St.
Dunsmuir St.
Alexander St.
Powell St.
Cordova St.
Hastings St.
Pender St.
Keefer St.

CHINATOWN

Hornby St.
Granville St.
Horner St.
Hamilton St.
Camble St.
Stadium

Livingstone Park

Abbott St.
Carrall St.
Columbia St.
Main St.
Gore Ave.
Dunley Ave.

Helmcken St.
Seymour St.
Nelson St.
Smithe St.
Beatty St.
Expo Blvd.

B.C. Place Stadium

Georgia St.
Prior St.

Davie St.
Hamilton St.
Mainland St.

YALETOWN

Pacific Blvd.

Creekside Park

Pacific Central Sta.

David Lam Park

Camble Bridge

False Creek

1st Ave.
2nd Ave.
3rd Ave.
4th Ave.
5th Ave.
6th Ave.
7th Ave.
8th Ave.

Industrial Ave.

Charleson Park
Charleson St.

Oak St.
Laurel St.
Willow St.
Heather St.
Ash St.
Camble St.
Yukon St.
Alberta St.
Columbia St.
Manitoba St.
Ontario St.
Quebec St.
Main St.
Scotia St.
Brunswick St.
Kingsway

10th Ave.
11th Ave.
12th Ave.

Broadway West

MOUNT PLEASANT

Marine Building
AXA Place
Cordova St.
Hastings St.
Commerce Place
Pender St.
Burrard St.
Benthell St.
Dunsmuir St.

Detail of Site 3

0   1/2 mi
0   1/2 km

While Vancouver may be better known as a business and quality-of-life capital, it's also home to a thriving arts scene and architects who are livening the city's heretofore dull, condo-heavy skyline with some standout modern buildings. This walking tour will take you to art sites big and small, from the top museums and galleries to the subtlest public-art installations. START: **Intersection of W. Georgia and Thurlow sts.**

A cornice on the facade of the Marine Building shows off some of the structure's intricate detailing.

1 ★★ **The Shangri-La.** Dominating Vancouver's modern skyline, this 61-story hotel/condo combo is the city's tallest building. Check out its minimalist, angular design, with its nearly weightless-looking glass-and-aluminum facade. ⏱ *5 min. 1120 W. Georgia St. www.shangri-la.com/en/property/vancouver/shangrila.*

2 ★ **The MacMillan Bloedel Building.** This 1970 building by Arthur Erickson (p 12) was designed in the "brutalist" style, its load-bearing exterior walls made from a checkerboard of cast, sandblasted concrete tapering 27 stories from base to roof. ⏱ *10 min. 1075 W. Georgia St.*

3 ★★ **Burrard Street's Architectural Landmarks.** From the intersection of West Georgia and Burrard streets, look right to see the classic profile of the grand dame **Fairmont Hotel** (p 126), then walk left (north) on Burrard. Ahead on your right, the 33-story, metal-and-glass **Benthell 5** (550 Burrard St.) is notable for its curving east and west facades. One block further, the **Commerce Place/CIBC building** (400 Burrard St.) is one of Vancouver's most striking, looking like a stack of mirrored boxes that form different patterns when viewed from different angles. Another block north, the bronze **AXA Place building** (999 W. Hastings St.) isn't particularly notable by itself, but its facade offers a beautiful reflection of the historic Marine Building (see 4) across the street. ⏱ *20 min.*

4 ★★★ **The Marine Building.** *See p 10, 4.*

5 ★★ **Bill Reid Gallery of Northwest Coast Art.** Entered via the lovely courtyard of the Cathedral Place office complex, this gallery celebrates the life work of Haida artist Bill Reid (p 51) through permanent and temporary exhibits of his totem poles, jewelry, bronze sculpture, wood carvings, and other objects. It's second only to the UBC Museum of Anthropology's amazing Reid collection (p 16, 6). ⏱ *45 min. 639 Hornby St. ☎ 604/682-3455. www.billreidgallery.ca. Admission C$10 adults, C$7 seniors, C$5 kids 5–17. Mon–Fri 10:30am–5pm, Sat–Sun 11am–5pm. Bus: 5. Sky-Train: Millennium or Expo lines to Burrard Station.*

6 ★ Pendulum Gallery. The seven-story glass atrium of the HSBC Building functions as half entranceway, half public art gallery. The highlight is Alan Storey's *Pendulum*, a 27m (90-ft.) brushed aluminum pylon that swings from the glass roof, detailing a slow, graceful arc that lines up at the end of each swing with a matching buttress on the atrium floor, appearing for a second to form an unbroken column. Other exhibits are installed around the gallery on a rotating basis. ⏱ *10–20 min. 885 W. Georgia St.* ☎ *604/250-9682. www. pendulumgallery.bc.ca. Free admission. Mon–Wed 9am–6pm, Thurs–Fri 9am–9pm, Sat–Sun 9am–5pm.*

The Italian-style **7 Caffè Artigiano** serves Vancouver's most elegantly poured cappuccinos and lattes, each with its own design in the foam. It's been the home of several Canadian Barista Champions. *763 Hornby St.* ☎ *604/694-7737. www.caffeartigiano.com. $.*

8 ★★ Vancouver Art Gallery. See p 11, 6.

9 ★ Robson Square. Across from the Art Gallery, enter architect Arthur Erickson's presciently "green" public plaza to see its mix of modernist concrete architecture with natural landscaping. And don't miss Alan Chung Hung's red, pop-art *Spring* sculpture on the Hornby Street side. You'll know it when you see it. *See p 11,* 7.

10 ★★ The Provincial Law Courts. See p 11, 8.

11 *Clouds.* Walking east along Nelson Street after exiting the courts, look left and up at the corner of Howe Street to see Alan Chung Hung's *Clouds* crowning two balconies atop a height-challenged

The soaring glass atrium of the Pendulum Gallery is highlighted by its namesake sculpture.

office building. Get it? It's not a skyscraper, so the architects brought the clouds to it. ⏱ *2 min. 983 Howe St. (just off Nelson).*

12 ★★ Vancouver Contemporary Art Gallery. A progressive contemporary art gallery programming world-class temporary exhibits in two large, high-ceilinged rooms. ⏱ *30 min. 555 Nelson St. (at Richards).* ☎ *604/681-2700. www. contemporaryartgallery.ca. Admission by voluntary donation. Wed–Sun noon–6pm.*

Continue along Nelson St. for 4 blocks, past Cambie St., and turn right onto:

13 Beatty Walk. In spring, this pretty residential street's trees bloom with vibrant pink flowers.

Art Galleries of Vancouver

Besides the Gallery Row galleries (p 31), other great nonprofit and commercial galleries around Vancouver include:

Access Gallery: New contemporary works, featuring local emerging artists. *206 Carrall St., Gastown.* ☎ *604/689-2907. www.vaarc.ca.*

Artspeak: Works that blur the line between writing and contemporary art. *233 Carrall St., Gastown.* ☎ *604/688-0051. www. artspeak.ca.*

ArtStarts: Works by children, created as part of a nonprofit school arts program. *808 Richards St., Downtown.* ☎ *888/878-7144 or 604/878-7144. www.artstarts.com.*

Buschlen Mowatt Gallery: Vancouver's most high-profile gallery, with a Robert Indiana *Love* sculpture out front. *1445 W. Georgia St., West End.* ☎ *604/682-1234. www.buschlenmowatt.com.*

Gallery Gachet: Works by artists "informed by mental health issues." *88 E. Cordova St., Gastown.* ☎ *604/687-2468. www. gachet.org.*

Grunt Gallery: An artist-run nonprofit featuring contemporary Canadian and International artists. *116-350 E. 2nd Ave., West Side.* ☎ *604/875-9516. www.grunt.ca.*

Jennifer Kostuik Gallery: Works by established and emerging contemporary artists. *1070 Homer St., Yaletown.* ☎ *604/737-3969. www.kostiukgallery.com.*

Or Gallery: Nonprofit gallery presenting experimental, challenging contemporary art. *555 Hamilton St., Downtown.* ☎ *604/683-7395. www.orgallery.org.*

For commercial galleries dealing in fine **Northwest Coast First Nations art,** see p 74.

Love sculpture by Robert Indiana, set in front of the Buschlen Mowatt Gallery.

Year-round, note the waterfall and leaf-shaped fountain at its southwestern end. ⏱ *5 min. Btw. Nelson St. & Pacific Blvd.*

From the fountain at Beatty Walk, turn left along Pacific Blvd. and look for the:

⑭ Cambie Bridge Ring Gear Monument.

Not really a sculpture at all, this 8m (26-ft.) red-orange circle is actually a gear from the truss swing span of the old 1911 Cambie Street Bridge. When the bridge was demolished in 1984, the gear was mounted here as a monument to Vancouver's bridge designers and builders. ⏲ *5 min. In the median on Pacific Blvd., near Cambie St. & the Cambie St. Bridge.*

Keep walking along Pacific Blvd. half a block, then turn right between 1010 and 1032 Pacific Blvd. into the unmarked:

⑮ ★ Cooper Mews.

Follow artist Alan Storey's serpentine pathway through the grass to the 12 wooden planks at the end. Stepping on any of the planks activates soft steam whistles in the five wooden barrels lined up on the galvanized steel track overhead. You can play a little tune by dancing on the boards. Planks 6 and 8 (north-south) make a particularly nice chord. ⏲ *10 min. Btw. Pacific Blvd. & Marinaside Crescent.*

Walk west around the curve of Marinaside Crescent, past the roundabout and out toward the next point on the False Creek shoreline to see:

⑯ Welcome to the Land of Light.

Along the walkway railing, artist Henry Tsang has installed aluminum letters spelling out phrases in English and Chinook. The work highlights intercultural communications in British Columbia, while use of Chinook, a 19th-century trade language that only had about 500 words, gives the sentiments great poetry. ⏲ *5 min. On the False Creek shoreline walkway btw. Davie & Drake sts.*

Walk the pedestrian path that runs from "Welcome to the Land

of Light" to Drake St., then follow Drake to Pacific Blvd. Cross Pacific and walk a few meters left to see:

⑰ ★ Footnotes & Password.

Gwen Boyle's *Footnotes* is a series of 57 unpolished black granite tiles set randomly into a brick sidewalk, marked with words and phrases evocative of the site. Alan Storey's *Password* is three sets of four large blocks, each block marked with a single letter on each side. Installed in air vents, the blocks turn with the vents' flow, spelling out random words for a split second at a time. ⏲ *5 min. In front of Governor's Tower, 1300 block of Pacific Blvd., on sidewalk btw. Homer & Drake sts.*

Keep walking west on Pacific and turn right at the next corner, onto Homer St.

⑱ ★ Collection.

Spaced along the sidewalk, artist Mark Lewis has installed three red, wedge-shape time capsules in concrete bases, each marked with a list of the random objects inside. How can I not love this? One of the objects is an old edition of *Frommer's Bulgaria on $5*

One of the three concrete blocks that make up Mark Lewis's Collection.

A ceramics exhibit at the Emily Carr University of Art + Design.

a Day. ⏱ *10 min. East side of Homer St. btw. Pacific Blvd. & Drake St.*

At the end of Homer, turn right onto Drake and continue across Pacific Blvd., turning left at the sign indicating "ROUNDHOUSE MEWS/ ROUNDHOUSE COMMUNITY CENTER."

⑲ *Terra Nova* & The Roundhouse. Follow the old train tracks to the Roundhouse to see Richard Prince's *Terra Nova*, a theatrical-looking piece mounted on and in front of the building's brick wall. Continue walking along the tracks through the Roundhouse, a classic, circular industrial building that was once the western terminus of the Canadian Pacific Railway. Today it's a community arts center. Look into the glass-walled pavilion to see the restored, gleaming Engine 374, which pulled the first transcontinental train into Vancouver in 1887. ⏱ *20 min.*

181 Roundhouse Mews. ☎ 604/ 713-1800. www.roundhouse.ca. Free admission.

At the foot of Davie St., walk to the end of the dock in Quayside Marina and catch the ferry to Granville Island. (Fares are C$3.50–C$4 adults, C$2 seniors/ kids. Departures every 15 min., 8:45am–9:15pm.)

Right at the dock, the **⑳ Granville Island Public Market** (p 33, ①) is a must stop for snacks, whether from one of the bakeries or produce stalls, or from one of the dozen-plus take-out restaurants on site. *$.*

Walk down Johnson St. to the:

㉑ ★ Emily Carr University of Art + Design. This prominent art school (opened in 1925 and named for the iconic Canadian painter) has three galleries on site showing work by both professional and student artists. ⏱ *30 min.–1 hr. 1399 Johnston St., Granville Island.* ☎ *604/ 844-3811. www.eciad.ca/resources/ galleries. Free admission. Mon–Fri noon–5pm, Sat–Sun 10am–5pm.*

㉒ Railspur Alley Artist Studios/Galleries. Granville Island is home to nearly four dozen artist/ artisan shops, many of them attached to the studios where the artwork, jewelry, prints, and other objects are made. The largest concentration of these gallery/ studios is along this small alley just steps from the Emily

A glass sculpture at the Diane Farris Gallery.

Robson Square mixes modern architecture with "green" landscaping.

Carr Institute. Others are scattered over the island; maps are available at the galleries and on the website below. ⏱ *30 min.–1 hr. Runs at an angle btw. Cartwright St. & Old Bridge St. www.granvilleislandartists. com.*

Go left onto Old Bridge St. and right onto Cartwright St. to Anderson St. Cross to Maritime Mews and arrive at the:

㉓ ★★ **Eagle Spirit Gallery.** This commercial gallery specializes in original, museum-quality (read: very pricey) Northwest Coast First Nations and Inuit art, including hand-carved masks, argillite stone carvings, and paintings. ⏱ *30 min. 1803 Maritime Mews.* ☎ *888/801-5277 or 604/801-5205. www.eaglespiritgallery.com. Thurs–Mon 11am–5pm.*

Touring Tip

Finish your art tour with dinner at **Boneta** in Gastown (p 93), which features works by important local artists. For an arty overnight, stay at the high-design **Opus Hotel** (p 128) or the **Listel** (p 127), which displays art from the Buschlen-Mowatt Gallery.

Exit Granville Island via the main Anderson St. entrance. Cross 4th Ave. and cut through the park to Granville St. and:

㉔ ★★ **South Granville's Gallery Row.** The stretch of Granville between 5th Avenue and Broadway is home to several significant galleries. Standouts for contemporary works by Canadian and international artists include the **Diane Farris Gallery,** 1590 W. 7th Ave. (☎ 604/737-2629; www.diane farrisgallery.com); **Equinox Gallery,** 2321 Granville St. (☎ 604/736-2405; www.equinoxgallery.com); **Monte Clark Gallery,** 2339 Granville St. (☎ 604/730-5000; www.monte clarkgallery.com); **Atelier Gallery,** 2421 Granville St. (☎ 604/732-3021; www.ateliergallery.ca); and **Jacana Gallery,** 2435 Granville St. (☎ 604/ 879-9306. www.jacanagallery.com). The **Douglas Reynolds Gallery,** 2335 Granville St. (☎ 604/731–9292; www.douglasreynolds gallery.com), deals in fine Northwest Coast Native art. ⏱ *1–2 hr. Most galleries open Tues–Sat 10am–5pm.*

Vancouver for Foodies

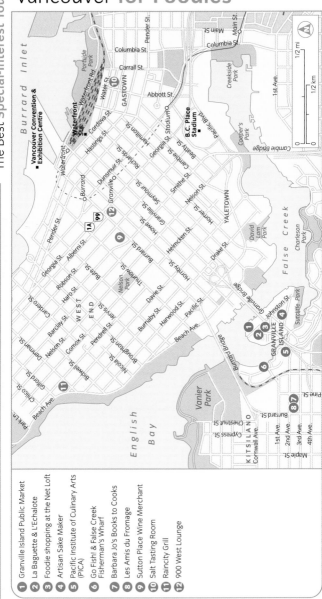

1 Granville Island Public Market
2 La Baguette & L'Echalote
3 Foodie shopping at the Net Loft
4 Artisan Sake Maker
5 Pacific Institute of Culinary Arts (PICA)
6 Go Fish! & False Creek Fisherman's Wharf
7 Barbara Jo's Books to Cooks
8 Les Amis du Fromage
9 Sutton Place Wine Merchant
10 Salt Tasting Room
11 Raincity Grill
12 900 West Lounge

V̲ancouver is one giant multicourse meal, a world-class smorgasbord laid out between mountains and sea. Ingredients: farm-fresh organic produce and sustainably harvested seafood. Philosophy: Buy local, eat seasonal. Seasoning: a staggering range of ethnic influences. Result? Yum. This tour takes you to some of the city's culinary high points, from hole-in-the-wall to haute. START: Granville Island.

The Granville Public Market is the best place in the city for picnic fare.

❶ ★★★ Granville Island Public Market. As English Bay Beach is to sunsets, the Public Market is to food: the undisputed heavyweight champ. Open 7 days a week, year-round, it offers three dozen indoor shops and stalls stuffed to the gills with fresh local produce, seafood, meats, artisanal cheeses, ethnic foods, grains, spices, sweets, rare teas and coffees, and fresh bread, bagels, and other baked goods. There are also 14 casual walk-up restaurants around a central seating area, and between June and October there's an outdoor Farmer's Market where regional growers bring fruits, vegetables, and plants fresh from the fields. Foodies can easily spend hours at the market, smelling the aromas and sampling the wares. Those who want to delve deeper can take a 3-hour chef-guided tour. ⏲ *2–3 hr. for foodies, 1 hr. for everyone else. 1689 Johnston St., at the Granville Island ferry dock.* ☎ *604/666-6477. www.granville island.com. Market daily 9am–7pm. Market tours offered through Edible British Columbia,* ☎ *604/812-9660. www.edible-britishcolumbia.com. Admission C$65. Tues, Thurs & Sat 8:30am.*

❷ La Baguette & L'Echalote. Just outside the Public Market, this bakery makes hearty breads and pastries, and keeps baskets of samples out for you to try. ⏲ *15 min. 1680 Johnston St., Granville Island.* ☎ *604/684-1351. www.labaguette bakery.com. Daily 7:30am–7:30pm.*

❸ Foodie Shopping at the Net Loft. Right across from the Public Market, the Net Loft building is home to numerous shops including the **Market Kitchen** for cookware and **Liberty Wine Merchants** for wine. There's also a **Barbara Jo's Books to Cooks,** but don't bother because you're going to their main shop in a few minutes. ⏲ *1666 Johnston St., Granville Island. Daily 10am–7pm.*

The hand-pressed sake made by Artisan Sake Maker comes in several varieties.

④ ★ Artisan Sake Maker.

Sake-maker Masa Shiroki's small establishment is the original Canadian small-batch sake winery, producing hand-pressed, hand-bottled sakes that complement the seasonal variations of BC's regional cuisine. Sake is available by the bottle or by the taste, the latter costs C$2 per glass. 🕐 *15 min. 1339 Railspur Alley, Granville Island.* ☎ *604/685-7253. www.artisansakemaker.com. Wed–Mon noon–6pm.*

Exiting Granville Island at Anderson St. (under the Granville Bridge), you'll see on your right the:

⑤ Pacific Institute of Culinary Arts (PICA).

Stop in for a snack at this culinary institute's bakeshop or to watch cakes being decorated in the glassed-in booth right at the entrance. 🕐 *10 min. 1505 W. 2nd Ave., West Side.* ☎ *604/734-4488. www.picachef.com. Mon–Sat 8am–7pm.*

From PICA, walk along serpentine Island Park Walk, which cuts right from Anderson St. along the waterfront. Beyond the PUBLIC FISH SALES sign you'll find a tiny blue tin shack surrounded by people. That's:

⑥ ★ Go Fish! & False Creek Fisherman's Wharf.

One of the city's most beloved fresh-seafood joints. Grab the catch of the day and settle into one of the outdoor seats, or head across the parking lot to Fisherman's Wharf, which offers fresh fish right off the boat. 🕐 *30 min. if you eat. Go Fish!, 1505 W. 1st Ave., West Side.* ☎ *604/730-5039. All items C$9–C$13. Cash only. Lunch Tues–Sun.*

Exit the parking lot and walk up 1st Ave. West, following it around the S-curve and making a left onto Pine St. Make the next right onto 2nd Ave. to reach:

⑦ ★★ Barbara Jo's Books to Cooks.

An absolutely huge selection of cookbooks, wine books, and periodicals from around the world, for both amateur and professional cooks. They offer cooking classes too at the open kitchen along the back wall, and the staff is 100% foodie. 🕐 *30 min.–1 hr. 1740 W. 2nd Ave. (btw. Burrard & Pine sts.).* ☎ *604/688-6755. www.books tocooks.com. Mon–Sat 9am–6pm.*

For a sweet treat, you can't beat a stop at the bakeshop of the Pacific Institute of Culinary Arts.

Foodies flock to Barbara Jo's Books to Cooks for its huge selection of cookbooks and culinary tools.

⑧ ★★ Les Amis du Fromage. Vancouver's best cheese shop, stocking between 400 and 500 cheeses at any given time. 🕐 15–30 min. 1752 W. 2nd Ave. (btw. Burrard & Pine sts.). ☎ 604/732-4218. www.buycheese.com. Mon–Wed & Sat 9am–6pm, Thurs–Fri 9am–6:30pm, Sun 9am–5pm.

From here, call a cab (p 191) and have it drop you off back Downtown, at:

⑨ ★★ Sutton Place Wine Merchant. Attached to the upscale Sutton Place Hotel, this upscale/rustic space offers a large selection (almost 500 labels) of British Columbia and international wines plus frequent wine tastings and seminars in their tasting room. Check the website for the latest schedule. 🕐 30 min., more if attending a tasting. 855 Burrard St. ☎ 604/642-2947. www.suttonplacewinemerchant.com. Mon–Sat 11am–10pm, Sun noon–7pm.

⑩ ★★ Salt Tasting Room. Consider this your pre-dinner meal. Secreted away in a grimy Gastown alley, Salt serves only artisanal cheese and cured meats, arranged in tasting plates of three, with three small sides and wine to complement them. The decor is brick-walled simplicity, and the day's selections are chalked on a blackboard. 🕐 1 hr. 45 Blood Alley. ☎ 604/633-1912. www.salttastingroom.com. Tasting plates C$15. Daily noon–midnight.

If it's still light, catch a taxi to English Bay Beach (Beach Ave. & Denman St.) and enjoy the sunset while you digest, then walk up Denman to:

⑪ ★★★ Raincity Grill. One of Vancouver's most influential farm-to-table restaurants. Order the "100 Mile Tasting Menu," built completely from ingredients sourced in the surrounding region. 🕐 1–2 hr. 1193 Denman St. ☎ 604/685-7337. www.raincitygrill.com. Dinner daily.

⑫ ★★ 900 West Lounge. End your foodie day with a nightcap and some quality jazz at this old-time-elegant lounge off the Fairmont Hotel lobby. It's regularly voted Vancouver's best wine bar. 🕐 30 min. to hours—your call. 900 W. Georgia St. ☎ 604/684-3131. www.fairmont.com/Hotel Vancouver. Sun–Thurs 11:30am–midnight, Fri–Sat 11:30am–1pm.

Vancouver with Kids

1. Vancouver Aquarium
2. Children's Farmyard
3. The Miniature Train
4. Concession Stand
5. Variety Kids Water Park
6. H.R. MacMillan Space Centre
7. Vancouver Maritime Museum
8. Science World at Telus World of Science

A central part of the "livability" for which Vancouver is so well known is its family-friendliness—as in, it's a good city in which to raise kids. Parks dot the landscape, cultural opportunities abound, and in neighborhoods like Yaletown it seems as if everything from Starbucks to the designer toddler shops is stroller-friendly. This tour takes in the city's kid-friendly high points, many of them located close together in Stanley Park (p 84). Depending on the age and stamina of your kids, you might want to break this tour over 2 days.
START: **Stanley Park.**

One of the Vancouver Aquarium's colorful jellyfish.

1 ★★★ **Vancouver Aquarium.** One of North America's largest and best, the Vancouver Aquarium focuses on Northwest species, with large pools for beluga whales, sea lions, Pacific white-sided dolphins, and sea otters, each of which offers views from both above and below water. There's also a jellyfish exhibit that's much more mesmerizing than you'd expect, plus tanks full of enormous freshwater fish, colorful tropical fish, frogs, piranhas, and sharks. Regular dolphin acrobatics shows and talks about various animals are held throughout the day, and those who want to shell out extra cash can go behind the scenes with the animal trainers and help feed the dolphins, belugas, sea lions, sea turtles, or (cutest of all, and cheapest) sea otters. ⏱ *2 hr. 845 Avison Way.* ☎ *604/659-FISH. www.vanaqua.org. Admission C$25 adults, C$20 seniors/teens, C$17 kids 4–12. "Animal encounters" C$25–C$195. Daily 9:30am–7pm summer, 9:30am–5pm winter. Bus: 19, plus no. 135 "around the park" shuttle in summer.*

2 ★ **Children's Farmyard.** An elaborate petting zoo set up like a rural farm, with barns and corrals, the Farmyard is home to more than

The Miniature Train at Stanley Park is a family favorite.

For kid-friendly watery fun, it's hard to beat the sprinklers and fountains at the Variety Kids Water Park.

200 animals, including sheep, goats, cows, potbellied pigs, ponies, and llama. Visitors are free to mingle with the smaller critters, but you'll need an attendant's supervision for reptiles and larger animals. ⏱ *1 hr. Off Pipeline Rd.* ☎ *604/257-8531. http:// vancouver.ca/Parks/parks/stanley/fun. htm. C$5.50 adults, C$3.75 seniors, C$2.75 kids 2–12. June–Aug daily 11am–4pm, Feb–May & early Sept weekends only 11am–4pm weekends only. Closed Jan & mid-Sept through Dec except for special events. Bus: 19, plus no. 135 "around the park" shuttle in summer.*

❸ ★ The Miniature Train.

Boarding near the farmyard, this minirailroad chugs along a 2km (1.25-mile) track though the park's forest, passing over trestles and through tunnels along the way. One of the engines is a replica of Engine 374, which pulled the first transcontinental train into Vancouver in 1887. (The original is at the Roundhouse in Yaletown, p 59, ❶⓭.) ⏱ *15 min. Address, rates & times same as Farmyard (❷), except July–Aug daily 10:30am–5pm. Bus: 19, plus no. 135 "around the park" shuttle in summer.*

Near the Miniature Train, one of Stanley Park's large ❹ **concession stands** sells burgers, hot

dogs, fish and chips, paninis, veggie dogs, veggie burgers, and other park food. *$.*

❺ Variety Kids Water Park. In

summer, kids can hop among the geysers, sprinklers, and water canons in this large play area. ⏱ *20 min.–2 hr., depending on your kids. Located at km 3.25 along Park Dr. Free admission. Late May to Labour Day daily. Bus: 19, plus no. 135 "around the park" shuttle in summer.*

The following attractions are all outside of Stanley Park, so if your kids are running on empty, end your tour here. If they still have energy to burn, take the False Creek Ferry (p 13, ⓭) to Vanier Park for two more stops.

❻ ★ H.R. MacMillan Space

Centre. Taking up half the big, cone-shaped building in Vanier Park, this very kid-friendly space museum offers a planetarium, a simulated space ride, displays on space flights, a theater for presentations on Canada's space program, and a room of interactive stations where you can, among other things, touch a moon rock, use a simulator to fly and dock the Space Shuttle, and prep a rocket for launch. ⏱ *1–2 hr. 1100 Chestnut St.* ☎ *604/738-7827. www.hr*

macmillanspacecentre.com. *C$15 adults, C$11 seniors & kids. Tues–Sun 10am–5pm (open Mon July–Aug & Christmas to New Year weeks only). Bus: 2, 22.*

7 ★ **Vancouver Maritime Museum.** For kids, the main attraction here is the chance to clamber around the Royal Canadian Mounted Police ship *St. Roch,* which sits in its entirety beneath a giant A-frame roof. There's also a children's discovery center with displays on why ships float, a model bridge where kids can act like captains, and displays of model ships created in the museum's open-view workshop. 🕐 *1¼ hr. 1905 Ogden Ave.* ☎ *604/257-8300. www. vancouvermaritimemuseum.com. C$10 adults, C$7.50 seniors & kids 6–19. Tues–Sat 10am–5pm, Sun noon–5pm. Bus: 2, 22.*

Last stop on your kids' tour is at the far eastern end of False Creek, an easy taxi or SkyTrain ride away.

8 ★★ **Science World at Telus World of Science.** Located near the Olympic Village, this huge, illuminated dome is a hands-on science center whose interactive exhibits include science projects, displays on

Kids can interact with watery environments at Science World at Telus World of Science.

how things work in the natural world and the human body, displays on creating a sustainable society, and a "Kidspace" learning environment with water, light, color, and movement themes geared to kids ages 2 to 6. There's also a large-screen Omnimax movie theater. 🕐 *2 hr. 1455 Quebec St., east end of False Creek.* ☎ *604/443-7443. www. scienceworld.ca. C$20 adults, C$17 seniors/teens, C$15 kids 4–12. Daily 10am–6pm. SkyTrain: Main Street/ Science World station.*

Interactive stations at the H.R. MacMillan Space Centre allow aspiring astronauts to dock a space shuttle, among other galactic experiences.

Multicultural Vancouver

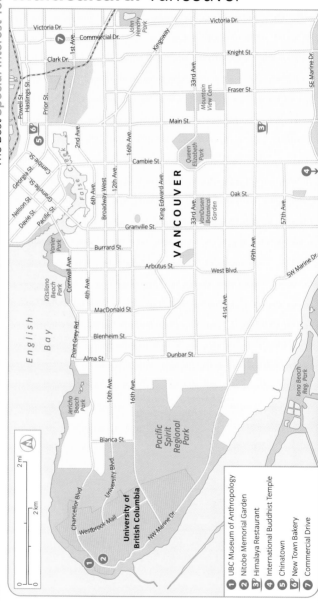

Victoria Dr.

Commercial Dr.

John Hendry Park

Victoria Dr.

Kingsway

Knight St.

1st Ave.

Clark Dr.

33rd Ave.

Mountain View Cem.

Fraser St.

SE Marine Dr.

Powell St.

Hastings St.

Prior St.

2nd Ave.

Main St.

Georgia St.

Cambie St.

False Creek

16th Ave.

Queen Elizabeth Park

Nelson St.

Davie St.

Granville St.

Pacific St.

6th Ave.

12th Ave.

Cambie St.

King Edward Ave.

33rd Ave.

VanDusen Botanical Garden

Oak St.

57th Ave.

VANCOUVER

Broadway West

Vanier Park

Kitsilano Beach Park

Burrard St.

Arbutus St.

West Blvd.

49th Ave.

SW Marine Dr.

Cornwall Ave.

4th Ave.

MacDonald St.

41st Ave.

E n g l i s h   B a y

Point Grey Rd.

Blenheim St.

Dunbar St.

Jericho Beach Park

Alma St.

10th Ave.

16th Ave.

Pacific Spirit Regional Park

Iona Beach Reg. Park

Blanca St.

University Blvd.

Chancellor Blvd.

Westbrook Mall

University of British Columbia

NW Marine Dr.

2 mi

2 km

1 UBC Museum of Anthropology
2 Nitobe Memorial Garden
3 Himalaya Restaurant
4 International Buddhist Temple
5 Chinatown
6 New Town Bakery
7 Commercial Drive

Vancouver is one of the most international cities you'll ever visit, its original Euro-American and First Nations populations now mixed with an enormous Chinese community (some 17% of the population) as well as people from India, Southeast Asia, Korea, Japan, Latin America, the Caribbean, and elsewhere. Mostly you'll just see these folks going about their day-to-day Canadian lives, but dotted around the city are monuments, touchstones, and other reminders of where they all came from. Because these sites are fairly far apart, a car is a great convenience, if not a must. START: **University of British Columbia campus, far west on the West Side.**

---

1 ★★★ University of British Columbia Museum of Anthropology. Vancouver's finest museum is dedicated primarily to British Columbia's astounding First Nations artistic traditions, with many works by the legendary Bill Reid. *See p 16, 6.*

The Raven and the First Men, at the UBC Museum of Anthropology.

2 ★★★ Nitobe Memorial Garden. Also on the UBC campus, the Nitobe is one of North America's finest classical Japanese gardens. *See p 17, 7.*

Set in Vancouver's tiny Punjabi Market district amidst sari shops, Indian jewelry, and bridal shops, the inexpensive **3 Himalaya Restaurant** offers a full menu and a huge selection of Indian sweets. *6587 Main St.* ☎ *604/324-6514. $.*

4 ★★★ International Buddhist Temple. Far from central Vancouver, near the southern end of neighboring (and 50% Asian) Richmond, is China—or it least it seems that way. The best example of Chinese imperial architecture in Canada, this temple's expansive grounds hold several pavilions and halls modeled after the Forbidden City in Beijing, with tiered roofs and flared eaves. Among them

are scholar's courtyards, murals, shrines, a classical Chinese garden with lotus pond, and many huge golden statues, including an 11m (35-ft.) Buddha Sakyamuni that's the largest Buddha in North America. Visitors are welcome. The weirdly cartoonish, Bambi-esque deer statues that dot the periphery of the grounds are a nod to Sarnath, the deer park where Gautama Buddha first proclaimed the Dharma. ⏱ *1 hr. 9160 Steveston Hwy. (btw. No. 3 Rd. & No. 4 Rd.), Richmond.* ☎ *604/274-2822. www. buddhisttemple.ca. Free admission. Daily 9:30am–5:30pm. Don't try to*

Entrance plaza at the Nitobe Memorial Garden.

A decorative dragon lamp post in Vancouver's Chinatown.

get here on public transit—it'd take hours.

⑤ ★★ Chinatown. Vancouver's Chinatown was first established in the 1880s by Chinese workers, many of whom had built the Canadian Pacific Railway. The area thrived as the center of Chinese life in Vancouver until the 1970s, when newer, wealthier immigrants began settling instead in Richmond and other suburbs. Today it's primarily a giant Chinese marketplace, its shops full of foodstuffs, traditional medicines, antiques, and knickknacks. *See p 52 for a full neighborhood tour.*

While you're in Chinatown, be sure to get in line with the old Chinese men and women at **⑥ New Town Bakery** for a steamed bun or sweet rice cake. *158 E. Pender St. ☎ 604/689-7835. $.*

⑦ ★ Commercial Drive. As immigrant communities become established, "ethnic neighborhoods" often shrink to ethnic streets, then to ethnic restaurants. So it is with Commercial Drive, one of Vancouver's funkiest shopping stretches. Once an enclave of Italian immigrants, the northern portion of "The Drive" is now an enclave of Italian restaurants acting as the old guard

to a newer wave of Ethiopian, Middle Eastern, Jamaican, Mexican, Thai, Vietnamese, and Indian joints. For a fine end to a multicultural day, try sipping cappuccino among the faux Roman statuary at **Caffè Calabria** (1745 Commercial Dr.; ☎ 604/253-7017), watching soccer on the giant TV at the **Abruzzo Cappuccino Bar** (1321 Commercial Dr.; ☎ 604/254-2641), choosing from among 218 flavors at **La Casa Gelato** (1033 Venables St., off the Drive; ☎ 604/251-3211; www.lacasagelato.com), or digging into dinner at one of several old-school restaurants. 🕐 *1–2 hr. or more. SkyTrain: Commercial Dr/Broadway Station.* ●

Customers can choose from 218 flavors at La Casa Gelato.

3 The Best
Neighborhood Walks

Coal Harbour, Downtown & the West End

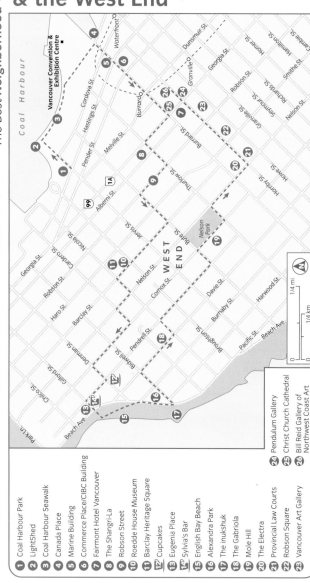

Previous page: Gold-Pots-on Marble is one piece of public art you'll find in Yaletown.

Comprising nearly all of Vancouver's central peninsula, these three neighborhoods virtually define Vancouver's international image: Downtown with its finance firms and skyscrapers, Coal Harbour with its ritzy condo buildings, and the West End with its tree-lined streets and mix of Victorian homes and low-rise residential buildings. This tour takes you on a route through all three, testing the walkability that's such a big part of Vancouver's famed livability. START: **Corner of Jervis and W. Hastings sts.**

Houseboats and yachts are equally at home in lovely Coal Harbor Park.

① ★ **Coal Harbour Park.** This small, circular park growing atop the Coal Harbour Community Centre lets on to a great view of the harbor marina, where funky houseboats are moored among luxury yachts and sailboats. Off to the west you can see Stanley Park as well as Deadman

Liz Magor's LightShed *is one of the city's best-known pieces of art.*

Island, a former Squamish burial ground that's now home to a Canadian Naval Reserves base. Across Burrard Inlet, Cypress Mountain, Grouse Mountain, and Mt. Seymour loom above the homes of North Vancouver. ⏲ *10 min. Corner of Jervis & W. Hastings sts. http://vancouver.ca/parks. Open 24 hr.*

Exit down the stairs on the east side of the park and walk east along the promenade to:

② ★ *LightShed.* One of Vancouver's most famous pieces of public art, this 2004 sculpture by Liz Magor is modeled on the wooden boat sheds that used to line this stretch of shoreline. It stands on stilts above the walkway, and glows softly at night. ⏲ *5 min. Northwest corner of Harbour Green Park.*

Boating on the Harbor

Got an interest in how the busiest port on the west coast works? **Harbour Cruises** offer 1-hour tours of Burrard Inlet (Apr–Oct), concentrating on the working port and areas around Stanley Park. There's also a 2½-hour sunset dinner cruise option from May to October. Ferries depart from a dock in Coal Harbor, near the foot of Denman Street. For info, call ☎ 604/688-7246 or check out www.boatcruises.com. One-hour tours cost C$25 adults, C$21 seniors and teens 12 to 17, C$10 kids 5 to 11. Sunset cruises cost C$70.

3 ★★★ Coal Harbour Seawalk. One of the city's loveliest urban promenades, the seawalk borders the water and the open fields of Harbour Green Park, with high-end condominiums towering just beyond. Besides *LightShed* (**2**), some other notables along its length include Sorel Etrog's seated *King & Queen* sculpture; the twin, sail-shaped Callisto and Carina condominium buildings behind; and a public square with a children's water park in summer and the popular Mill Marine Bistro (p 104) year-round. ⏲ *30 min. The seawall stretches from Stanley Park in the west to the Convention Centre in the east.*

4 ★★ Canada Place. This two-building convention center, cruise ship terminal, and hotel/office complex was originally built as the Canada pavilion for World Expo '86 and was home to the world's first permanent IMAX 3-D theater. The newer western building, with its monumental green roof, was built in preparation for the 2010 Olympics, for which it will function as the media center. ⏲ *20 min. See p 9,* **2**.

After emerging at the intersection of Burrard and Cordova sts., walk south 1 block on Burrard to W. Hastings St. to see:

5 ★★★ The Marine Building. This gem of 1930s Art Deco, set in the midst of Vancouver's ultramodern Downtown, often serves as a film and TV backdrop (it currently

Stroll along the scenic Coal Harbor Seawalk for great people-watching opportunities.

The reflective exterior of the CIBC Building, one of the most architecturally significant buildings in the city.

subs in as the *Daily Planet* building on the TV series *Smallville*). If you walk south from its entrance, and turn around between W. Hastings Street and W. Pender Street, you can see its reflection in the bronze AXA Place building. *See p 10,* **4**.

6 ★★ Commerce Place/CIBC Building. The most beautiful modern building on a stretch that has a wealth of them, this 1986 gem is clad in silver reflective glass and is so jagged it offers 12 corner offices on every floor—and looks different from every angle. ⏱ *5 min. 400 Burrard St.*

7 ★★ Fairmont Hotel Vancouver. The sandstone carvings and gargoyles on the facade of this 1939 landmark took 10 international craftsmen an entire year to create. ⏱ *20 min. See p 10,* **5**.

From here, walk down W. Georgia St. to see Vancouver's tallest building:

8 ★★ The Shangri-La. *See p 26,* **1**.

Walk up Thurlow St. to:

9 ★★★ Robson Street. One of Canada's hottest shopping stretches is named for John Robson (1824–92), the premier of British Columbia from 1889 to 1892. In addition to major-league shopping, it's also home to a plethora of dining and people-watching opportunities. ⏱ *30 min., more if you shop or people-watch. See p 11,* **9**.

Walk west on Robson St. and make left onto Bute St., passing Haro St. and crossing a small pocket-park to Barclay St. You're now officially in the West End, central Vancouver's quintessential residential neighborhood. Turn right (west) on Barclay and walk 3 blocks past Broughton St. to the:

10 ★ Roedde House Museum. Built in 1893 for German immigrants Gustav and Matilda Roedde, this modest but handsome Queen Anne Revival home was designed by Francis Rattenbury, architect of the magnificent Vancouver Art Gallery (p 11, **6**). Today its interiors reflect the house's original 1893–1925 period, during the Roeddes' residence. On Sunday afternoons (2–4pm) tours are followed by tea and cookies. ⏱ *30–45 min. 1415 Barclay St. ☎ 604/684-7040. www.roeddehouse.org. Admission C$6 Sun, C$5 other days. Tues–Fri 1:30–4pm (Tues–Sat 1–5pm in summer), Sun 2–4pm.*

11 ★ Barclay Heritage Square. Roedde House (**10**) is only one of several historic structures on this 2.3-acre (1 hectare), block-square park, with its manicured central lawn and walking paths, century-old trees and flower beds, and eight heritage homes. If you're interested in late-19th-century home and landscape architecture, grab a free walking tour map at Roedde House and

One of the heritage homes that make up Barclay Heritage Square.

take a detour. 🕑 *30–45 min. Btw. Barclay, Broughton, Haro & Nicola sts.*

Now zigzag through the West End, turning left from Barclay onto Nicola St., walk 1 block, and turn right onto Nelson St. Walk 1 more block and turn left onto Cardero St. Walk 1 block and turn right onto Comox St., then walk 2 blocks to busy Denman St.

The cutest of Denman Street's dozens of snack, meal, and caffeine options is 12 **Cupcakes,** which serves just that—in mini, regular, and "Big One" sizes, and almost 20 different flavors. *1168 Denman St.* ☎ *604/974-1300. www.cupcakes online.com. $.*

Cut across the intersection of Denman and Morton sts., then walk through the small triangular park toward the beach. At mid-park, look right to see:

13 **Eugenia Place.** One of Vancouver's most famous residential buildings, notable primarily for the 35-foot Oregon pin oak that grows from its circular rooftop terrace, 180 feet above street level. The building's architect, Richard Henriquez, included it as a tribute to the old-growth Douglas fir that once covered this area, and which grew as high as the Eugenia's top branches. 🕑 *5 min. 1919 Beach St.*

Thirsty? In the vine-covered Sylvia Hotel, 14 **Sylvia's Bar** is Vancouver's oldest cocktail lounge, a woody, comfortable spot offering great views over the bay. There's also a light afternoon snack menu. *1154 Gilford St.* ☎ *604/681-9321. www.sylviahotel.com. $.*

15 ★★★ **English Bay Beach.** The logs along this beach (also known as First Beach) are a natural theater for Vancouver's famous sunsets, while the park that runs its length is a haven for joggers, strollers, and picnickers. 🕑 *30 min., or as long as you want to linger. See p 12,* 12.

Walk east on Beach St. to:

16 **Alexandra Park.** Front and center of this pretty, triangular park is a little fountain dedicated to Joe Fortes, a Barbadian sailor who

Shopping addicts can get their retail fix (and then some) on Robson Street. See p 47.

The early-20th-century homes that make up Mole Hill are the only intact structures that date back to the original settlement of the West End. See p 50.

moved to the city in 1885, lived in a cottage on English Bay Beach, and became its unofficial (and later official) lifeguard and swimming instructor, teaching all the local kids. When he died in 1922, Vancouver held the largest public funeral in its history in his honor. The memorial is inscribed "Little Children Loved Him." At the center of the park, the Haywood Bandstand gazebo offers free concerts on Sunday afternoons (1–3pm), from June to August. ⏱ *10 min. On Beach Ave. btw. Burnaby & Bidwell sts.*

From the southeast edge of the park, at Bidwell, walk down to the waterline to see:

⑰ ★ The Inukshuk. Abstract human forms with outstretched arms, inuksuit have long been used by the Inuit as landmarks and navigation aids. More recently, they've become regional symbols of hospitality and are used as the emblem of the Vancouver 2010 Olympic Winter Games. This one, made by Alvin Kanak of Canada's northern Nunavut Territory, stands about 6m (20 ft.) tall and weighs almost 31,500kg (70,000 lb.). It was built for Expo '86, Vancouver's World's Fair. ⏱ *15 min. Located on English Bay, at Bidwell St.*

From here, walk up Bidwell St. 2 blocks and make a right onto Davie St., then walk another 2 blocks to:

⑱ The Gabriola. This mansion was the finest in the West End when it was built for sugar magnate B. T. Rogers in 1900. Twenty-five years later the neighborhood became less tony and it was turned first into an apartment house, then a restaurant. What was once a stately manor is

The immense inukshuk, symbol of the city's hospitality, was built for the 1986 World's Fair.

The glass-roofed atrium of the Provincial Law Courts.

now a Romano's Macaroni Grill. O fate! 🕐 *5 min. 1531 Davie St.*

Cut through the Gabriola's side garden to Nicola St., walk through the pocket park, make a right onto Pendrell St., and walk 3 blocks. At Bute St., follow the curve of the road left and walk 1 block to Comox St. Cross the block to the corner of Nelson Park and look down Comox (right) to see:

⑲ **Mole Hill.** This block, between Bute and Thurlow sts., opposite Nelson Park, contains the only intact stretch of houses dating from the original development in the West End, providing a view of what the whole area looked like in the early 20th century. Built primarily as rooming houses for laborers, the block's 36 homes are now run as a joint venture between BC Housing, the city, and the Mole Hill Community Housing Society, providing 168 rental units for low- and medium-income residents. The modern four-story building at the end of the block is the Dr. Peter Centre, BC's only day-health program and care residence for people with HIV/AIDS. 🕐 *15 min.*

Turn left on Thurlow St. and make a right on Nelson St., walking to Burrard St. and:

⑳ ★ **The Electra.** The former headquarters of BC Electric (today it houses mostly condos) is one of the great examples of 1950s West Coast modern architecture. 🕐 *10 min. 970 Burrard St.*

㉑ ★★ **The Provincial Law Courts.** One of Vancouver's most beautiful modern buildings, it's home to galleries, 35 courtrooms, and a number of public spaces. Its crowning glory (literally) is its glass roof, which covers an area nearly the size of an acre. 🕐 *15 min. See p 11,* ⑧.

㉒ ★ **Robson Square.** Part of the same complex as the Law Courts, this public plaza and garden helped define Vancouver's modern look. 🕐 *10 min. See p 11,* ⑦.

㉓ ★★ **The Vancouver Art Gallery.** Vancouver's premier fine art museum, originally a courthouse designed by Francis Rattenbury (1867–1935) and built between 1905 and 1913. The wide staircase, expansive lawn, and elaborate modern fountain at its West Georgia Street entrance are the site of frequent

Bill Reid

Born to a European-Canadian father and a Haida mother, Victoria native Bill Reid (1920–98) was the most famous Northwest Coast First Nations artist of the latter 20th century. Beginning as a jewelry-maker, Reid spent the 1950s rediscovering the complex principles of the region's traditional art, which at that time were all but lost. His subsequent works, including both jewelry and monumental bronze and cedar sculptures, are among the best known in the First Nations oeuvre. Some may be in your pocket right now: Four of his works are pictured on the C\$20 bill. Many of his best works are on display at the UBC Museum of Anthropology (p 16, ⑥) and the Bill Reid Gallery (p 26, ⑤).

protests and rallies. ⏱ *15 min. to see the building, 1½ hr. to see the art. See p 11,* ⑥.

Right across W. Georgia St. is:

㉔ ★ **The Pendulum Gallery.** A bit of well-known modern art and rotating temporary exhibitions. ⏱ *10–20 min. See p 27,* ⑥.

㉕ **Christ Church Cathedral.** Built between 1891 and 1895, this Anglican church was considered for demolition in the early 1970s to make room for a modern high-rise, but public outcry resulted in the Gothic Revival cathedral being named a city and provincial heritage building instead. Take a look inside to see its elaborate cedar wood beams and ceiling. ⏱ *15 min. 690 Burrard St. www.cathedral.vancouver.bc.ca.*

㉖ ★★ **The Bill Reid Gallery of Northwest Coast Art.** Master-works by Vancouver's most noted First Nations artist (1920–98), housed in a lovely courtyard setting. ⏱ *45 min. See p 26,* ⑤.

The elaborate stained-glass windows at Christ Church Cathedral depict various biblical scenes and Christian saints.

Gastown, Chinatown & Yaletown

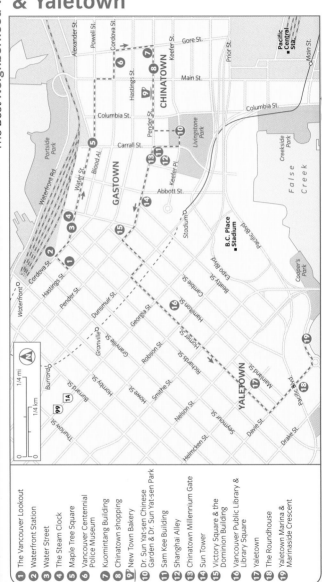

1 The Vancouver Lookout
2 Waterfront Station
3 Water Street
4 The Steam Clock
5 Maple Tree Square
6 Vancouver Centennial Police Museum
7 Kuomintang Building
8 Chinatown shopping
9 New Town Bakery
10 Dr. Sun Yat-sen Chinese Garden & Dr. Sun Yat-sen Park
11 Sam Kee Building
12 Shanghai Alley
13 Chinatown Millennium Gate
14 Sun Tower
15 Victory Square & the Dominion Building
16 Vancouver Public Library & Library Square
17 Yaletown
18 The Roundhouse
19 Yaletown Marina & Marinaside Crescent

In ultramodern Vancouver, this is as close as you get to seeing what the city was like more than a century ago. Gastown is its oldest section, with many buildings dating to the 1880s. Both Chinatown and Yaletown grew in the 1890s, the former as home to Chinese laborers who built the railroads, the latter as a commercial and industrial district around the Canadian Pacific's western terminus. Today Gastown is touristy, Chinatown gritty, and Yaletown yuppie—but a time machine nonetheless. START: **Corner of W. Hastings and Seymour sts.**

1 ★ The Vancouver Lookout. An enclosed, circular observation deck on the 28th floor of the Harbour Centre building (one of the city's tallest at 177m/581ft.), the Lookout offers 360-degree views of the city: East Vancouver, Gastown, and the rail yards to the east; Yaletown to the south; the mountains and Burrard Inlet to the north; and Downtown, English Bay, Stanley Park, and the distant coastal mountains to the west. ⏱ *45 min. 555 W. Hastings St.* ☎ *604/689-0421. www. vancouverlookout.com. C$13 adults, C$11 seniors, C$9 teens 13–18, C$6 kids 6–12. Mid-Oct to late Apr daily 9am–9pm, late Apr to mid-Oct daily 8:30am–10:30pm.*

Walk 1 block north on Seymour St. to:

2 Waterfront Station. Built by the Canadian Pacific Railway between 1912 and 1914, this handsome Beaux Arts building was converted in the late 1970s into a full-service, intermodal station where passengers can board the SeaBus ferries to North Vancouver and the SkyTrain and West Coast Express trains to the near and distant 'burbs. Duck inside to see its classic "Age of Rail" interior, with its high ceiling and supporting columns. Up near the ceiling, paintings depict scenes you might have witnessed when taking the train across Canada 100 years ago. Just ignore the Starbucks and Subway down at floor level. ⏱ *10 min. 601 W. Cordova St.*

Walk east on W. Cordova St. and bear left onto:

3 ★ Water Street. The central avenue of Gastown, Water Street is tourist central but it's also one of the city's oldest streets, lined with brick buildings that mostly date to the aftermath of the great 1886 fire

The Vancouver Lookout offers unparalleled 360-degree views of the city.

Exhibits at the Vancouver Centennial Police Museum range from weapons to uniforms to an old autopsy room!

that destroyed most of the city. In addition to kitschy souvenir shops, Water Street is also home to several notable galleries selling pricey First Nations art, including the Inuit Gallery, Marion Scott Gallery, and Spirit Wrestler Gallery (p 75). ⏱ *30–45 min. Btw. Richards & Carrall sts.*

❹ ★ **The Steam Clock.** This bit of street furniture draws its power from an underground steam system that heats many area buildings. Designed by local "horologist" Raymond L. Saunders and erected in 1977, it hoots a version of the Westminster chimes every 15 minutes as

Gastown's iconic Steam Clock vents every 15 minutes.

steam vents from its top. ⏱ *30 sec. if you're there when it whistles, longer if you have to wait. Northwest corner of Water & Cambie sts.*

❺ ★ **Maple Tree Square.** The central square (triangle, actually) of Gastown was named for the maple tree that stood here in the town's early days, but burned in the 1886 fire. Look here for a statue of Gassy Jack Deighton (the barkeep who gave the neighborhood its name) standing atop a whiskey barrel. Behind the statue is the Byrnes Block (2 Water St.), a brick Victorian Italianate building erected in 1886–87 by Victoria realtor George Byrnes. It's one of the oldest buildings in Vancouver. Across the square, the Hotel Europe (43 Powell St.) was the city's first reinforced-concrete building, dating to 1908–09. It's notable for its wedge shape, its large cornice, and its original Italian tilework. ⏱ *15 min. Intersection of Water, Carrall, Alexander & Powell sts.*

Walk 2 blocks east on Powell St., turn right onto Main, then left onto Cordova St. to the:

❻ ★ **Vancouver Centennial Police Museum.** Housed in the 1932 Coroner's Courtroom and Laboratory building, this old-fashioned little museum traces the history of the Vancouver Police Department back to May 1886, when John Stewart became the city's first constable. Displays contain every variety of weapons, drug paraphernalia, counterfeit currency, and police uniforms, but the creepy highlights are the old morgue and autopsy rooms, whose macabre displays will give you the willies. Weirdly, this is where Errol Flynn's autopsy was done, after he dropped dead after partying with his very young girlfriend in 1959. ⏱ *30–45 min. 240 E. Cordova St.* ☎ *604/665-3346. www.vancouverpolice museum.ca. C$7 adults, C$5 seniors & kids 6–18, kids under 6 free. Mon–Sat 9am–5pm.*

Continue east on Cordova and make a right onto Gore Ave. In another block you'll cross West Hastings St., which, between Gastown and Chinatown is grim and awful and full of crackheads, heroin and meth addicts, and other questionable characters. Busy enough that it's more-or-less safe in daylight hours, the street is still just soul-suckingly unpleasant, so cross it as fast as you can and try not to focus on the details. Continue to the corner of W. Pender St. and the:

The statue of Gassy Jack Deighton, Gastown's namesake, in Maple Tree Square.

A supermarket crammed with Chinese foodstuffs in Chinatown.

❼ Kuomintang Building. Also known as the Nationalist League building, this structure was built in 1920 as the western Canadian headquarters of Kuomintang, a Chinese political party that ruled much of China from 1928 until 1949, when it was defeated by the communists and retreated to Taiwan, forming that island's separate Chinese government. Note the Taiwanese flags on the roof. The building today marks the eastern edge of Vancouver's Chinatown. ⏱ *5 min. 296 E. Pender St.*

❽ ★ Chinatown shopping. Vancouver's Chinatown (centered on E. Pender and Keefer sts. btw. Carrall St. and Gore Ave.) is one of the largest in North America. Even though most of Vancouver's huge Asian population has moved out, many return here to shop, keeping the area vital and lively. Along Pender between Gore Street and Main Street, low-rise buildings house dozens of open-air shops selling dried seafood and fruit, teas, herbs, and other foodstuffs. Look for bins of lizard-on-a-stick. The **Kiu Shun Trading Co.** (269 E. Pender St.) is known for its traditional herbal cures. From Main Street to Columbia Street you'll find many shops selling Chinese knickknacks, housewares, and other items. The best of the bunch is **Bamboo Village** (135 E. Pender St.), stuffed to the rafters with Chinese lanterns, hats, furniture, antiques, etc. 🕐 *1 hr. E. Pender St., btw. Gore Ave. & Columbia St.*

For a quick bite, get in line with the old Chinese men and women at **9 New Town Bakery** for a steamed bun or sweet rice cake. *158 E. Pender St.* ☎ *604/689-7835. $.*

Continue west on Pender St. On the left, between Columbia and Carrall sts., you'll see an ornate, three-panel Chinese gate fronting the courtyard at the Chinese Cultural Centre. At the far end of the courtyard is the entrance to the:

10 ★★★ Dr. Sun Yat-Sen Chinese Garden & Dr. Sun Yat-Sen Park. Named in honor of "The Father of Modern China" and first president of the Republic of China, this classical garden and attached public park are the cultural highlight of Chinatown and one of Vancouver's best sites. 🕐 *1 hr. 578 Carrall St. See p 16,* **4**.

Continue west on Pender. Just beyond Carrall St., on the left, you'll see:

11 The Sam Kee Building. Called the world's narrowest (or more precisely, "least deep") commercial building, this thin slice of early Chinatown is some 95 ft. (29m) long but only 6 ft. (1.8m) front to back. It was built in 1913 by merchant Chang Toy (who owned the Sam Kee Company) to frustrate a rival businessman. The glass bricks in the sidewalk illuminate what was once a public bath house. 🕐 *5 min. 8 W. Pender St.*

12 Shanghai Alley. Shanghai Alley was the original street from which Chinatown grew in the late 19th century. Though not much to look at today, it was once home to more than 1,000 Chinese residents. At the end of the alley, the West Han Dynasty Bell was a gift from Vancouver's "twin" city of Guangzhou. The bell weighs in at just under a ton and bronze bands at its top bear the names of early residents. 🕐 *5 min. Off W. Pender St., btw. Carrall & Taylor sts.*

Just west of Shanghai Alley, on Pender St., is the:

13 Chinatown Millennium Gate. A symbol of Chinatown's past and future, this traditional ornamental gate (incorporating both eastern and western themes) was

The Dr. Sun Yat-Sen Chinese Garden is a beautiful haven no matter what time of year you visit.

The ornamental Chinatown Millennium Gate.

erected at the turn of the 20th century. Walk through it and then turn back around to get the intended "now entering Chinatown" effect— then say goodbye to Chinatown. ◷ *5 min. Pender St.*

Continue along a gritty stretch of Pender St. to the foot of Beatty St. and the:

⓮ **Sun Tower.** The one-time home of the *Vancouver World* and later the *Vancouver Sun* newspapers, this 17-story beaux-arts tower was, at its 1912 opening, the tallest building in the British Empire. Look up its hexagonal tower to the domed, green-patina roof, which was designed to be seen from every point where the *Vancouver World* was sold. Below, topping the main body of the building, is a cornice supported by nine topless muses. They caused quite a scandal back in the day. ◷ *5 min. Corner of W. Pender & Beatty sts.*

Continue 1 block further west on Pender St. to:

⓯ **Victory Square & the Dominion Building.** Site of BC's provincial courthouse until 1912, Victory Square was home to a recruiting center during World War I and is now dominated by a cenotaph erected in 1924 to commemorate Vancouver's war dead. At the park's northern edge, the 14-story, Second Empire–style Dominion Building was, like the newer Sun Tower, the British Empire's tallest when it went up in 1910. It was also the city's first steel-framed building, and is notable for its three-story mansard roof and sculpted terracotta detailing. ◷ *10 min. Park btw. W. Pender, Cambie, Hamilton & W. Hastings sts. Dominion Building at 207 W. Hastings.*

Chinatown's Night Market

On weekend nights in summer, Chinatown's Keefer Street (btw. Gore Ave. and Columbia St.) is transformed into a prototypical outdoor Asian market, lined with stalls selling clothing, food, jewelry, music, and other bargain merchandise. Feel free to bargain. For more information, call ☎ 604/682-8998. It's open Friday to Sunday 6:30pm to 11pm, mid-May through early September.

The elliptically shaped main branch of the Vancouver Public Library holds more than 1.3 million items in its collection.

Turn left onto Hamilton St. at the west end of the park. Turn right at Dunsmuir St., then left onto Homer St. At the next corner, cross the intersection to the:

16 ★ Vancouver Public Library & Library Square. One of the city's most distinctive and well-used public spaces, the library (designed by renowned Israeli-Canadian architect Moshe Safdie and opened in 1995) looks like a skewed Roman coliseum, one wall breaking free of

Victory Square, with the Dominion Building in the background.

the building's otherwise circular shape and spinning out in a wider arc, like the tail of a hurricane. A concourse takes up the space created by that errant wall, and is filled with cafes and shops; the library itself offers numerous workstations with free Internet access. ⏱ *10–15 min. 350 W. Georgia St.* ☎ *604/331-3603. www.vpl.ca/branches/details/central_library. Mon–Thurs 10am–9pm, Fri–Sat 10am–6pm, Sun noon–5pm.*

Exit at the other end of the library concourse, at the corner of Homer and Robson sts. Continue walking 2 blocks south on Homer to Nelson St. You're now at the northwest corner of:

17 ★★ Yaletown. This former warehouse district (centered on Hamilton, Mainline, and Davie sts.) is now Vancouver's trendiest neighborhood, mixing high-rise residential towers with old warehouse buildings that have been converted into restaurants, bars, galleries, offices, and many interesting shops and boutiques. It's the neighborhood where young urban professionals go to spawn, so expect lots of attractive young couples pushing baby carriages, and lots of high-style baby-gear shops. ⏱ *At least*

1 hr., more if you want to poke around all the options.

Walk south on either Hamilton St. or Mainline St. and make a left onto Davie St., walking past Pacific Blvd. to:

⑱ ★ **The Roundhouse.** This classic, circular industrial building was once the western terminus of the Canadian Pacific Railway, and today functions as a community arts and recreation center. A glass-walled pavilion at its western end holds Engine 374, a perfectly preserved steam locomotive that pulled the first transcontinental train into Vancouver in 1887. The engine retired in 1945, and was restored between 1983 and 1986. ⏱ *20–30 min. 181 Roundhouse Mews.* ☎ *604/713-1800. www.roundhouse.ca. Free admission, except for performances. Mon–Fri 9am–10pm, Sat–Sun 9am–5pm.*

Exit the Roundhouse and walk half a block further southeast to:

⑲ ★ **Yaletown Marina & Marinaside Crescent.** A lovely spot surrounded by high-rise condos, this is where Yaletown's well-heeled seamen keep their boats and where you can catch the ferry to Granville Island, if the mood strikes. At the

The Roundhouse's Engine 374, a perfectly preserved steam locomotive.

entrance to the Marina, Bernie Miller and Alan Tregebov's *Street Light* sculpture (1997) is an assembly of bronze I-beams supporting panels with images from Vancouver's past. On the anniversary of the events depicted, the sun's rays cast appropriate shadow images on the sidewalk. For other public art in this area, see p 29, ⑯–⑲. ⏱ *15–30 min. Intersection of Davie St. & Marinaside Crescent.*

The lovely Yaletown Marina is a great place for strolling, sunbathing, and taking in top-notch public art.

Kitsilano & Granville Island

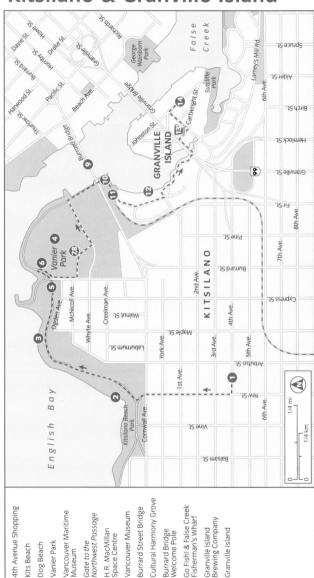

1 4th Avenue Shopping
2 Kits Beach
3 Dog Beach
4 Vanier Park
5 Vancouver Maritime Museum
6 Gate to the Northwest Passage
7 H.R. MacMillan Space Centre
8 Vancouver Museum
9 Burrard Street Bridge
10 Cultural Harmony Grove
11 Burrard Bridge Welcome Pole
12 Go Fish! & False Creek Fisherman's Wharf
13 Granville Island Brewing Company
14 Granville Island

The Downtown peninsula may be the city's heart, but it's not the be-all and end-all. Immediately across English Bay, Kitsilano (aka "Kits") is home to the city's most popular beach, great shopping, and fantastic restaurants. Between Kits and Downtown, the old industrial site of Granville Island is now packed with markets, art studio/galleries, shopping, comedy clubs, and theaters. START: **4th Ave. and Cypress St. (just west of Burrard St.).**

1 ★ 4th Avenue Shopping.
The 4 blocks of 4th Avenue between Cypress and Vine sts. (uphill in this direction) comprise one of Vancouver's densest and most enjoyable shopping stretches. Highlights include the inimitable Zulu Records (p 77), Ming Wo Cookware (p 76), Duthie Books (p 71), Coast Mountain Sports (p 77), and Wanderlust, selling travel gear, books, and maps (p 72). ⏲ *At least 1 hr.*

Après shopping, head north (downhill) on Yew St. to Cornwall Ave. and the entrance to:

2 ★★ kids Kits Beach. That's English Bay out in front of you, on the other side of all the sunbathers, joggers, volleyball and tennis players, and sun-seeking Vancouverites. To your left is the saltwater Kitsilano Pool, at 137 meters the largest of its kind in Canada. Beyond the water you can see the West End, with the snowcapped North Vancouver mountains far off in the distance. Start following the walking path east (right) along the sand, where logs have been placed for you to sit on. ⏲ *1 hr. The beach runs roughly from Yew to Maple St. Kits Pool is at 2305 Cornwall Ave.* ☎ *604/731-0011. Open mid-May to mid-Sept. Hours vary. Pool fees C$5 adults, C$3.45 seniors, C$3.70 teens, C$2.50 kids 6–12.*

Continue east along the path that edges the beach, following it around a wide, tree-lined curve. On your left you'll see:

Kits Beach is a wonderful place to soak up some sun while taking in gorgeous mountain views.

3 ★ Dog Beach. One of the happiest places in Vancouver, where the city's dog people bring their pups to chase each other around the sand, swim, and dig holes. ⏲ *30 min. for pugs, 8 hr. for Labs. Near the intersection of Maple St. & Ogden Ave., just before Vanier Park. http://vancouver.ca/parks/info/dog parks/index.htm.*

4 ★★ kids Vanier Park. Located just east of Kits Beach, Vanier Park feels miles removed from busy Downtown. Popular year-round with kite flyers, it gets very busy in summer when Bard on the Beach sets up its tents for the season (p 113). The park is also home to three major museums (see **5**–**7**). ⏲ *30–45 min. 1000 Chestnut St.* ☎ *604/257-8400. Bus: 2, 22. Also accessible*

Alan Chung's iconic Gate to the Northwest Passage.

from downtown via False Creek ferries from the Aquatic Centre, 1050 Beach Ave., at Thurlow.

5 ★ Vancouver Maritime Museum. Make sure to look at the museum's Small Boat Repair Dock, home to several historic boats and ships. This is also where you can catch the ferry to Downtown. *See p 20,* **4**.

Just beyond the museum, on the park's main lawn, you'll see:

6 ★ Gate to the Northwest Passage. This 4.6m (15-ft.) square of weathered Corten steel, peeled back from itself at its base, commemorates the arrival of Captain George Vancouver, the first European to explore the area, in 1792. Created by artist Alan Chung Hung and installed in 1980, the piece frames English Bay and the mountains beyond. ⏲ *5 min.*

7 ★ H.R. MacMillan Space Centre. *See p 38,* **6**.

8 The Vancouver Museum. In the same cone-shaped building as the Space Centre, the Vancouver Museum is literally that: a museum of Vancouver and its history from the boom years of the early 20th century up until today. The story is told through artifacts, dioramas, movies, photos, and objects set up in themed rooms, including one dedicated to the '50s and another to Vancouver's hippie era. Temporary displays focus on specific

A giant steel crab fountain (a Haida symbol of protection) marks the entrance to the H.R. MacMillan Space Centre.

Walking the Burrard Street Bridge at sunset is a quintessential Vancouver experience.

aspects of the city, past and present. ⏰ *45 min. 1100 Chestnut St.* ☎ *604/736-4431. www.vanmuseum. bc.ca. C$11 adults, C$9 seniors, C$7 kids 5–17. Tues–Sun 10am–5pm (until 9pm Thurs; open Mon July–Aug).*

Return to the shore walk and continue east into the parking lot, past the public boat ramp and the gray Canadian Coast Guard station. Take a look up as you pass below the:

⑨ ★ Burrard Street Bridge. Completed in 1932 and designed as a ceremonial gateway to the city (beyond its function of connecting the peninsula to the West Side), the bridge mixes a utilitarian steel span with large concrete towers embellished with Art Deco sculptural details. Walk across the bridge some other day (south to north) if you have time, preferably at sunset. ⏰ *2 min.*

After passing under the bridge, you'll see the:

⑩ Cultural Harmony Grove. This small park is planted with trees honoring winners of the city's Cultural Harmony Awards, which honor individuals and organizations that "display a significant and sustained commitment to the promotion of cultural harmony in the City of Vancouver." ⏰ *5 min. East of the Burrard Marina, at the south foot of the Burrard Street Bridge.*

Just a little farther along the path, on the right, you'll find the:

⑪ Burrard Bridge Welcome Pole. This totem pole depicts a traditional grandfatherly welcome figure of the Squamish people, his arms outstretched toward Granville Island and Yaletown. The Squamish village of Snauq once stood near this site. ⏰ *2 min. East of the Burrard Marina, at the south foot of the Burrard Street Bridge.*

Around the curve of the path, climb the stairway to the left (at the orientation sign) and walk along the path that runs between the parking lot and the parking garage of The Clipper building. At the end of the walkway, go up the short stairway into Creekside Park, a privately maintained park with a nice view of the marina and Downtown. Walk past the fountain and take the stairs down to the T intersection of 1st Ave. and Creekside Drive. Walk left past the blue tin shack into the parking lot for:

Chow down on some of the city's freshest seafood at Go Fish!

⑫ ★ Go Fish! & False Creek Fisherman's Wharf. *See p 34, ⑥.*

Continue along the pathway past Go Fish! and two residential buildings fronted by private lagoons. At Anderson St., follow the blue railing to the left onto Granville Island, the make a right onto Cartwright St.

Granville Island is home to a variety of street performers . . . and a lot of pigeons.

Drop in for a pint at the ⑬ **Granville Island Brewing Company,** probably Vancouver's best microbrewery. If you time it right, you can also take a tour of the brewery and taste four of their beers, including their current limited-release brew. *1441 Cartwright St.* ☎ *604/687-2739. www.gib.ca. Taproom daily noon–8pm. Tours at noon, 2pm & 4pm daily, C$9.75.*

The rest of your tour is free time on:

⑭ ★★★ **Granville Island.** Foodies can browse the giant Public Market (p 33, ①); art lovers can see the galleries at the Emily Carr Institute of Art & Design and along Railspur Alley (p 30, ㉑ and ㉒); shoppers can indulge at dozens of boutiques, knickknack shops, boating equipment suppliers, and other options; and everyone can enjoy the great post-industrial-but-somehow-natural location, the street performers, and the flocks of pigeons who circle the square outside the Public Market, descending when they spot a likely mark. ⏱ *2 hr., more if you take in a show. See p 13, ⑭.* ●

The Best Shopping

Vancouver **Shopping**

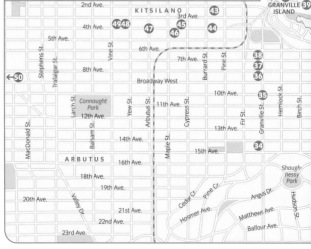

Previous page: Punjabi Market sells a variety of Indian merchandise, from saris to handbags.

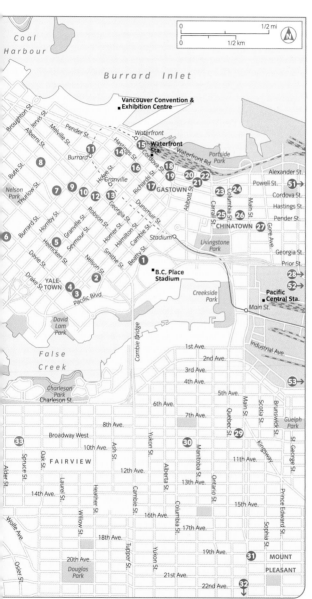

Coal Harbour

Burrard Inlet

Vancouver Convention & Exhibition Centre

Waterfront

Waterfront Sta.

Waterfront Rd

Portside Park

Alexander St.

Powell St. **51**→

Cordova St.

Hastings St.

Pender St.

23

24

GASTOWN

CHINATOWN **27**

15

14

11

Pender St.

Hastings St.

Cordova St.

Burrard

Broughton St.

Jervis St.

Melville St.

Alberni St.

Bute St.

8

Nelson Park

Thurlow St.

7

9

10

12

13

Howe St.

Granville

Richards St.

16

17

18

19

20

21

22

Abbott St.

Carrall St.

Columbia St.

Main St.

Gore St.

25

26

Georgia St.

Dunsmuir St.

Robson St.

Georgia St.

Homer St.

Hamilton St.

Cambie St.

Beatty St.

Stadium

Prior St.

28→

52→

Burrard St.

Hornby St.

Granville St.

Seymour St.

Smithe St.

Nelson St.

5

6

Davie St.

Helmcken St.

YALE-TOWN

4

3

2

1

B.C. Place Stadium

Livingstone Park

Creekside Park

Pacific Central Sta.

Main St.

Drake St.

Pacific Blvd.

David Lam Park

Cambie Bridge

False Creek

1st Ave.

2nd Ave.

3rd Ave.

4th Ave.

5th Ave.

6th Ave.

7th Ave.

8th Ave.

10th Ave.

Industrial Ave.

53→

Charleson Park

Charleson St.

Broadway West

33

FAIRVIEW

12th Ave.

Oak St.

Spruce St.

Alder St.

Wolfe Ave.

Osler St.

Ash St.

Heather St.

Laurel St.

Willow St.

Cambie St.

Yukon St.

14th Ave.

16th Ave.

18th Ave.

20th Ave.

Douglas Park

Tupper St.

Yukon St.

Alberta St.

Manitoba St.

Ontario St.

Columbia St.

Quebec St.

Main St.

Scotia St.

Brunswick St.

Kingsway

Prince Edward St.

Sophia St.

St. George St.

Guelph Park

11th Ave.

13th Ave.

15th Ave.

17th Ave.

19th Ave.

21st Ave.

22nd Ave.

29

30

31

MOUNT PLEASANT

32↓

0   1/2 mi

0   1/2 km

Shopping Best Bets

Best Place **to Prep for an Indian Wedding**
★ Punjabi Market, *Main St., btw. 49th & 50th sts. (p 69)*

Best **Radical Bookstore**
★ People's Co-Op Bookstore, *1391 Commercial Dr. (p 72)*

Best Place **for Chinese Herbal Cures**
★★ Kiu Shun Trading Co., *261–269 Keefer St. (p 73)*

Best Store **for a Rainy Day**
★★ The Umbrella Shop, *1106 W. Broadway (p 74)*

Best Place **for Recycled Furniture**
★★ Industrial Artifacts, *132 Powell St. (p 71)*

Bamboo Village is covered from floor to ceiling with Chinese knickknacks.

Best **Big-Name, Big-Label Shopping**
★★★ Robson Street, *btw. Hornby & Jervis sts. (p 69)*

Best Place **for First Nations Art**
★★★ Water St., *in Gastown (p 70)*

Best Shop **for Outdoors & Sports Gear**
★★★ Coast Mountain Sports, *2201 West. 4th Ave. (p 77)*

Best **Rock/Pop Record Shop**
★ Zulu Records, *1972 W. 4th Ave. (p 77)*

Best Place **for Cookbooks**
★★★ Barbara Jo's Books to Cooks, *1740 W. 2nd Ave. (p 71)*

Best Place **for Skateboards**
★★ Shops at intersection of Fourth & Burrard sts. *(p 78)*

Best **Camera Shop**
★★★ Leo's Camera Supply, *1055 Granville St. (p 72)*

Best **Canadian Kitsch Outlet**
Hudson House Trading Co., *321 Water St. (p 72)*

Best **for Pampering**
★★ Farfalla, *57 E. Cordova St. (p 76)*

Best **Classic Department Store**
★ The Bay, *674 Granville St. (p 76)*

Best **Chinese Cookware**
★ Ming Wo Cookware, *23 E. Pender St. (p 76)*

Best **for High-Design Chinese Furniture & Gifts**
★★ Peking Lounge, *83 E. Pender St. (p 73)*

Best **for Chinese Knickknacks**
★ Bamboo Village, *135 E. Pender St. (p 73)*

Vancouver Shopping A to Z

A-List Shopping Neighborhoods

★★ Commercial Drive EAST VANCOUVER
Lest you leave Vancouver thinking it's all high-end swank and trendy coffee bars, visit Commercial Drive, where old and new counterculture mix with old-world Italian cafes, Jamaican food stores, Portuguese social clubs, and a slew of interesting boutiques and shops. *Btw. E. 6th Ave. & Venables St. SkyTrain: Broadway Station. Bus: 99B, 10, 16. Map p 66.*

★★ 4th Avenue KITSILANO
Vancouver's original hippie neighborhood grew up a long time ago, and now offers a wonderful 6-block shopping stretch full of new and used clothing shops, bookstores, and furniture and housewares stores for the happy West Sider—plus lots of coffee shops and restaurants. *Btw. Balsam & Burrard sts. www.kitsilano4thavenue.com. Bus: 4, 7, 44. Map p 66.*

★★★ Granville Island
See p 13, ⑭. Bus: 50. Ferries: Aquabus or False Creek (p 13, ⑬). Map p 66.

★★ Main Street EAST VANCOUVER
Head to Main Street (on the border between East Van and the West Side) for funky clothing boutiques and the city's "Antique Row" stores (p 70), all crammed into a 10-block stretch. *Main St., btw. 19th & 29th aves. Bus: 3. Map p 66.*

★ Punjabi Market WEST SIDE
Canada gives way to India along 2 short blocks on an otherwise uninteresting stretch of Main St. Shops selling Indian ethnic clothing, jewelry, bridal goods, housewares, and knickknacks are interspersed with Hindi video stores, cafes, and

For unique boutique shopping and interesting food options, head for Commercial Drive.

restaurants. *Main St., btw. 49th & 51st aves. Bus: 3. Map p 66.*

★★★ Robson Street WEST END
This is the best location in town for big-name, big-label shopping, with dozens of shops crammed into just a few blocks. Expect lots of clothing (Ferragamo, Bebe, Roots, Armani, Hilfiger, etc.), big music retailers such as HMV, and lots of places to caffeinate. *Robson St., btw. Hornby & Jervis sts. Bus: 5. Map p 66.*

★★★ South Granville Rise
SOUTH GRANVILLE High-end shops stand shoulder to shoulder along 11 blocks of Granville St., south of False Creek. Expect lots of housewares (from Oriental rugs to kitchen gear), clothing boutiques, and interesting knickknack shops. Vancouver's "Gallery Row" (p 31, ㉔) stretches from 5th Ave. to Broadway,

Vancouver's Antique Row

On the West Side, the stretch of Main Street between 16th and 33rd avenues is Vancouver's number-one neighborhood for antiques, from traditional 18th- and 19th-century furniture through trendy modern retro items from the 1950s, '60s, and '70s. Standouts include **A Baker's Dozen** (3520 Main St.; ☎ 604/879-3348), **Vancouver Architectural Antiques** (north of the main row at 2403 Main St.; ☎ 604/872-3131), **Sugar Barrel Antiques** (4514 Main St.; ☎ 604/876-5234), and **Second Time Around** (4428 Main St.; ☎ 604/879-2313). Bus: 3.

with numerous world-class art galleries. *Granville St., btw. 5th & 16th aves. www.southgranville.org Bus: 98B, 10. Map p 66.*

★★★ **Water Street** GASTOWN Water St. is basically a funnel into which the cruise ships that dock at Canada Place pour their passengers, but it still offers more than the usual tourist shops. It's got several of the best shops in town selling quality First Nations art (p 74), plus numerous interior design and clothing shops catering to Vancouver's moneyed professionals. *Water St., btw. Waterfront Station & Carrall St. Bus: 50. SkyTrain: Waterfront Station. Map p 66.*

Antiques & Recycled Furniture

★ **A Baker's Dozen Antiques** EAST VANCOUVER   One of the city's "Antique Row" shops, specializing in 19th-century furniture, paintings, folk art, and antique toys. *3520 Main St. ☎ 604/879-3348. AE, MC, V. Bus: 3. Map p 66.*

★★★ **Antique Market Warehouse** EAST VANCOUVER   This Antique Row mainstay moved north a while back, into larger digs that can better accommodate its huge stock of antique furniture, architectural salvage (stained-glass windows, wrought iron gates, etc.), Chinese

For a good assortment of 19th-century furniture and art, try A Baker's Dozen Antiques.

antiques, etc. *1324 Franklin St.* ☎ *604/875-1434. www.anantique market.com. MC, V. Bus: 10, 16, 4, 7. Map p 66.*

★★ Industrial Artifacts GAS-TOWN   One of a growing number of shops that are taking the detritus of civilization (crosswalk lights, gears, reclaimed wood) and recycling it into remarkable high-design furniture and housewares. *132 Powell St.* ☎ *604/874-7797. www.industrialartifacts. com. AE, MC, V. Bus: 50. Map p 66.*

★★ Mihrab SOUTH GRANVILLE   This gallery of Eastern exotica features antiques, furniture, architectural pieces, and modern design pieces from India and Indonesia, all personally selected by the owners. *2229 Granville St.* ☎ *604/879-6105. www.mihrabgallery.com. AE, MC, V. Bus: 98B, 10. Map p 66.*

★★★ Shaughnessy Antique Gallery SOUTH GRANVILLE   One of Vancouver's best-known antique outlets, with displays of China, furniture, silver, Asian pieces, 1950s–'70s retro, and general knickknacks from some 30 different dealers. *3025 Granville St.* ☎ *604/739-8413. www.shaughnessy antiquegallery.com. MC, V. Bus: 98B, 10. Map p 66.*

Books
★★★ Barbara Jo's Books to Cooks WEST SIDE   A cookbook mecca, stocking thousands of cookbooks, wine books, and periodicals from around the world, for both amateurs and professionals. Cooking classes and recipe demos from featured books are presented in the open kitchen along the back wall. *1740 West 2nd Ave.* ☎ *604/688-6755. www.bookstocooks.com. Second location in the Net Loft building on Granville Island. AE, MC, V. Bus: 44 (for 2nd Ave. shop). Map p 66.*

Browse the selections at Duthie Books if you want to shop for general interest books in a comfy and informal atmosphere.

★ Bibliophile Bookshop EAST VANCOUVER   Cozy used bookstore along Commercial Drive, with a resident cat to keep things earthy. *2010 Commercial Dr.* ☎ *604/254-5520. MC, V. Bus: 99B, 10, 16. SkyTrain: Broadway Station. Map p 66.*

★★ Duthie Books KITSILANO   Established in 1957, Duthie's offers a good general selection in a comfortable, uncluttered atmosphere along Kitsilano's main shopping stretch. *2239 W. 4th Ave.* ☎ *604/732-5344. www.duthiebooks.com. AE, MC, V. Bus: 4, 7, 44. Map p 66.*

★★ Kidsbooks KITSILANO   Vancouver's largest and most interesting selection of children's books, plus toys, games, craft kits, and puppets. Check their website for a schedule of readings. *3083 W. Broadway.* ☎ *604/738-5335. www.kidsbooks.ca. AE, MC, V. Bus: 99B, 9. Map p 66.*

MacLeod's Books DOWNTOWN   One of those dusty, totally chaotic, books-stacked-everywhere used-tome shops—the kind book lovers can dig through for hours. *455 W. Pender St.* ☎ *604/681-7654. MC, V. Bus: 6. Map p 66.*

Leo's Camera Supply has been catering to shutterbugs for more than 50 years.

★ People's Co-Op Bookstore

EAST VANCOUVER   Open since 1945, this little shop carries books and periodicals dealing with left-leaning politics, social justice, environmental responsibility, and related topics. Viva la revolucion! *1391 Commercial Dr.* ☎ *604/253-6442. www. peoplescoopbookstore.com. MC, V. Bus: 99B, 10, 16. Map p 66.*

★ Wanderlust, the Traveler's Store
KITSILANO   This exceptionally large travel store stocks Frommer's, of course, but it also stocks a huge selection of travel literature, phrase books, and many, many specialized local and regional guides—plus luggage, maps, and travel accessories too. *1929 W. 4th Ave.* ☎ *604/739-2182. www. wanderlustore.com. AE, DC, MC, V. Bus: 4, 7, 44. Map p 66.*

Cameras
★ Dunne & Rundle
DOWNTOWN Large selection of digital and film cameras, plus lenses, bags, tripods, and other accessories. *595 Burrard St., in the Bentall Shopping Centre.* ☎ *604/681-9254. www.dunneand rundle.com. AE, DC, MC, V. Bus: 2, 22. SkyTrain: Burrard Station. Map p 66.*

★★★ Leo's Camera Supply

DOWNTOWN   In business for more than 50 years, Leo's has a reputation as one of western Canada's very best photo shops, with everything from point-and-shoots to large-format film cameras and darkroom equipment. *1055 Granville St.* ☎ *604/685-5331. www.leoscamera.com. MC, V. Bus: 50. Map p 66.*

Canadian Kitsch
Hudson House Trading Co.

GASTOWN   What corny Canadian item do you want? Maple syrup and cookies? Smoked salmon? Toy inuk-suit? Moose teddy bears? Pretty much any item of clothing emblazoned with a maple leaf? Look no further. *321 Water St.* ☎ *604/687-4781. AE, DC MC, V. Bus: 50. SkyTrain: Waterfront Station. Map p 66.*

Michelle's Import Plus
GASTOWN   Hudson House doesn't have that moose T-shirt in your size? Try here. Their selection is nearly identical. *73 Water St.* ☎ *604/687-5930. AE, MC, V. Bus: 50. SkyTrain: Waterfront Station. Map p 66.*

If you're looking for that perfect kitschy souvenir, you can't do better than Hudson House.

Mounted Police Post GASTOWN
This little shop near Waterfront Station stocks all things Royal Canadian Mounted Police: clothing, books, teddy bears (in RCMP uniforms, of course), knickknacks, etc. Too corny. Too cute. *767 W. Cordova St. ☎ 604/605-5557. www.mountieshop.com. AE, MC, V. Bus: 50. SkyTrain: Waterfront Station. Map p 66.*

Chinese Goods

★ **Bamboo Village** CHINATOWN
Chinatown's best selection of Chinese stuff: lanterns, furniture, antiques, Mao kitsch, china, drums and gongs, and thousands of other items, crammed floor to rafters into a long storefront. *135 E. Pender St. ☎ 604/662-3300. AE, MC, V. Bus 19, 22. Map p 66.*

★★ **Kiu Shun Trading Co.**
CHINATOWN Back bothering you? Sore throat? Chi a little off? Kiu Shun might be able to help. Established here in 1977 (but extending back more than 130 years as a family business), it advocates a holistic approach to health, seeking to keep all the body's functions in balance. Staff will recommend herbal treatments for what ails you, and there's also an acupuncturist working on site. *261–269 Keefer St. ☎ 604/682-2621 MC, V. Bus 19, 22. Map p 66.*

★★ **Peking Lounge** CHINATOWN
Much more high-style than your average Chinatown shop, Peking Lounge is a place where century-old furniture is displayed beside pieces by modern Chinese designers—from modern reinterpretations of traditional lanterns to Buddha throw pillows in bright, Pop Art colors. *83 E. Pender St. ☎ 604/844-1559. www.pekinglounge.com. MC, V. Bus 19, 22. Map p 66.*

All are encouraged to try on the many options for sale at the very fun Edie Hats.

Clothing, Shoes & Accessories

★ **Basquiat** YALETOWN Like its namesake artist Jean-Michel Basquiat (though unlike his graffiti art), this chic boutique offers upscale European and American fashion that's "classic with an edge," with clothing and accessories for both men and women. *1189 Hamilton St. ☎ 604/688-0828. AE, MC, V. Bus: 6, C21, C23. Map p 66.*

★ **Edie Hats** GRANVILLE ISLAND
Hat shops are almost inherently fun, and this one definitely is, with an interior like a little social parlor and hats for men and women stacked everywhere. Go ahead—try one on. *The Net Loft Building, 1666 Johnston St. ☎ 604/683-4280. http://ediehats. com. AE, MC, V. Bus: 50. Ferries: Aquabus or False Creek (p 13, ⑬). Map p 66.*

★ **Gravity Pope Tailored Goods** KITSILANO Shoes and clothing for men and women by hard-to-find and independent designers. The space is totally hip and minimalist, with a white Carrara marble floor and lighting fixtures from a 1920s ocean liner. *2203 4th*

Ave. ☎ 604/731-7647. www.gravity
pope.com. AE, DC, MC, V. Bus: 4, 7,
44. Map p 66.

★★ John Fluevog Boots &
Shoes GASTOWN   Vancouver's
own avatar of funky footwear
opened this over-the-top store in
2008, a cavernous space with a
glass roof 14m (45 ft.) up, brick
walls to either side, and views of the
North Vancouver mountains out the
back. The main floor could fit 10,000
shoes instead of the few carefully
chosen and oh-so-hip pairs on display. The second floor contains the
Fluevog Design Studio. *65 Water St.*
☎ *604/688-6228. www.fluevog.com.
AE, MC, V. Bus: 50. SkyTrain: Waterfront Station. Map p 66.*

★ Livestock GASTOWN   A youth-
oriented store selling colorful limited-
edition sneakers plus custom T-shirts,
hoodies, and accessories. *239 Abbott
St.* ☎ *604/685-1433. www.dead
stock.ca. AE, MC, V. Bus: 50. SkyTrain:
Waterfront Station. Map p 66.*

★★ Maiwa Handprints
GRANVILLE ISLAND   Imported, natu-
rally dyed, and block-printed silk,
linen, and cotton clothing for women,
plus embroidered handbags, amazing
bedding, and other textiles. The company is run on an ethical business
model, with artisans paid a large
advance and given full artistic control
over their work. *Net Loft Building,
1666 Johnston St.* ☎ *604/669-3939.
www.maiwa.com. MC, V. Bus: 50.
Ferries: Aquabus or False Creek
(p 13, ⑬). Map p 66.*

★ Tilley Endurables SOUTH
GRANVILLE   Long-wearing and func-
tional (if not particularly fashionable)
travel clothing and accessories for
men and women. Need a UPF 50+
sun hat, zip-off trekking pants, or
quick-dry travel underwear? Here ya
go. *2401 Granville St.* ☎ *604/732-
4287. www.tilleyvancouver.com. AE,
MC, V. Bus: 98B, 10. Map p 66.*

★★ The Umbrella Shop
GRANVILLE ISLAND   Established in
1932 by Polish immigrant Isadore
Flader, Vancouver Umbrella (this
store's parent company) is both a
manufacturer and retailer, with
several stores selling all different
designs—from the most staid black
bumbershoot to the most colorful
floral print. *Factory Store 1106 W.
Broadway.* ☎ *604/669-9444. www.
theumbrellashop.com. Second location on Granville Island, in front of
Kids Market (*☎ *604/697-0919). AE,
MC, V. Bus: 9, 17. Map p 66.*

Cigars & Tobacco
★ La Casa del Habano DOWN-
TOWN   You're in Canada. Cuban
cigars are legal here—hundreds of
different kinds. Go to town. *402
Hornby St.* ☎ *604/609-0511. www.
havanahouse.com. AE, DC, MC, V.
Bus: 2, 22. Map p 66.*

★ Vancouver Cigar Co. DOWN-
TOWN   Another major Cuban cigar
importer, selling Cohibas, Monte-
cristos, and all the others that send
U.S. conservatives into a Cold War
tizzy. *780 Beatty St.* ☎ *604/685-0445.
www.vancouvercigar.com. AE, DC,
MC, V. Bus: C21, C23, 15. Map p 66.*

First Nations Art
★★ Coastal Peoples Fine Arts
Gallery YALETOWN/GASTOWN
Museum-quality sculpture, masks,
glasswork, jewelry, and more by
Northwest Coast First Nations and
Inuit artists—both older carvers and
younger artists who are pushing traditional forms. *1024 Mainland St.*
☎ *604/685-9298. Also at 312 Water
St.* ☎ *604/684-9222. www.coastal
peoples.com. AE, MC, V. Bus: 6. Map
p 66.*

★★ Douglas Reynolds Gallery
SOUTH GRANVILLE   Historic and
contemporary Northwest Coast
First Nations Art, nestled among the

contemporary art galleries of Gallery Row (p 31, ㉔). *2335 Granville St. ☎ 604/731–9292. www.douglas reynoldsgallery.com. AE, MC, V. Bus: 98B, 10. Map p 66.*

★★★ Eagle Spirit Gallery

GRANVILLE ISLAND   This museum-like gallery specializes in original (and very pricey) Northwest Coast First Nations and Inuit art, including hand-carved masks, argillite stone carvings, and paintings. *1803 Maritime Mews. ☎ 604/801-5205. www.eaglespiritgallery.com. AE, MC, V. Bus: 50. Ferries: Aquabus or False Creek (p 13, ⑬). Map p 66.*

Hills Native Art GASTOWN   More touristy than the other galleries listed here, Hill's stocks both quality First Nations artwork and cheaper pieces such as mini–totem polls. *165 Water St. ☎ 604/685-4249. www.hills nativeart.com. AE, DC, MC, V. Bus: 50. SkyTrain: Waterfront Station. Map p 66.*

★★★ Inuit Gallery of Vancouver

GASTOWN   Another of Vancouver's top galleries for First Nations art, the Inuit Gallery specializes in fine Inuit sculpture from the Arctic regions, plus Inuit prints and original drawings and traditional and contemporary works by Northwest Coast First Nations artists. *206 Cambie St. ☎ 604/688-7323. www.inuit.com. AE, MC, V. Bus: 50. SkyTrain: Waterfront Station. Map p 66.*

★★★ Marion Scott Gallery

GASTOWN   Founded in 1975, the Marion Scott Gallery is another of Vancouver's best, mounting shows by First Nations artists from Canada's northern territories and publishing exhibit catalogs that are first rate. *308 Water St. ☎ 604/685-1934. www.marionscottgallery.com. AE, MC, V. Bus: 50. SkyTrain: Waterfront Station. Map p 66.*

★ Spirit Wrestler Gallery

GASTOWN   Spirit Wrestler is different than the city's other galleries in that it displays museum-quality works from New Zealand Maori artists as well as Inuit and Northwest Coast First Nations art. *47 Water St. ☎ 604/669-8813. www.spirit wrestler.com. AE, MC, V. Bus: 50. SkyTrain: Waterfront Station. Map p 66.*

Gifts, Housewares & Knickknacks

Ainsworth Custom Design

GRANVILLE ISLAND   Interesting modern knickknacks, handcrafted jewelry, cards, and accessories from local designers. *1243 Cartwright St. ☎ 604/682-8838. MC, V. Bus: 50. Ferries: Aquabus or False Creek (p 13, ⑬). Map p 66.*

★★ Chachkas SOUTH GRANVILLE

A wonderful store stocking refined, high-design home and kitchenware, jewelry, handbags, handmade glass, and other objets d'art. *2423 Granville St. ☎ 604/688-6417. www.chachkas. ca. AE, MC, V. Bus: 98B, 10. Map p 66.*

The Marion Scott Gallery is a first-rate choice for those seeking pieces by First Nations artists.

★ Circle Craft Co-Operative

GRANVILLE ISLAND Works by 200 craftspeople from across British Columbia are for sale here, everything from blown glass and handmade jewelry to dolls and toys. *Net Loft Building, 1666 Johnston St.* ☎ *604/669-8021. www.circlecraft. net. AE, MC, V. Bus: 50. Ferries: Aquabus or False Creek (p 13, ⑬). Map p 66.*

★★ Farfalla GASTOWN What

began as a monogramming shop has expanded into a full-service pampering center, offering handmade Italian soaps, French linens, Russian tea, European bath and beauty items, woven goods, and more. There's even an on-site tearoom. *57 E. Cordova St.* ☎ *604/215-8707. www.shop farfalla.ca. MC, V. Bus: 50. SkyTrain: Waterfront Station. Map p 66.*

★ Inhabit YALETOWN This high-

end "Yaletown lifestyle" shop offers high-design home furniture and accessories, primarily targeted toward couples and their urban kids. *1188 Hamilton St.* ☎ *604/662-7408. www.inhabitshop.com. AE, MC, V. Bus: 6. Map p 66.*

For cute accessories targeted at urban families, march your credit card to Inhabit.

★ Ming Wo Cookware CHINA-

TOWN/KITSILANO Opened as a hardware store in 1917, family-owned Ming Wo turned exclusively to cookware in the mid-1960s and now offers an amazing variety of Asian and Western kitchen supplies for both home and professional cooks. *23 E. Pender St.* ☎ *604/683-7268. www. mingwo.com. Also at 2170 W. 4th Ave., Kitsilano (*☎ *604/737-2624). MC, V. Bus 19, 22. Map p 66.*

★★ Vancouver Art Gallery

Shop DOWNTOWN Off the Art Gallery's main lobby, this store stocks works related to the museum's current exhibits as well as paper goods, jewelry, designer giftware, and art books. *750 Hornby St.* ☎ *604/662-4706. www.vanartgallery.bc.ca. AE, MC, V. Bus: 5. Map p 66.*

Jewelry

★★★ Birk's DOWNTOWN Sort of the Tiffany's of Canada, Birks is a beloved institution that's also got some conscience: It has a policy against "conflict diamonds," sourced in war zones to finance the fighting. Its classic, Romanesque Vancouver store dates to 1913. *698 W. Hastings St.* ☎ *604/669-3333. www.birks.com. AE, MC, V. Bus: 10, 6. SkyTrain: Granville Station. Map p 66.*

Markets, Malls & Department Stores

★ The Bay DOWNTOWN The department store arm of the centuries-old Hudson's Bay Company, The Bay is an old-fashioned, full-service department store occupying a grand city-block-sized building dating to 1927, its terra cotta exterior sporting dozens of Corinthian columns. The store's "Hudson's Bay Traditional Point Blanket" has been on sale since 1779. *674 Granville St.* ☎ *604/681-6211. www.thebay.com. AE, MC, V. Bus: 50. SkyTrain: Granville Station. Map p 66.*

★★★ **Granville Island Public Market** GRANVILLE ISLAND   See p 33, **1**. *Map p 66.*

★★ **Kids Market** GRANVILLE ISLAND   Like a little mall for kids, this market is home to 25 different shops selling toys, crafts, kids' books, and other stuff, plus play areas, a train caboose, a pond, a next-door water park, and such services as a kids' hairdresser. *1496 Cartwright St.* ☎ *604/689-8447. www.kidsmarket. ca. Shops accept major credit cards. Bus: 50. Ferries: Aquabus or False Creek (p 13, **13**). Map p 66.*

★ **Pacific Centre Mall** DOWN-TOWN   This huge Downtown complex contains more than 100 stores, including H&M, Holt Renfrew, Hugo Boss, Club Monaco, Crabtree & Evelyn, and Coach. *700 W. Georgia St. www.pacificcentre.ca. Shops accept major credit cards. Bus: 50. Map p 66.*

Music (Recorded)

★ **Audiopile** EAST VANCOUVER   New and used CDs, LPs, and music memorabilia, with a helpful, knowledgeable staff. *2016 Commercial Dr.* ☎ *604/253-7453. www.audiopile. com. AE, MC, V. Bus: 99B, 10, 16. Sky-Train: Broadway Station. Map p 66.*

Highlife Records & Music EAST VANCOUVER   This little place stocks world music, jazz, and select "other" styles, plus a small selection of instruments and accessories (guitar strings, picks, etc.). *1317 Commercial Dr.* ☎ *604/251-6964. www.highlife world.com. MC, V. Bus: 99B, 10, 16. Map p 66.*

★ **HMV** DOWNTOWN   The big commercial record store in town, with all the hits, the back catalog, and lots of DVDs. *788 Burrard St.* ☎ *604/669-2289. www.hmv.ca. AE, MC, V. Bus: 5, 6. Map p 66.*

You can still get an actual LP at Zulu Records, one of the city's best music stores.

★ **Red Cat Records** EAST VANCOUVER   One of those great little independent shops beloved of music-heads, Red Cat stocks an eclectic selection of current releases plus new and used older CDs and LPs. *4307 Main St.* ☎ *604/708-9422. www.redcat.ca. AE, MC, V. Bus: 3. Map p 66.*

★ **Zulu Records** KITSILANO   Always on the "city's best" lists, Zulu stocks CDs and LPs with a pop/rock focus and a drizzling of R&B, electronica, jazz, and others for good measure. *1972 W. 4th Ave.* ☎ *604/ 738-3232. www.zulurecords.com. AE, MC, V. Bus: 4, 7, 44. Map p 66.*

Outdoor & Sporting Gear
★★★ **Coast Mountain Sports** KITSILANO   One of Vancouver's best stores for outdoor gear, with a massive selection, great quality, and a helpful staff. *2201 W. 4th Ave.* ☎ *604/731-6181. www.coast mountain.com. AE, MC, V. Bus: 4, 7, 44. Map p 66.*

Board in Vancouver

Skateboarders and snowboarders should head to the corner of W. 4th and Burrard St. on the West Side, which has been taken over completely by shops selling boards, clothing, and accessories. Major stores here include **Comor** (1980 Burrard St.; ☎ 604/736-7547; www. comorsports.com), **Pacific Boarder** (1793 W. 4th Ave.; ☎ 604/734-7245; www.pacificboarder.com), **Westbeach** (1766 W. 4th Ave.; ☎ 604/731-6449; www.westbeach.com), and **The Boardroom** (1745 W. 4th Ave.; ☎ 604/734-7669; www.boardroomshop.com).

★★★ Mountain Equipment Co-op
WEST SIDE MEC is the largest retail co-operative in Canada, selling its own gear plus hardcore and leisure gear from other top manufacturers. Their store takes up a city block, and the area around it has sprouted so many like-minded stores it's become known as "fleece row." *130 W. Broadway.* ☎ *604/872-7858. www.mec.ca. MC, V. Bus: 9. Map p 66.*

Wine
★ Marquis Wine Cellars
DOWNTOWN Located in the heart of Vancouver's gay community, Marquis is a good neighborhood wine shop with a large selection of BC wines. *1034 Davie St.* ☎ *604/684-0445. www.marquis-wines.com. AE, MC, V. Bus: 6. Map p 66.*

★★ Sutton Place Wine Merchant
DOWNTOWN *See p 35,* ⑨. *Bus: 2, 22. Map p 66.*

★ Taylorwood Wines
YALETOWN A good assortment of BC wines and complimentary tastings every Thursday and Sunday highlight this shop's solid general selection and comfortable atmosphere. *1185 Mainland St.* ☎ *604/408-9463. www.taylorwood wines.com. AE, MC, V. Bus: 6. Map p 66.* ●

Attend a complimentary tasting before snapping up some great BC vintages at Taylorwood Wines.

The Great Outdoors

West Side Parks & Gardens

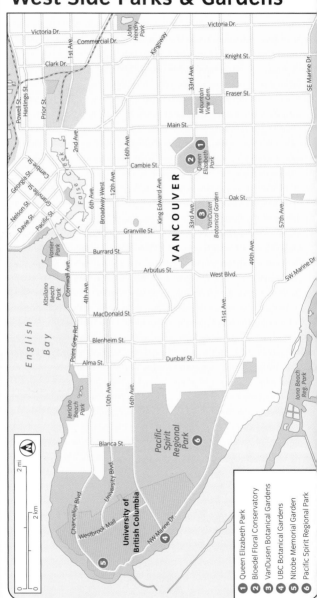

1. Queen Elizabeth Park
2. Bloedel Floral Conservatory
3. VanDusen Botanical Gardens
4. UBC Botanical Gardens
5. Nitobe Memorial Garden
6. Pacific Spirit Regional Park

Previous page: A view of the North Shore mountains from the Stanley Park Seawall.

Vancouver has more than 200 parks in total, from m. such as Stanley Park to little city-block parks like Barclay He. itage Square (p 47, ⑪). By far the largest number is located in the city's West Side, stretching from Queen Elizabeth Park in the east to the University of British Columbia gardens in the west. Serious park-and garden-hounds can hit several of the top spots in 1 day. Stops 1, 2, and 3 are all located within easy walking distance of each other, while stops 4, 5, and 6 are bunched within a short drive or bus ride to the west. START: **Queen Elizabeth Park.**

① ★★ Queen Elizabeth Park.
What was once a basalt quarry gar-den (whose rock was used to create many of the city's roads) has been transformed over decades into a beautiful, flower-filled municipal park. Note that it's not named for Queen Elizabeth II, as many pre-sume, but for her mother, who visited Vancouver with King George VI in 1939 and helped dedicate the site. *See p 21,* ⑧. *Bus: 15.*

② ★ Bloedel Floral Conservatory. Spend some time smelling the flowers and spotting the numerous birds that live in this huge plexiglass dome. *See p 22,* ⑨. *Bus: 15.*

③ ★★★ VanDusen Botanical Gardens. Created between 1971 and 1975 on part of the old Shaugh-nessy Golf Course grounds, this

The VanDusen Botanical Gardens are home to more than 7,500 plant types from around the world.

gorgeous botanical garden is home to more than 255,000 plants, includ-ing a first-rate collection of rhodo-dendrons. *See p 22,* ⑩. *Bus: 15.*

The plexiglass dome of the Bloedel Floral Conservatory overlooks some of the tulip gardens in Queen Elizabeth Park.

Tourist Trap Alert

You'll see tourist lit about the **Capilano Suspension Bridge** (www.capbridge.com)—a wobbly 135m (443-ft.) wooden-plank span suspended by steel cables high above the Capilano River in North Vancouver—all over town. I say "don't bother."

4 ★★ **UBC Botanical Garden.**
Located along the southern coast of the University of British Columbia campus, this 43-hectare (106-acre) expanse includes several distinct gardens (alpine, Asian, BC native, food, medicinal, and winter gardens) containing some 8,000 different plant types. This is a true horticulturist's garden, home to extensive research, preservation, and development activities. For a bird's-eye view of the forest canopy there's a system of eight platforms linked by a 308m (1,000-ft.) walkway, suspended some 18m (57 ft.) above the David C. Lam Asian Garden. Less thrilling but still excellent is the garden store, which sells plants, seeds, books, and gardening tools.
⏱ *1–2 hr. 6804 SW Marine Dr. (near 16th Ave).* ☎ *604/822-9666. www.ubcbotanicalgarden.org. Open daily 9am–5pm. Adults C$8, seniors & teens C$6, kids 12 & under free. Bus: 4, 17 to the UBC transit center, then walk or take C20 shuttle.*

The African Garden at the UBC Botanical Garden.

5 ★★★ **Nitobe Memorial Garden.** So authentic is this traditional Japanese garden that the future Emperor of Japan remarked, "I am in Japan," when he walked through. *See p 17,* **7**.

If you still have time at the end of the day, you might spend some time exploring:

6 ★★ **Pacific Spirit Regional Park.** Whereas the five parks and gardens above represent man's attempt to mold nature to his own taste, Pacific Spirit is an altogether wilder beast. Separating the University of British Columbia from the rest of the West Side, it's Vancouver's largest park at 763 hectares (1,885 acres), offering an expanse of rainforest, marsh, and beaches joined by

Ascending Grouse Mountain

It has a major tourist vibe, but Grouse Mountain (www.grousemountain.com) might be worth your time. The highest point in Vancouver, it offers ski trails in winter and ziplines, hiking trails, wildlife shows, and other activities in summer. An aerial tram takes you to the mountain's 1,110m (3,642-ft.) summit, or you can do as intrepid locals do and hike or run the **Grouse Grind,** a rugged trail that offers an elevation gain of 853m (2,800 ft.) over just 3km (1¾ miles). There's a pub at the top so you can reward yourself with beer.

Kayaking False Creek & English Bay

Water is so intrinsic to the Vancouver experience that getting out on it is a must. Most folks take the ferries (p 13, ), but do-it-your-selfers might prefer renting a kayak and really seeing things from the waterline. **Ecomarine Ocean Kayak Centre** (☎ 888/425-2925 or 604/689-7575; www. ecomarine.com) has two locations from which you can rent stable single or double sea kayaks. Their Granville Island location—at 1668 Duranleau St., next to the boatyard—puts you right onto the calm waters of False Creek. It's open daily 10am to 6pm September to May. In summer they open an hour earlier and stay open 'til 9pm Tuesday, Friday, and Saturday.

To truly get in touch with the city's love of water, take a kayak out onto English Bay.

A second shop, at the English Bay Bath House in the West End (1700 Beach Ave., at the corner of Denman and Davie sts. and Beach Ave.), is open June to August only, 11am to dusk Monday to Friday, 9am to dusk Saturday and Sunday. Rental rates at both outlets start at C$34 for a single kayak (C$46 for a double) for 2 hours.

more than 73km (45 miles) of hiking, biking, and horseback trails. ⏰ *1–8 hr. Visitor Centre located on 16th Ave. between Blanca St. and Westbrook*

Mall. ☎ *604/224-5739. www.metro vancouver.org/services/parks_lscr/ regionalparks/Pages/PacificSpirit.aspx.*

For a small sampling of Japanese tranquillity, relax in the haven of greenery that is the Nitobe Memorial Garden.

The Great Outdoors

Stanley Park

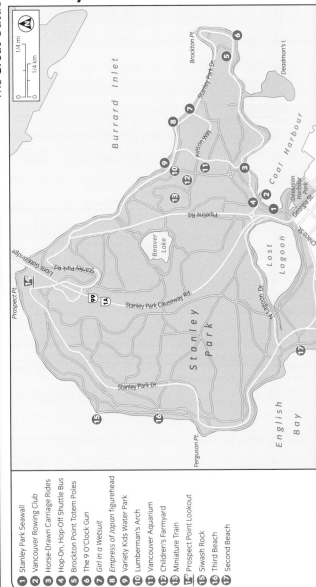

1. Stanley Park Seawall
2. Vancouver Rowing Club
3. Horse-Drawn Carriage Rides
4. Hop-On, Hop-Off Shuttle Bus
5. Brockton Point Totem Poles
6. The 9 O'Clock Gun
7. *Girl in a Wetsuit*
8. *Empress of Japan* figurehead
9. Variety Kids Water Park
10. Lumberman's Arch
11. Vancouver Aquarium
12. Children's Farmyard
13. Miniature Train
14. Prospect Point Lookout
15. Siwash Rock
16. Third Beach
17. Second Beach

Vancouver would not be Vancouver without Stanley Park—without the great arm of green that holds Coal Harbour in a mother's embrace; without the dense wall of trees that caps the West End with living nature; without the trails, lawns, beaches, gardens, and forests that let Vancouverites escape so quickly from their urban lives. Extending over 404 hectares (1,000 acres), the park is only about 25% smaller than the city's Downtown, West End, and Coal Harbour neighborhoods combined, and offers not only nature but some of the city's best views, family attractions, and historic sites. START: **Enter Stanley Park via W. Georgia St., at the western end of Coal Harbour. Bus 19 from the city center takes you to the park, where a number of other transportation options are available.**

Travel Tip

Stanley Park information is available by calling ☎ **604/257-8400,** or surfing the Web to **www.city. vancouver.bc.ca/parks/parks/ stanley/index.htm**.

❶ ★★★ Stanley Park Seawall.

One of the great outdoor experiences of Vancouver, the 10.5km (6.5-mile) Seawall rings the entirety of Stanley Park, with separate lanes for walkers/runners and bicyclists. You'll get fantastic views of the sea, the city skyline, the North Shore Mountains, and the distant peaks of Vancouver Island, plus easy access to most of the park's major sights, including most on this tour. (You'll

have to head inland for a few of the kid-friendly attractions.) ⏱ *1½ hr., depending how many of the park's attractions you check out. Main entrances are via W. Georgia St. & Beach Ave. Bike rentals are available from C$9.50/hr. (C$26 half-day) at Spokes, 1798 W Georgia St. at Denman.* ☎ *604/688-5141. www. vancouverbikerental.com. Bus: 19.*

❷ Vancouver Rowing Club.

This rustic-style heritage building is nestled on the edge of Coal Harbour and surrounded by piers and boats. The club was chartered in April 1899 and is the oldest social club in Vancouver. The clubhouse itself dates to September 1911. ⏱ *2 min. 450 Stanley Park Dr.* ☎ *604/687-3400. www.vancouverrowingclub.ca.*

The Vancouver Rowing Club, the city's oldest social club, occupies an enviable position right on the edge of Coal Harbour.

The Brockton Point Totem Poles are actually reproductions of the First National originals.

③ ★ kids Horse-Drawn Carriage Rides. A nicely old-fashioned way to see the park, these hour-long tours by old-style tram car meander along the park's eastern edge, stopping at the Brockton Point Totem poles (**⑤**) and several other historic and natural sights. ⏲ *1 hr. Ticket kiosk is located approx. 90m (300 ft.) beyond the rowing club, just next to an information booth.* ☎ *604/681-5115. www.stanleyparktours.com. Adults C$27. Seniors & students C$25. Kids 3–12 C$15. Departures every 20–30 min., 9:40am–4pm (Mar & Oct), 9:40am–5pm (April–June & Sept), 9:40am–5:30pm (July–Aug).*

④ Hop-On, Hop-Off Shuttle Bus. In summer, Stanley Park offers a free shuttle service that stops at 15 popular locations all around the park. The shuttle runs every 12 to 15 minutes; shuttle stops are clearly marked, and you can hop on or off at your leisure. ⏲ *45 min. for the full circuit, longer if you get off. The nearest stops to the park entrance are near Lost Lagoon and the Rowing Club. Look for the green and gold signs. www.city.vancouver.bc.ca/parks/parks /stanley/shuttle.htm. Available 10am– 6:30pm, mid-June to late Sept.*

⑤ ★★ Brockton Point Totem Poles. Between 1920 and 1936, the city purchased a number of totem poles from First Nations peoples in Alert Bay, the Queen Charlotte Islands, and Rivers Inlet with the idea of constructing an "Indian Village" display in Stanley Park. Some poles dated to the 1880s, which explains why the eight poles you see here today are reproductions—totem poles just don't last very long out in the elements. The originals were sent to museums for preservation. ⏲ *15 min. Located near Brockton Point, the park's easternmost spit.*

⑥ The 9 O'clock Gun. Cast in England in 1816, this 12-pounder muzzle-loaded naval cannon was brought to Canada 40 years later and installed in Stanley Park around 1894. It's acted as a signal cannon from that day onward, first to alert fishermen and later as a daily 9pm signal by which Vancouverites on ship and shore could set their clocks! Boom! It's 9pm. You also get a wonderful view of the city from here. ⏲ *2 min. Located just beyond the totem poles, in a roofed glass booth at waterside.*

⑦ *Girl in a Wetsuit.* This iconic Vancouver sculpture—of a young

Elrek Imrady's iconic Girl in a Wetsuit.

woman in a scuba suit, sitting atop a rock in the water—was inspired by Copenhagen's famous *Little Mermaid* sculpture, and created in 1972 by sculptor Elek Imredy. ◷ *2 min. Located in the water, about .5km (⅓ mile) past Brockton Point.*

8 ***Empress of Japan* figurehead.** The *Empress of Japan* was a clipper-bowed, steam-driven ocean liner that made 315 trips between Vancouver and Hong Kong from 1891 until 1922, carrying passengers and mail. Scrapped in 1926, her ornate, dragon-shaped figurehead was mounted in Stanley Park the following year. When it began to deteriorate in 1960, it was replaced with the fiberglass recreation you see today. The original, now restored, is on display at the Vancouver Maritime Museum (p 20, ④). ◷ *2 min. Located near* Girl in a Wetsuit.

9 kids Variety Kids Water Park. There's no swimming pool in sight, but your offspring will have no problems getting wet and cooling off at Vancouver's largest water spray facility. *See p 38, ⑤.*

10 Lumbermen's Arch. Erected in 1952 to honor British Columbia's lumber industry, this simple arrangement of one enormous log supported at an angle by two stubbier ones frames a walking path that leads to the next three attractions. ◷ *2 min. Located just beyond the 3km point on Stanley Park Dr., across from the water park.*

11 ★★★ kids Vancouver Aquarium. Canada's first public aquarium (opened in 1956) is one of North America's largest and best, with displays that focus on life in British Columbia's waters. *See p 37, ①.*

12 ★ kids Children's Farmyard. *See p 37, ②.*

13 ★ kids Miniature Train. *See p 38, ③.*

The basalt Siwash Rock is the only one of its kind in Vancouver.

If you're walking or biking the Seawall, stop for some refreshment at the **14 Prospect Point Lookout,** perched on a cliff top at the highest point in the park, near the foot of the Lion's Gate Bridge. There's a cafe serving a large menu of comfort food, a bar and grill, ice cream, and great views of the bridge, built in 1937 by the Guinness family (of Irish beer fame), who owned much of the land on the other side. *2099 Beach Ave.* ☎ *604/669-2737. www.prospect point.ca. $.*

15 Siwash Rock. Formed some 32 million years ago when volcanic activity pushed molten magma to the surface, this basalt sea stack (roughly 18m/60 ft. in height) is the only one of its kind in the Vancouver area. Roughly conical in shape, it sprouts at the water's edge a few meters from the Seawall path, and has a tree growing out of its crown. ◷ *2 min. Located 1 km (½ mile) SW of Prospect Point.*

16 kids Third Beach. Though Stanley Park has numerous natural beaches, especially at low tide, only

The heated pool at Second Beach is a magnet for local families.

two are suitable for swimming. Third Beach is the quieter and more northerly one, surrounded by forest and offering a snack stand, washrooms, and lifeguards from late May

to early Sept. 🕐 *Depends on your sun tolerance. Located at Ferguson Point. Parking C$2/hr.*

17 **kids** **Second Beach.** The busier of the park's two beaches, Second Beach is extremely family friendly, with a playground, a large grassy area, a snack stand, washrooms, lifeguards (late May to early Sept), and a large, heated outdoor pool with one section for lap swimmers and another for folks who just want to cool off. (FYI: For those keeping score, "First Beach" is located down around Denman St., where it's more commonly known as English Bay Beach.) 🕐 *15 min. to 5 hr., depending on your sun tolerance. Located at North Lagoon Dr. Parking C$2/hr. Pool fees C$4.95 adults, C$3.45 seniors, C$3.70 teens, C$2.50 kids.* ●

Lighthouse Park

You'll need a car to reach this spot in West Vancouver, but it's worth it if you try. Secluded among quiet residential streets, quiet, rustic **Lighthouse Park** (☎ 604/925-7270) contains 10km (6.2 miles) of groomed hiking trails that wind among some of the largest and oldest trees on the Lower Mainland. One trail leads to the Point Atkinson Lighthouse, which has warned ships away from the point since 1912. (An older light, dating to 1881, was responsible for the forests here never being clear-cut: The 65 hectares/160 acres of Douglas fir and other growth were the requisite dark background that would make the light visible.) From the Lighthouse Viewpoint, you can see across the Georgia Strait to Vancouver Island. Nearby Arbutus Knoll provides a giant rock on which to picnic while taking in views of the city. It's located at the end of Beacon La., off Marine Dr. in West Vancouver, about 8km (5 miles) west of the Lions Gate Bridge.

The Point Atkinson Lighthouse.

The Best Dining

Vancouver **Dining**

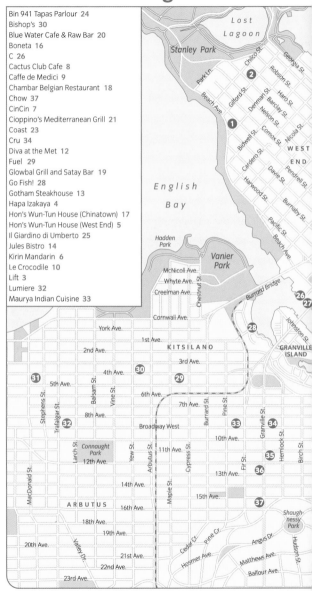

Previous page: The delicate seafood dishes at Blue Water Cafe & Raw Bar are the best of their type in the city.

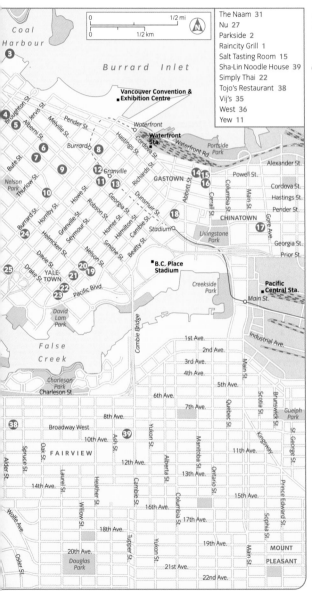

The Naam 31
Nu 27
Parkside 2
Raincity Grill 1
Salt Tasting Room 15
Sha-Lin Noodle House 39
Simply Thai 22
Tojo's Restaurant 38
Vij's 35
West 36
Yew 11

Dining Best Bets

Best **BC Regional Cuisine**
★★★ West $$$$ *2881 Granville St. (p 98)*

Best **Seafood**
★★★ Blue Water Cafe $$$ *1095 Hamilton St. (p 93)*

Best **Outdoor Seafood**
★ Go Fish! $ *1505 West 1st Ave. (p 95)*

Best **Romantic Dining**
★★★ Raincity Grill $$ *1193 Denman St. (p 97)*

Best **Italian**
★★★ Cioppino's Mediterranean Grill $$$ *1133 Hamilton St. (p 94)*

Best **French**
★★★ Le Crocodile $$$ *100–909 Burrard St. (p 96)*

Best **Informal Arty Restaurant**
★★ Boneta $$ *1 W. Cordova St. (p 93)*

Best **Small-Plate Restaurant**
★ Bin 941 $ *941 Davie St. (p 93)*

Best **Wine, Meat & Cheese**
★★ Salt Tasting Room $ *45 Blood Alley (p 97)*

Best **Japanese**
★★★ Tojo's $$$ *1133 W. Broadway (p 98)*

Best **Chinese**
★★★ Kirin Mandarin $$$ *1166 Alberni St. (p 96)*

Best **Indian**
★★★ Vij's $$ *1480 W. 11th Ave. (p 98)*

Best **Steakhouse**
★★★ Gotham Steakhouse $$$ *615 Seymour St. (p 95)*

Best **Casual Chain**
★ Cactus Club Cafe $$ *588 Burrard St. (p 94)*

Best **View**
★★ Lift $$$ *333 Menchions Mews (p 96)*

Best **Service**
★★★ Bishop's $$$ *2183 W. 4th Ave. (p 93)*

Best **Open-View Kitchen**
★★★ Fuel $$$ *1944 4th Ave. (p 95)*

Most **Stylish Hotel Restaurant**
★★ Yew $$ *791 W. Georgia St. (p 98)*

Gotham Steakhouse boasts a chic dining room and the best steaks in town.

Dine on award-winning Italian cuisine in elegant surroundings at CinCin.

★ Bin 941 Tapas Parlour

DOWNTOWN *TAPAS/ECLECTIC* It's tiny, crowded, full of attitude, and doesn't take reservations, but the seafood, Moroccan, and other small plates here are amazing. I'd go again just for the Navajo fry bread. *941 Davie St.* ☎ *604/683-1246. www. bin941.com. All items C$5–C$15. MC, V. Dinner daily. Bus: 2, 22, 44. Map p 90.*

★★★ Bishop's KITSILANO *BC REGIONAL* One of Vancouver's best and classiest restaurants since 1985, focusing on local organic ingredients in a creative seasonal menu. Atmosphere is elegant and intimate, and service is friendly and attentive. *2183 West 4th Ave.* ☎ *604/738-2025. www.bishopsonline.com. Entrees C$35–C$40. AE, DC, MC, V. Dinner daily. Bus: 4, 7. Map p 90.*

★★★ Blue Water Cafe & Raw Bar YALETOWN *SEAFOOD* Vancouver's A-1 pick for seafood from wild and sustainable fisheries. The regular dishes are prepared with a delicate touch, and the sushi and sashimi are perfecto. *1095 Hamilton St.* ☎ *604/688-8078. www.blue watercafe.net. Entrees C$31–C$45. AE, DC, MC, V. Dinner daily. Bus: 6, C21, C23. Map p 90.*

★★ Boneta GASTOWN *ECLECTIC* A little gem, arty Boneta mixes a creative, seasonal West Coast menu; great service and cocktails; and a cool/casual atmosphere. It's one of the best informal bets in town. *1 W. Cordova St.* ☎ *604/684-1844. www. boneta.ca. Entrees C$25–C$29. AE, MC, V. Lunch & dinner Tues–Sat. Bus: 50. Map p 90.*

★★★ C FALSE CREEK NORTH *SEAFOOD* A longtime seafood favorite, featuring local fish and recipes from around the world. An outdoor patio on False Creek makes for wonderful sunset meals. *2-1600 Howe St.* ☎ *604/681-1164. www. crestaurant.com. Entrees C$37–C$50. AE, DC, MC, V. Lunch Mon–Fri, dinner daily. Bus: C21, C23, 98b, 10. Map p 90.*

★ **Cactus Club Cafe** DOWNTOWN *ECLECTIC/CASUAL* Fashion-model waitstaff and a chic decor mix with an inexpensive West Coast menu, bar TVs for sporting events, and outdoor seating under funky giant umbrellas. *588 Burrard St. ☎ 604/682-0933. www.cactusclubcafe.com. Entrees C$12–C$34. AE, MC, V. Lunch & dinner daily. Bus: 2, 22, 44. Map p 90.*

★★ **Caffé de Medici** WEST END *ITALIAN* A longtime favorite (3 decades and counting) serving traditional northern Italian in an elegant dining room and outdoor patio, with attentive service. *109-1025 Robson St. ☎ 604/669-9322. www.caffede medici.com. Entrees C$20–C$39. AE, DC, MC, V. Lunch Mon–Fri, dinner daily. Bus: 5. Map p 90.*

★★ **Chambar Belgian Restaurant** DOWNTOWN *BELGIAN* A stylish (if loud) spot offering legendary *moule frites* (mussels) along with other seafood, meats, Moroccan influences, lots of paprika, and Belgian beers. *562 Beatty St. ☎ 604/879-7119. www.chambar.com. Entrees C$25–C$29. AE, MC, V. Dinner daily. Bus: 15. Map p 90.*

Belgian dishes with a Middle Eastern twist is what you'll get at Chambar Belgian.

★★ **Chow** WEST SIDE *BC REGIONAL* Chic but unpretentious, this "farm-to-table" restaurant serves seasonal menus based on organic local ingredients, including pork raised on a Vancouver Island farm. *3121 Granville St. ☎ 604/608-2469. http://chow-restaurant.com. Entrees C$15–C$29. AE, DISC, MC, V. Dinner Mon–Sat. Bus: 98b, 10. Map p 90.*

★★★ **CinCin** WEST END *ITALIAN* An Italian villa with an outdoor terrace, serving both classic and modern dishes with a seasonal focus. The open kitchen is built around a huge wood-fired oven. *1154 Robson St. ☎ 604/688-7338. www.cincin.net. Entrees C$23–C$47. AE, DC, MC, V. Dinner daily. Bus: 5. Map p 90.*

★★★ **Cioppino's Mediterranean Grill** YALETOWN *ITALIAN/MEDITERRANEAN* The seasonal menu at the city's best formal Italian restaurant is prepared with a light touch. The wine list is enormous, and the vibe is warm and low-lit. *1133 Hamilton St. ☎ 604/688-7466. www.cioppinosyaletown.com. Entrees C$23–C$48. AE, DC, MC, V. Dinner Mon–Sat. Bus: 6, C21, C23. Map p 90.*

★★★ **Coast** YALETOWN *SEAFOOD* A hip, minimalist hot-spot featuring local and international seafood and seasonal produce. The "community table" offers tasting menus prepared on the spot. *1257 Hamilton St. ☎ 604/685-5010. www.coast restaurant.ca. Entrees C$19–C$34. AE, DC, MC, V. Dinner daily. Bus: 6, C21, C23. Map p 90.*

★★ **Cru** WEST SIDE *BC REGIONAL* Small, minimalist, and intimate, Cru serves West Coast small-plates and a wine list color-coded for food pairings. The staff knows their wines, and the prices are low-ish. *1459 W. Broadway. ☎ 604/677-4111. www.cru.ca. Small plates C$9–C$16, 3-course prix* fixe C$42. AE, MC, V. Dinner daily. Bus: 98B, 10. Map p 90.

★★ Diva at the Met DOWNTOWN
BC REGIONAL A stylish, multi-tiered room serving regional and world cuisine to seriously delicious effect. The wine list wins raves, as does the Chef's Table fronting the open-view kitchen. *In the Metropolitan Hotel, 645 Howe St.* ☎ 604/602-7788. www.metropolitan.com/Diva. Entrees C$28–C$48. AE, DC, DISC, MC, V. Breakfast, lunch & dinner daily. Bus: 4, 7. Map p 90.

★★★ Fuel KITSILANO
BC REGIONAL Get a bar seat for a view of the open kitchen, then order some locally sourced, perfectly prepared regional cuisine from the weekly changing menu. The creative wine list changes seasonally too. *1944 4th Ave.* ☎ 604/288-7905. www.fuel restaurant.ca. Entrees C$28–C$35. AE, DC, MC, V. Lunch Mon–Fri, dinner daily. Bus: 4, 7. Map p 90.

The menu changes weekly, but the regionally inspired food is always perfectly prepared at Fuel.

★★ Glowbal Grill and Satay Bar YALETOWN ECLECTIC
Satay (plus fusion meat and seafood) is the thing at this trendy Yaletown spot, which has a sleek modern interior, open kitchen, and buzz-heavy atmosphere. *1079 Mainland St.* ☎ 604/602-0835. www.glowbalgrill.com. Entrees C$18–C$34. AE, DC, MC, V. Lunch & dinner daily, brunch Sat–Sun. Bus: 6. Map p 90.

★ Go Fish! WEST SIDE SEAFOOD
A tin shack on the water, Go Fish! has limited hours and you'll have to sit outside (even in winter). But that's half the charm. The other half? The fresh, delicious seafood. *1505 West 1st Ave. (at False Creek Fisherman's Wharf).* ☎ 604/730-5039. All items C$9–C$13. Cash only. Lunch Tues–Sun. Bus: 50. Map p 90.

★★★ Gotham Steakhouse
DOWNTOWN STEAK Vancouver's best restaurant for carnivores combines serious steak-and-cocktails decor with 28-day dry-aged Canadian Prime beef. In good weather you can dine on the outdoor patio. *615 Seymour St.* ☎ 604/605-8282. www.gothamsteakhouse.com. Entrees C$27–C$50. AE, DC, MC, V. Dinner daily. Bus: 5, 6. Map p 90.

★ Hapa Izakaya WEST END JAPANESE
Everything's loud and hectic, but that's part of the izakaya (Japanese pub food) shtick. Expect speedy service, a mostly Asian clientele, and meats, seafood, and hot pots. *1479 Robson St.* ☎ 604/689-4272. www.hapaizakaya.com. Entrees C$9–C$15. AE, MC, V. Dinner daily. Bus: 5. Map p 90.

Hon's Wun-Tun House CHINATOWN/WEST END CHINESE
It's chaotic, loud, and decor-free, but Hon's is an institution for reliably good, solid Hong Kong–food served in huge portions from the longest menu you've ever seen. *Chinatown: 268 Keefer St.* ☎ 604/688-0871. *West End: 1339 Robson St.* ☎ 604/685-0871. www.hons.ca. Everything C$5–C$12. MC, V. Lunch & dinner daily. Bus: 22 (Chinatown), 5 (Robson). Map p 90.

★★ Il Giardino di Umberto Ristorante FALSE CREEK NORTH ITALIAN
A lovely classic Italian restaurant, with rustic beams, white tablecloths, a tile floor, and a menu full of classics, game, pastas, and seasonal ingredients. *1382 Hornby*

Rustic French dishes rule the menu at Jules Bistro.

St. ☎ 604/669-2422. www.hotelvilla delia.com/restaurant_ilgiardino.cfm. Entrees C$33–C$40. AE, DC, MC, V. Lunch Mon–Fri, dinner Mon–Sat. Bus: C21, C23. Map p 90.

★ **Jules Bistro** GASTOWN *FRENCH* This cute-as-a-button bistro has tile floors, brick walls, sidewalk dining, and rustic French food—think coq au vin, escargots, and French onion soup. *216 Abbott St.* ☎ *604/669-0033. http://julesbistro.ca. Entrees C$14–C$26. AE, MC, V. Lunch & dinner Mon–Sat. Bus: 50. Map p 90.*

★★★ **Kirin Mandarin** WEST END *CHINESE* Dine on upscale northern Chinese, accompanied by wonderful service, in an elegant two-level venue. The Peking duck is a favorite at dinner, while fresh dim sum is the thing for lunch. *1166 Alberni St.* ☎ *604/682-8833. www.kirin restaurant.com. Entrees C$15–C$25. AE, MC, V. Lunch & dinner daily. Bus: 5. Map p 90.*

★★★ **Le Crocodile** DOWNTOWN *FRENCH* This elegant, intimate room seems perpetually bathed in a sunny glow. Expect classic French cuisine and style with a dash of West Coast, plus doting service.

100–909 Burrard St. ☎ *604/669-4298. www.lecrocodilerestaurant. com. Entrees C$27–C$42. AE, MC, V. Lunch Mon–Fri, dinner Mon–Sat. Bus: 2, 22, 44. Map p 90.*

★★ **Lift** COAL HARBOUR *BC REGIONAL* Perched over Coal Harbour, Lift has knockout views, a modern design, and beautiful servers. The menu is French-accented West Coast, and the upstairs patio is to die for. *333 Menchions Mews.* ☎ *604/689-5438. www.liftbarandgrill.com. Entrees C$29–C$49. AE, DC, MC, V. Lunch & dinner daily. Bus: 19. Map p 90.*

★★★ **Lumiere** KITSILANO *FRENCH* Super-elegant French dining, with a subtly luminous decor, simple yet exquisite French/West Coast dishes, and very high prices. *2551 W. Broadway.* ☎ *604/739-8185. www.lumiere. ca. Prix-fixe menus C$85–C$180. AE, DC, MC, V. Dinner Tues–Sun. Bus: 99B. Map p 90.*

★★ **Maurya Indian Cuisine** WEST SIDE *INDIAN* Authentic, traditional North Indian cuisine served in a gorgeous, woody, high-ceilinged space with draped floor-to-ceiling

The kitchen at Kirin Mandarin puts out the best Chinese cuisine in Vancouver.

Foodies will rejoice in the award-winning array of artisanal cheeses, cured meats, and wines at Salt Tasting Room.

windows. The chefs go lighter than usual on the butters and creams, yet retain all the flavor. There's a great weekday lunch buffet, plus streetside patio dining in nice weather. *1643 W. Broadway.* ☎ *604/742-0622. www. mauryaindiancuisine.com. Entrees C$13–C$30; buffet C$13. AE, MC, V. Lunch & dinner daily. Bus: 10, 98B, 99B. Map p 90.*

The Naam KITSILANO *VEGETARIAN* An updated '60s holdover open 24-hours, mixing Asian, Indian, Mexican, and Canadian/American faves. There's local art on the walls, and live music at night. *2724 W. 4th Ave.* ☎ *604/738-7151. www.thenaam. com. All items C$5–C$13. AE, MC, V. Open daily 24 hrs. Bus: 4, 7. Map p 90.*

★★ Nu FALSE CREEK NORTH *ECLECTIC* Right on False Creek, this farm-to-table French/West Coast spot goes for the hip jugular with a retro-groovy decor, great cocktails, and a lovely waterside patio. *1661 Granville St.* ☎ *604/646-4668. www.whatisnu. com. Entrees C$25–C$37. AE, DC, MC, V. Lunch & dinner daily. Bus: 98b, 10, C21, C23. Map p 90.*

★★★ Parkside WEST END *FRENCH/ MEDITERRANEAN* Local ingredients, informal but elegant service, one of the city's loveliest courtyard patios, and an always-changing menu—all just blocks from Stanley Park. *1906 Haro St., in the Buchan Hotel.* ☎ *604/683-6912. www. parksiderestaurant.ca. 3-course prix-fixe menu C$65. MC, V. Dinner Wed–Sun. Bus: 5. Map p 90.*

★★★ Raincity Grill WEST END *BC REGIONAL* Raincity and its "100-mile tasting menu" set the bar for Vancouver's fresh local food movement. Expect exceptional organic cuisine, friendly service, and a killer view of the English Bay sunset (from both the interior dining room and the patio). *1193 Denman St.* ☎ *604/685-7337. www.raincitygrill.com. Entrees C$27–C$32. AE, DC, MC, V. Lunch Mon–Fri, brunch Sat–Sun, dinner daily. Bus: C21, C23, 6, 5. Map p 90.*

★★ Salt Tasting Room GASTOWN *CHARCUTERIE/CHEESE* Select three cured meats and/or artisanal cheeses, three perfect condiments, and then top it off with wine. Yum. The day's selections are chalked on a blackboard. *45 Blood*

The well-prepared Thai cuisine at Simply Thai is as colorful as it is tasty.

Alley. ☎ 604/633-1912. www.salt
tastingroom.com. Tasting plates
C$15. AE, MC, V. Lunch & dinner
daily. Bus: 50. Map p 90.

Sha-Lin Noodle House WEST
SIDE *CHINESE* This typical-looking
storefront Chinese is a longtime
favorite for cheap workingman's
dishes, with noodles made from
scratch while you watch. *548 W.
Broadway.* ☎ *604/873-1816. All
items C$10 or less. No credit cards.
Lunch & dinner daily. Bus: 15, 99B.
Map p 90.*

★ **Simply Thai** YALETOWN *THAI*
Chef Siriwan "Grace" Rerksuttisiri-
dach offers a modern, trendy take
on Thai cuisine, served in a hip,
crowded, and moderately upscale
atmosphere. There's an open
kitchen, friendly service, and an outdoor patio for nice weather. *1211
Hamilton St.* ☎ *604/642-0123.
www.simplythairestaurant.com.
Entrees C$14–C$19. AE, DC, MC, V.
Dinner daily, lunch Mon–Fri. Bus: 6,
C21, C23. Map p 90.*

★★★ **Tojo's Restaurant** WEST
SIDE *JAPANESE* A perennial "best
Japanese" winner, Tojo's offers legendary sushi and sashimi created
with fresh, seasonal ingredients,
plus *omakase* tasting menus. *1133
W. Broadway.* ☎ *604/872-8050.*

*www.tojos.com. Entrees C$18–C$38,
omakase C$55–C$110. AE, DC, MC,
V. Dinner Mon–Sat. Bus: 99B, 9. Map
p 90.*

★★★ **Vij's** WEST SIDE *INDIAN*
Stratospherically inventive Indian
cuisine, mixing classic dishes with
seasonal local meats, seafood, and
produce. No reservations are taken,
so arrive early. *1480 W. 11th Ave.*
☎ *604/736-6664. www.vijs.ca.
Entrees C$22–C$28. AE, DC, MC, V.
Dinner daily. Bus: 98b, 10. Map p 90.*

★★★ **West** WEST SIDE *BC
REGIONAL* Perennially named Vancouver's best restaurant, it's stylish
yet relaxed, of-the-moment but not
trendy, and offers perfect service
and contemporary seasonal cuisine.
2881 Granville St. ☎ *604/738-8938.
www.westrestaurant.com. Entrees
C$40–C$47. AE, DC, MC, V. Dinner
daily. Bus: 98b, 10. Map p 90.*

★★ **Yew** DOWNTOWN *CONTEMPO-
RARY* Stylish in both menu and
decor, Yew has a high ceiling, central sandstone fireplace, and a wine
bar with an enormous by-the-glass
list. *In the Four Seasons, 791 W.
Georgia St.* ☎ *604/689-9333. www.
fourseasons.com/vancouver/dining.
html. Entrees C$18–C$35. AE, DC,
DISC, MC, V. Breakfast, lunch & dinner daily. Bus: 4, 7. Map p 90.* ●

*The stylish dining room at West provides a perfect backdrop for its award-winning
regional cuisine.*

Vancouver **Nightlife**

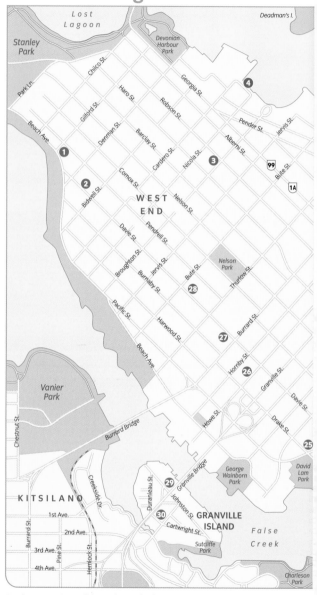

Previous page: Some of the coolest cocktails in Vancouver are found at the Opus Bar.

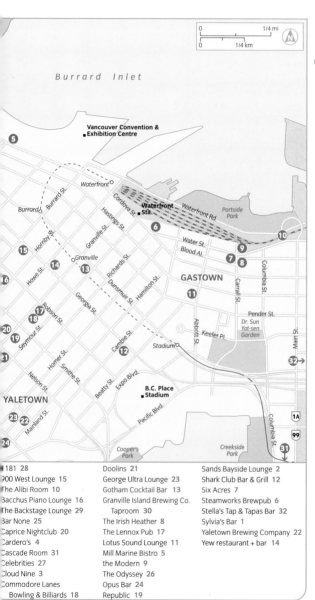

Burrard Inlet

Vancouver Convention &
Exhibition Centre

0   1/4 mi
0   1/4 km

⑤

Waterfront

Cordova St.

Waterfront Sta.

Waterfront Rd.

Portside Park

Burrard

Burrard St.

Hastings St.

Water St.
Blood Al.

⑥

⑦ ⑧

⑨

⑩

Hornby St.

Granville

Granville St.

Richards St.

GASTOWN

⑮

Howe St.

⑭

⑬

Dunsmuir St.

Hamilton St.

⑪

Carrall St.

Columbia St.

⑯

Georgia St.

Pender St.
Dr. Sun
Yat-sen
Garden

Robson St.

⑰
⑱

Cambie St.

Abbott St.

Keefer Pl.

Main St.

⑳

⑲

Seymour St.

Stadium

㉜ →

㉑

Homer St.

Smithe St.

Beatty St.

Expo Blvd.

Nelson St.

YALETOWN

B.C. Place
Stadium

㉓ ㉒

Mainland St.

Pacific Blvd.

Columbia St.

1A

99

㉔

Cooper's
Park

Creekside
Park

㉛

181 28
900 West Lounge 15
The Alibi Room 10
Bacchus Piano Lounge 16
The Backstage Lounge 29
Bar None 25
Caprice Nightclub 20
Cardero's 4
Cascade Room 31
Celebrities 27
Cloud Nine 3
Commodore Lanes
Bowling & Billiards 18

Doolins 21
George Ultra Lounge 23
Gotham Cocktail Bar 13
Granville Island Brewing Co.
Taproom 30
The Irish Heather 8
The Lennox Pub 17
Lotus Sound Lounge 11
Mill Marine Bistro 5
the Modern 9
The Odyssey 26
Opus Bar 24
Republic 19

Sands Bayside Lounge 2
Shark Club Bar & Grill 12
Six Acres 7
Steamworks Brewpub 6
Stella's Tap & Tapas Bar 32
Sylvia's Bar 1
Yaletown Brewing Company 22
Yew restaurant + bar 14

The Best Nightlife

Nightlife Best Bets

Best Model-Friendly Hipster Lounge
★★★ Opus Bar, *322 Davie St. (p 107)*

Best Wine Bar
★★★ 900 West Lounge, *900 W. Georgia St. (p 105);* and ★★★ Yew, *791 W. Georgia St. (p 106)*

Best Piano Bar
★★★ Bacchus Piano Lounge, *845 Hornby St. (p 106)*

Best Bar with a View
★ Sylvia's Bar, *1154 Gilford St. (p 105);* and ★ Sands Bayside Lounge, *1755 Davie St. (p 104)*

Best Outdoor Bar
★ Mill Marine Bistro, *1199 W. Cordova St. (p 104)*

Best for Beer Connoisseurs
★★ Six Acres, *203 Carrall St. (p 104);* and ★★ Stella's Tap & Tapas Bar, *1191 Commercial Dr. (p 105)*

Best Brewpub
★ Granville Island Brewing Co. Taproom, *1441 Cartwright St. (p 103)*

Best Subterranean Bowling
★★ Commodore Lanes Bowling and Billiards, *838 Granville St. (p 103)*

Best Irish Pub
★★★ The Irish Heather, *210 Carrall St. (p 103)*

Best Cozy After-Work Scene
★ Cardero's, *1583 Coal Harbour Quay (p 103)*

Best Sports Bar
★ Shark Club Bar & Grill, *180 W. Georgia St. (p 104)*

Best Old-School Cocktails
★★★ George Ultra Lounge, *1137 Hamilton St. (p 107)*

Best Classic Hotel Lounge
★★★ 900 West Lounge, *900 W. Georgia St. (p 105)*

Best Gay Bar
★★★ 1181, *1181 Davie St. (p 107);* and ★★ The Odyssey, *1251 Howe St. (p 107)*

Best Music Bar
★★★ The Backstage Lounge, *1585 Johnston St. (p 103)*

Best Dance Club
★★★ Celebrities, *1022 Davie St. (p 107);* and ★★ the Modern, *7 Alexander St. (p 108)*

1181 is Vancouver's most stylish and most popular gay bar.

Vancouver Nightlife A to Z

Bowling, Billiards & Booze
★★ Commodore Lanes Bowling & Billiards DOWNTOWN
Located under the Commodore Ballroom (p 116), this place has been drawing local friends, groups, and folks on active dates since 1930. Your options are 5-pin bowling, billiards, arcade games, and beer—though the latter is allowed only in a designated area behind the lanes, to avoid stickiness. *838 Granville St.* ☎ *604/681-1531. Bus: 5, 50. Map p 100.*

Casual Bars
★★ The Alibi Room GASTOWN
A sleek, almost minimalist room in a century-old building facing Gastown's railyards, serving a rotating list of craft beers and well-mixed martinis. *157 Alexander St.* ☎ *604/623-3383. www.alibi.ca. Bus: 50. SkyTrain: Waterfront Station. Map p 100.*

★★★ The Backstage Lounge
GRANVILLE ISLAND Located under the Granville Bridge, this super-comfortable lounge has a waterfront patio with views, and a stage that presents local bands at night. The clientele is part art student (the Emily Carr Institute is nearby) and part theater people coming from the next-door Arts Club Theatre (p 113). *1585 Johnston St. (near the Public Market).* ☎ *604/687-1354. www.thebackstage lounge.com. Bus: 50. Map p 100.*

★ Cardero's COAL HARBOUR
Set on pilings over the water, this half-restaurant, half-bar (split down the middle) has a great old woody decor and a nautical theme, and gets a fun after-work crowd. *1583 Coal Harbour Quay.* ☎ *604/669-7666. www. vancouverdine.com/carderos/home. html. Bus: 19. Map p 100.*

The sleek Alibi Room is a self-described "modern tavern" that pours a very good selection of craft beers.

★ Doolin's DOWNTOWN
Settle in and enjoy this Irish pub's atmosphere, with gleaming woodwork, dart boards, and pub grub. There's music (from Irish to DJ) nightly. *654 Nelson St.* ☎ *604/605-4343. www. doolins.ca. Bus: 50. Map p 100.*

★ Granville Island Brewing Co. Taproom GRANVILLE ISLAND
Probably the best of Vancouver's few microbreweries. The taproom is almost cavernous (no coziness here), but there are limited-edition brews on tap, you can see the works, and they do tours daily at noon, 2pm, and 4pm ($9.75 per person, including four tastings). *1441 Cartwright St.* ☎ *604/687-2739. www.gib.ca. Bus: 50. Map p 100.*

★★★ The Irish Heather GASTOWN
Vancouver's classic, old-time, authentic Irish bar—just like home, only with better conversation and colder beer—recently moved from its original home to a similar space across the street, which retains much of the old ambience but with a larger, less labyrinthine layout. *210 Carrall St.* ☎ *604/688-9779.*

Want to hang out at an authentic Irish pub while in Vancouver? Doolin's is a good choice.

www.irishheather.com. Bus: 50. Sky-Train: Waterfront Station. Map p 100.

★ **The Lennox Pub** DOWNTOWN This centrally located pub has a comfortable bar atmosphere, a good beer list, a pub menu, and an outdoor patio. Oh, and they tune in all the Canucks' games. *800 Granville St.* ☎ *604/408-0881. Bus: 5. Map p 100.*

★ **Mill Marine Bistro** COAL HARBOUR This place doesn't look like much when it's cold or rainy, but bring out the sun and it blooms from a smallish, almost underground

Young professionals flock to Stella's Tap & Tapas Bar for its great mix of food and craft beers.

bar/restaurant into Vancouver's largest outdoor dining and drinking spot, with wonderful views of the harbor and North Vancouver mountains. *1199 W. Cordova St.* ☎ *604/687-6455. www.millbistro.ca. Bus: 19. Map p 100.*

★ **Sands Bayside Lounge** WEST END Located on the second floor of the Best Western Sands by the Sea, this circular bar offers stunning English Bay views and a cocktail vibe that comes off as more authentic than retro. *1755 Davie St.* ☎ *604/682-1831. www.bestwesternbc.com/hotels/best-western-sands. Bus: 5, 6. Map p 100.*

★ **Shark Club Bar & Grill** DOWNTOWN Located close to Vancouver's two main team-sports venues, GM Place and BC Place, this giant chain sports bar has the requisite TVs (about three dozen of them), sports memorabilia, and tall tables for good views, but it's also got DJ entertainment after the game, and dancing on weekends. *180 W. Georgia St.* ☎ *604/687-4275. www.sharkclubs.com. Bus: 15, 17. SkyTrain: Stadium/Chinatown Station. Map p 100.*

★★ **Six Acres** GASTOWN This stylish little spot, with exposed brick walls and a woody atmosphere, keeps about three dozen carefully chosen bottled beers from all over the world on tap for the connoisseur. There's also a menu of "nibbles, dips, salads, and shares." *203 Carrall St.* ☎ *604/488-0110. www.sixacres.ca. Bus: 50. SkyTrain: Waterfront Station. Map p 100.*

★ **Steamworks Brewpub** GAS-TOWN A favorite of cruise-ship passengers coming from nearby Canada Place, this huge place has different themed rooms for different tastes, from pub to wine bar to oyster bar. *375 Water St.* ☎ *604/689-2739. www. steamworks.com. Bus: 50. SkyTrain: Waterfront Station. Map p 100.*

★★ **Stella's Tap & Tapas Bar** EAST VANCOUVER The name says it all: For eats, its young professional crowd can indulge in a huge tapas menu; for drink, they've got a rotating menu of ten craft brews on draft, plus two dozen others in bottles, including many Belgian labels. *1191 Commercial Dr.* ☎ *604/254-2437. www.stellasbeer.com. Bus: 10, 16. Map p 100.*

★ **Sylvia's Bar** WEST END Vancouver's oldest cocktail lounge (it opened in 1918) is a woody, cozy, comfortable spot off the lobby of the vine-covered Sylvia Hotel. The view of English Bay through their big picture windows is sublime, especially at sunset. *1154 Gilford St.* ☎ *604/ 681-9321. www.sylviahotel.com. Bus: 5, 6. Map p 100.*

★**Yaletown Brewing Company** YALETOWN This big, boisterous brewpub opened in 1994 when Yaletown was still in its warehouse-frontier stage. Today it's an institution, its big barroom offering a fireplace, pool tables, TVs, and a selection of its own microbrews. A separate dining room caters to families. In spring and summer, take in the neighborhood scene at one of the outdoor tables. *1111 Mainland St.* ☎ *604/681-2739. Bus: 6, C21, C23. Map p 100.*

Wine Bars

★★★ **900 West Lounge** DOWNTOWN Regularly voted Vancouver's best wine bar, 900 West is a classic hotel bar in the lobby of the grande dame Fairmont Hotel Vancouver. The chairs are plush and deep, the wine list is impressive (the martinis rate, too), there's a pianist in the evenings, and a jazz trio plays late on Friday and Saturday nights. *900 West Georgia St.* ☎ *604/684-3131. www. fairmont.com/hotelvancouver/Guest*

If you're a fan of hockey (the Canucks!) and beer, the Lennox Pub is a great place to drink.

The Cascade Room generally hosts a cool crowd looking for classic cocktails.

Services/Restaurants/900WestLounge. htm. Bus: 2, 22. SkyTrain: Burrard Station. Map p 100.

★★★ Yew restaurant + bar

DOWNTOWN The bar at the Four Seasons' stylish restaurant (p 98) offers 150 wines by the glass—they'll open any bottle as long as you commit to buying two glasses. *791 W. Georgia St., in the Four Seasons Hotel.* ☎ *604/689-9333; www.four seasons.com/vancouver/dining.html. Bus: 2, 22. SkyTrain: Burrard Station. Map p 100.*

Lounges & Cocktail Bars

★★★ Bacchus Piano Lounge

DOWNTOWN A carved limestone fireplace, burgundy velvet banquettes, and cherrywood paneling set a mood that's as ornate and gilded as everything else at the tony Wedgewood. A hot spot for cocktail hour, the Bacchus transforms at night into an elegant piano bar. *845 Hornby St., in the Wedgewood Hotel.* ☎ *604/ 689-7777. www.wedgewoodhotel. com. Bus: 5. Map p 100.*

★★ Cascade Room EAST VAN-

COUVER This one-time brewery turned upscale British-style pub is a magnet for fashionable types of the 30-ish, hipster, "right way to make a cocktail" persuasion. Exposed wood beams, horseshoe-shaped leather booths, and drinks made with fresh-squeezed juices set the mood. *2616 Main St.* ☎ *604/709-8650. www.the cascade.ca. Bus: 3. Map p 100.*

★ Cloud Nine WEST END Every

city needs a revolving cocktail lounge at the top of a skyscraper. Ride the Empire Landmark Hotel's elevator to the 42nd floor, get out, and you're in for one amazing view. Grab a cocktail, pretend it's the swingin' '70s, and enjoy. There's live jazz on Friday and

The very chic Yew restaurant + bar has one of the best wine lists in the city.

The George Ultra Lounge is where Vancouver's beautiful people meet up for cocktails.

Saturday evenings. *1400 Robson St. ☎ 604/687-0511. www.empire landmarkhotel.com. Bus: 5. Map p 100.*

★★★ George Ultra Lounge

YALETOWN Old-school cocktails, super-stylish decor, and beautiful people dominate the menu at this Yaletown chic-spot. There's a good tapas menu, but all that fresh fruit at the bar goes into the drinks. *1137 Hamilton St. ☎ 604/628-5555. www. georgelounge.com. Bus: 6, C21, C23. Map p 100.*

★★★ Gotham Cocktail Bar

DOWNTOWN The decor says power suit—as do the power suits on most of the clientele. Part of the Gotham Steakhouse (p 95), the lounge mixes a good martini, and jazz-age art, low lighting, and leather and velvet seating help complete the mood. *615 Seymour St. ☎ 604/605-8282. www. gothamsteakhouse.com. Bus: 5, 6. Map p 100.*

★★★ Opus Bar YALETOWN Like

the namesake hotel in whose lobby it lives, the Opus Bar is all about style in that sleek, of-the-moment, high-design kind of way. A mix of local and international DJs provides the sound,

and a mix of stylish locals and international visitors give the eye something to do. *322 Davie St., in the Opus Hotel. ☎ 866/642-6787 or 604/ 642-6787. www.opushotel.com. Bus: C21, C23, 6. Map p 100.*

Gay Bars & Clubs

★★★ 1181 WEST END The city's

most stylish gay bar, with the requisite polished concrete floors, cushy seating, and shoulder-to-shoulder bar area. It's known for its sexy cocktails and creative martinis. *1181 Davie St. ☎ 604/689-3991. www.tightlounge. com. Bus: 6. Map p 100.*

★★★ Celebrities WEST END

Vancouver's largest gay dance club attracts a mostly young crowd and lives up to its name with guests such as Boy George, Janet Jackson, and various gay porn stars. *1022 Davie St. ☎ 604/681-6180. www.celebrities nightclub.com. Cover charge most nights. Bus: 6, 2, 22. Map p 100.*

★★ The Odyssey DOWNTOWN

Possibly the gayest place in town, with themed nights and a high-energy dance floor. Sunday nights

You'll find the style conscious—both local and not—grooving to a mix of sounds while tossing back tapas and cocktails at Opus Bar.

The Best Nightlife

host Vancouver's longest-running drag show. Thursdays offer "Shower Power," with naked studs showering above the dance floor. *1251 Howe St.* ☎ *604/689-5256. www.theodyssey nightclub.com. Cover charge most nights. Bus: 4, 10, 6. Map p 100.*

Dance Clubs/Nightclubs

★ **Bar None** YALETOWN   A very Yaletown dance club, with an exposed-brick vibe, a 20- and 30-something clientele, and both live-music and DJ entertainment. *1222 Hamilton St.* ☎ *604/689-7010. www. donnellynightclubs.com/home.asp? barNone. C$12 cover on some nights. Bus: 6. Map p 100.*

★★ **Caprice Nightclub** DOWN-TOWN   A very young, very popular club where getting in is supposed to mean something. Look like Paris Hilton? Welcome to the club. *965 Granville St.* ☎ *604/685-3288. www. capricenightclub.com. C$10–C$15 cover most nights. Bus: 50. Map p 100.*

★★ **Lotus Sound Lounge** GAS-TOWN   Located in a basement below the Honey restaurant/lounge, this underground club doesn't open until midnight and doesn't close until the sun is up. *455 Abbott St.* ☎ *604/ 685-7777. www.markjamesgroup. com/restbrew/honey/flash.html. C$12 cover charge most nights. Bus: 50. SkyTrain: Waterfront Station. Map p 100.*

★★ **the Modern** GASTOWN   A nightclub for trendy 20-somethings, with great decor; high-tech sound and lighting; and an elevated, glowing dance floor. *7 Alexander St.* ☎ *604/647-0121. www.donnellynightclubs.com/ home.asp?theModern. C$15–18 cover charge most nights. Bus: 50. SkyTrain: Waterfront Station. Map p 100.*

★★ **Republic** DOWNTOWN   This two-level club has a dance floor packed with 20- and 30-something scenesters and an almost room-length bar on one level, and a comfortable lounge on the other. The space itself is beautiful, and the cocktail list is inventive. *958 Granville St.* ☎ *604/669-3266. www.donnelly nightclubs.com/home.asp?republic. C$8–C$18 cover charge most nights. Bus: 50. Map p 100.* ●

If you're young, trendy, and like your techno surroundings, you'll fit right in at the Modern.

Vancouver **Arts & Entertainmen**

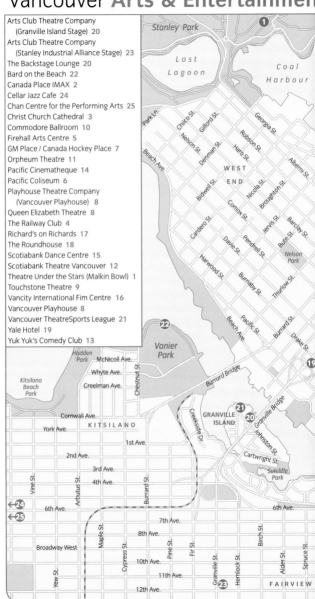

Previous page: The Vancouver Opera presents both classic works and collaborations with First Nations artists.

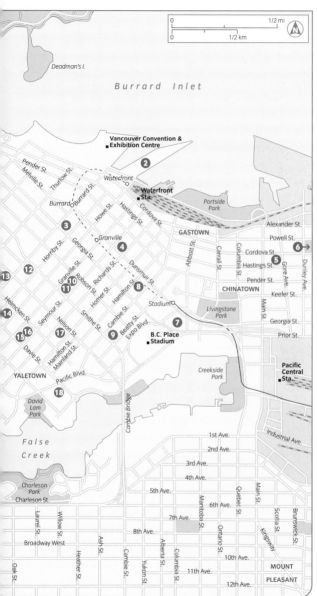

0   1/2 mi
0   1/2 km

Deadman's I.

Burrard Inlet

Vancouver Convention &
Exhibition Centre

2

Waterfront

Waterfront
Sta.

Portside
Park

Pender St.
Melville St.
Thurlow St.
Burrard St.
Burrard St.
Howe St.
Hastings St.
Cordova St.

GASTOWN

Alexander St.

Powell St.

6

3

Granville

Georgia St.
Hornby St.
Granville St.
Robson St.
Richards St.
Dunsmuir St.

4

Cordova St.

5

Hastings St.

Abbott St.
Carrall St.
Columbia St.
Gore Ave.
Dunlevy Ave.

Pender St.

CHINATOWN

Keefer St.

13

12

10

11

Homer St.
Hamilton St.

8

Stadium

Livingstone
Park

Main St.

Georgia St.

14

Helmcken St.
Seymour St.
Smithe St.
Cambie St.
Beatty St.
Expo Blvd.

7

Prior St.

15

16

17

Nelson St.

9

B.C. Place
Stadium

Pacific
Central
Sta.

Davie St.
Hamilton St.
Mainland St.

Pacific Blvd.

Creekside
Park

YALETOWN

18

David
Lam
Park

Cambie Bridge

Industrial Ave.

False
Creek

1st Ave.

2nd Ave.

3rd Ave.

4th Ave.

Charleson
Park

5th Ave.

Manitoba St.
Quebec St.
Main St.
Scotia St.
Brunswick St.

Charleson St.

6th Ave.

7th Ave.

Laurel St.
Willow St.
Ash St.
Heather St.
Cambie St.
Yukon St.
Alberta St.
Columbia St.
Ontario St.
Kingsway

8th Ave.

Broadway West

10th Ave.

MOUNT

Oak St.

11th Ave.

PLEASANT

12th Ave.

Arts & Entertainment Best Bets

Best Theater Company
★★★ Arts Club Theatre Company, *various locations (p 113)*

Best Outdoor Theater Experience
★★★ Bard on the Beach, *Vanier Park (p 113)*

Best Jazz Club
★★★ Cellar Jazz Cafe, *3611 W. Broadway (p 116)*

Best Rock Venue
★★ Commodore Ballroom, *868 Granville St. (p 116)*

Best for High Cs
★★★ Vancouver Opera, *600 Hamilton St. (p 119)*

Best Art-House Movie Theater
★★ Vancity International Film Centre, *1181 Seymour St. (p 115)*

Best Classic Art Deco Theater
★★★ Stanley Industrial Alliance Stage, *2750 Granville St. (p 113)*

Most Essential Local Sports Experience
★★★ Vancouver Canucks at GM Place, *800 Griffiths Way (p 120)*

Best Improv Comedy
★★ Vancouver TheatreSports League, *1601 Johnston St. (p 115)*

Best for Harmony
★★ Vancouver Chamber Choir, *locations vary (p 119)*

Best Place for All Things Dance
★★★ Scotiabank Dance Centre, *677 Davie St. (p 120)*

Best Blues Club
★★ Yale Hotel, *1300 Granville St. (p 117)*

Best Casual Music Lounge
★★★ The Backstage Lounge, *1585 Johnston St. (p 116)*

Best Music Bar
★ The Railway Club, *579 Dunsmuir St. (p 117)*

Best Giant Festival
★★★ Vancouver International Film Festival, *various venues (p 115)*

The Arts Club Theatre Company stages the city's best productions year-round.

Vancouver Arts & Entertainment A to Z

The Playhouse Theatre Company focuses on the works by Canadian playwrights.

Theater

★★★ Arts Club Theatre Company GRANVILLE ISLAND and WEST SIDE   Founded as an actual private club in 1958, the Arts Club began operating professionally in 1964 and has been at it ever since, staging professional musicals, classics, contemporary comedies, and other new works year-round at two theaters, and also staging touring productions. Their 650-seat Stanley Industrial Alliance Stage is a recently renovated grand Art Deco theater dating to 1931, while their 450-seat Granville Island Stage is a more intimate venue right in the heart of Granville Island. ☎ *604/687-1644. www.artsclub.com. Granville Island Stage, 1585 Johnston St. Stanley Industrial Alliance Stage, 2750 Granville St. Tickets C$55–C$65. Bus: 50 to Granville Island; 98B to Stanley Stage. Map p 110.*

★★★ Bard on the Beach WEST SIDE   Every year from June through September, this nonprofit group stages daily Shakespeare plays and related dramas in two large tents in Vanier Park, right across False Creek from Downtown. In the main tent, actors perform against a backdrop of mountains, sea, and sky. *Vanier Park (at Whyte Ave.).* ☎ *877/739-0559 or 604/739-0559. www.bardonthebeach.org. Tickets C$18–C$35. Bus: 2, 22. Also via False Creek Ferries from the Aquatic Centre, 1050 Beach Ave., at Thurlow, Downtown. Map p 110.*

★★ Firehall Arts Centre EAST VANCOUVER   Housed in a 1906 firehouse, this theater presents about 300 performances a year, balancing its offerings between contemporary theater and dance, often by Canadian playwrights and choreographers. *280 E. Cordova St.* ☎ *604/689-0926. www.firehallartscentre.ca. Tickets C$20–C$28. Bus: 7, 8, 10. Map p 110.*

★★ Playhouse Theatre Company DOWNTOWN   Formed in

The Firehall Arts Centre focuses most of its performances on contemporary theater and dance.

1963, this professional theater company presents six Canadian and international plays each year. *600 Hamilton St.* ☎ *604/665-3034. www.vancouverplayhouse.com. Tickets C$33–C$63. Bus: 5, 6. Sky-Train: Granville Station. Map p 110.*

★★ **Theatre Under the Stars** STANLEY PARK From mid-July to mid-August, this organization presents popular musicals such as *Grease, Annie Get Your Gun,* and *Oklahoma!* at Stanley Park's outdoor Malkin Bowl. *Malkin Bowl, Stanley Park (near the Vancouver Aquarium).* ☎ *604/684-2787. www.tuts.ca. Adults C$31–C$36. Kids 5–15 C$29–C$34. Bus: 19. Map p 110.*

★★ **Touchstone Theatre** DOWNTOWN This group has been presenting Canadian works for more than 30 years. Most of its productions are premieres by local playwrights, productions of works previously premiered elsewhere in Canada, and collective projects developed by the company members. *873 Beatty St.* ☎ *604/709-9973. www.touchstonetheatre.com. Tickets C$26 adults, C$24 seniors, C$20 students. Bus: 6, C21, C23. Map p 110.*

The popular Theatre Under the Stars stages musicals each summer in Stanley Park.

Cinema

★ **Canada Place IMAX** DOWNTOWN   The first permanent IMAX theater in the world was built here for Vancouver's Expo '86 fair, and it's still a major draw, showing nature documentaries and remastered Hollywood blockbusters on its immense high-resolution screen. *At Canada Place, northern end of Burrard & Hornby sts.* ☎ *800/582-4629 or 604/682-IMAX. www.imax.com/vancouver. Adults C$12, seniors and kids 3–12 C$11. SkyTrain: Waterfront Station. Bus: 4, 7. Map p 110.*

★★ **Pacific Cinematheque** DOWNTOWN   Founded in 1972, this nonprofit society is dedicated to advancing cinema as an art. They screen retrospectives, documentaries, and independent films daily. *1131 Howe St.* ☎ *604/688-3456. www.cinematheque.bc.ca. Adults C$9.50, seniors/students C$8. Bus: 4, 6, 7. Map p 110.*

Scotiabank Theatre Vancouver DOWNTOWN   The largest and most centrally located theater in Downtown, showing mainstream new releases on nine large screens. *900 Burrard St.* ☎ *604/630-1407. www.cineplex.com. Aged 14 and over C$13, seniors & under 14 C$10. Bus: 2, 22. Map p 110.*

★★ **Vancity International Film Centre** DOWNTOWN   The folks behind the Vancouver International Film Festival (see below) need something to do during the rest of the year, so they present a year-round series of great new films from around the world, all in a super-comfortable environment with state-of-the-art projection. *1181 Seymour St.* ☎ *604/683-3456. www.viff.org. Adults C$9.50, senior/students C$7.50. Bus: 4, 6, 7. Map p 110.*

★★★ **Vancouver International Film Festival** DOWNTOWN & WEST SIDE   The VIFF is Vancouver's

The Vancity International Film Theatre is one of the best places in the city to see a movie.

number-one giant annual event, drawing some 150,000 attendees (including celebs) to see 350 films from around the world. It's held for 2 weeks each year in late September and early October, at venues around the city, including the Vancity International Film Centre and Pacific Cinematheque. ☎ *604/685-0260. www.viff.com. Adults C$10, seniors C$8, matinees C$8. No one under 18 may attend. Bus: 4, 6, 7. Map p 110.*

Comedy

★★ **Vancouver TheatreSports League** GRANVILLE ISLAND   Vancouver's most popular improv comedy troupe presents solo and team improv every week, Wednesday through Saturday. *1601 Johnston St., in the northeast end of the Public Market building.* ☎ *604/738-7013. www.vtsl.com. Adults C$16–C$18, seniors/students C$12–C$15. Anyone under age 19 must be accompanied by an adult. Bus: 50. Map p 110.*

★ **Yuk Yuk's Comedy Club** DOWNTOWN   Name comedians play this popular comedy club, located in the basement of the Century Plaza Hotel, from Thursday to Saturday, and there's amateur standup on Tuesday and Wednesday. *1015 Burrard St.* ☎ *604/696-9857. www.yukyuks.com. Tickets*

Film-lovers from all over the world flock to the ultrapopular Vancouver International Film Festival each fall.

C$5 Tues–Wed, C$10 Thurs, C$15 Fri, C$18 Sat. Bus: 2, 22. Map p 110.

Popular Music

★★★ The Backstage Lounge
GRANVILLE ISLAND   A great, casual spot to hear small-scale, upbeat, and eclectic live music. *See p 13, ⑭. 1585 Johnston St. (near the Public Market).* ☎ *604/687-1354. www.thebackstagelounge.com. Bus: 50. Map p 110.*

★★★ Cellar Jazz Cafe KITSILANO
Vancouver's #1 jazz club (and 1 of the 100 best in the world, according to a *Downbeat* poll) presents both local talent and international stars in a comfortable small-room atmosphere. *3611 W. Broadway.* ☎ *604/738-1959. www.cellarjazz.com. Most shows C$10–C$15, plus C$10–C$15 minimum food/beverage charge. Bus: 99B. Map p 110.*

★★ Commodore Ballroom
DOWNTOWN   This classic space first opened in 1929 as a dance hall and music venue, and it's still going strong, presenting big-time rock, hip-hop, reggae, and other popular music acts. *868 Granville St.* ☎ *604/739-4550. www.livenation.com/venue/getVenue/venueId/2559.*

Vancouver's Favorite Music Festivals

Throughout the year, Vancouver boasts a number of major music festivals and many more minor ones. Among the biggest is the **Vancouver International Jazz Festival** (☎ 888/438-JAZZ or 604/872-5200; www.coastaljazz.ca), which brings in some 1,800 well-known and lesser-known musicians for some 400 concerts from June through July. The 3-day **Vancouver Folk Festival** (☎ 800/883-3655; http://thefestival.bc.ca) offers folk traditions and stylistic updates from Canada and around the world.

Tickets approximately C$13–C$35. Bus: 5. Map p 110.

★ **The Railway Club** DOWN-TOWN A true music bar, the Railway has a comfortable, lived-in atmosphere, lots of good beer on tap, great pub food, and live music (mostly of the rock and rock-ish variety) nightly. *579 Dunsmuir St. ☎ 604/ 681-1625. www.therailwayclub.com. Admission usually C$6–C$10. Bus: 4, 6, 7. Map p 110.*

★★ **Richard's on Richards** DOWNTOWN Is it a live music venue, a nightclub, or a dance club? A little bit of each, actually, and with a long-running hip-hop night every Saturday. *1036 Richards St. ☎ 604/ 687-6794. www.richardsonrichards. com. Tickets approximately C$12– C$45. Bus: 4, 6, 7. Map p 110.*

★★ **Yale Hotel** DOWNTOWN Vancouver's only real blues and R&B club, housed in a former Canada Pacific Railway bunkhouse from the 1880s. There's music every night of the week from both big-name and lesser-known talent. *1300 Granville St. ☎ 604/681-9253. www.theyale.ca. No cover some nights, others C$12– C$30. Bus: 4, 6, 7. Map p 110.*

Both local and international jazz stars take the stage at the Cellar Jazz Cafe, the city's best jazz venue.

Classical Music & Opera
★★ **Vancouver Bach Choir** DOWNTOWN This award-winning choir (it gave its first concert in 1930) presents five concerts annually, including a popular sing-along of Handel's *Messiah*. (See, they don't just do Bach.) ☎ *604/921-8012. www. vancouverbachchoir.com. Concerts at the Orpheum Theatre, 601 Smithe St. Tickets for most performances C$24–C$45. Bus: 4, 6, 7. Map p 110.*

A longtime fixture on the performing arts scene, the Vancouver Symphony Orchestra performs more than 150 concerts a year.

Vancouver's Classical Performance Venues

As in most major cities, many of Vancouver's chamber, choir, and other classical music and dance groups present their performances in a variety of venues. These are the major ones:

Orpheum Theatre, 884 Granville St. (☎ 604/876-3434; http://vancouver.ca/theatres/orpheum/orpheum.html): Built as a vaudeville house in 1927, this 2,800-seat theater is the city's top concert hall.

Queen Elizabeth Theatre, Hamilton and Dunsmuir sts. (☎ 604/665-3050; http://vancouver.ca/theatres/QET/qet.html): Built in 1959, this 2,900-seat theater presents everything from classical and opera to rock and Broadway on its wide stage.

Vancouver Playhouse, Hamilton and Dunsmuir sts. (☎ 604/873-3311; http://vancouver.ca/Theatres/play/play.html): This intimate, 700-seat theater is part of the Queen Elizabeth Theater complex. It's home to the Playhouse Theatre Company and also presents recitals.

Chan Centre for the Performing Arts, 6265 Crescent Rd., University of British Columbia campus (☎ 604/822-9187; www.chancentre.com): This distinctive, cylindrical, zinc-clad building houses a 1,200-seat main theater and several smaller halls.

The Roundhouse, 181 Roundhouse Mews (☎ 604/713-1800; www.roundhouse.ca): This former railroad roundhouse (p 59, ⑱) functions as a venue for concerts as well as workshops and classes.

Christ Church Cathedral, 690 Burrard St. (☎ 604/682-3848; www.cathedral.vancouver.bc.ca): Built between 1891 and 1895, this Anglican church presents frequent choir, orchestra, recital, and organ concerts.

Christ Church Cathedral's excellent acoustics are put to use throughout the year during numerous recitals and organ concerts.

★★ Vancouver Cantata Singers VARIOUS LOCATIONS

While specializing in music of the Baroque era, this choir also performs new works from regional and international composers. Performances take place in different venues around the city, including the Orpheum Theatre and the Roundhouse. ☎ 604/730-8856. www.vancouvercantatasingers.com. Tickets for most performances C$12–C$45. Map p 110.

★★ Vancouver Chamber Choir

VARIOUS LOCATIONS   This award-winning 20-person group has a diverse repertoire, from chant to avant-garde, folksong to jazz. Concerts take place at various venues, including the Orpheum Theatre and Christ Church Cathedral. ☎ 604/738-6822. www.vancouverchamberchoir.com. Tickets for most performances $C24–C$45. Map p 110.

★★★ Vancouver Opera DOWNTOWN

Founded in 1958, the Vancouver Opera is the second largest opera company in Canada, presenting great works from the canon as well as variations such as 2007's The Magic Flute, created in collaboration with a team of First Nations artists. ☎ 604/683-0222. www.vancouveropera.ca. Performances take place at the Queen Elizabeth Theatre, 600 Hamilton St. Tickets C$24–C$170 Bus: 5, 6. Map p 110.

★★ Vancouver Recital Society

VARIOUS LOCATIONS   This society began life in 1980 and brings classical music stars and emerging international artists (Yo-Yo Ma and Joshua Bell, to name just a few) to Vancouver for performances in various venues, including the Vancouver Playhouse and the Orpheum Theatre. ☎ 604/602-0363. www.vanrecital.com. Tickets for most performances C$31–C$45; special events up to $175. Map p 110.

★★ Vancouver Symphony Orchestra DOWNTOWN & VARIOUS

Vancouver's big-time orchestra, founded in 1919, presents more than 150 concerts a year at various venues, including its main home, the Orpheum Theatre. ☎ 604/876-3434. www.vancouversymphony.ca. Tickets C$25–C$78. Map p 110.

Dance
★★ Ballet British Columbia DOWNTOWN

A relatively young company, the BBC mixes popular

The annual Dancing on the Edge Festival celebrating contemporary dance is one of the city's most prestigious events.

ballet (the obligatory *Nutcracker* and *Swan Lake*) with newer works, including works by Canadian choreographers and collaborations with visual artists, theatre directors, and others. ☎ *604/732-5003. www. balletbc.com. Most performances take place at the Queen Elizabeth Theatre. Tickets C$32–C$85. Bus: 5, 6. Map p 110.*

★★ **Dancing on the Edge Festival** VARIOUS LOCATIONS   Held each July, this 10-day festival presents some 30 works by choreographers from Vancouver and elsewhere. ☎ *604/689-0926. www.dancingontheedge.org. Performances at various venues, including the Firehall Arts Centre and Scotiabank Dance Centre. C$250 Gold Pass allows unlimited attendance; C$150 Flex Pass gives admission to 8 performances; C$75 Flex gives admission to 4 performances; individual performance tickets C$20. Map p 110.*

If you visit Vancouver during hockey season, a trip to GM Place to watch the Canucks is de rigueur . . . if you can score the hard-to-get tickets.

★★ **Firehall Arts Centre** EAST VANCOUVER   *See p 113. Map p 110.*

★★★ **Scotiabank Dance Centre** DOWNTOWN   Opened in 2001, this space is the hub of Vancouver's dance scene, offering performances, classes, workshops, rehearsal space, and other dance events year-round. *677 Davie St.* ☎ *604/606-6400. www.thedance centre.ca. Tickets for most performances C$12–C$26. Bus: 4, 6, 7. Map p 110.*

Spectator Sports
★★★ **GM Place** DOWNTOWN   Canada = Hockey and Vancouver = the Vancouver Canucks, the city's National Hockey League team. This C$150 million arena (opened in 1995) is the Canucks' home. Take in a game if you can get tickets, but they often sell out fast. *Note:* For the 2010 Olympic Winter Games, the venue has been temporarily renamed Canada Hockey Place. *800 Griffiths Way. www.generalmotors place.com. For Canucks' information, see http://canucks.nhl.com. Get tickets throughTicketmaster at* ☎ *888/663-9311 or 604/280-4400. Tickets C$55–C$130. Bus: C21, C23. SkyTrain: Stadium/Chinatown Station. Map p 110.*

★ **Pacific Coliseum** EAST VANCOUVER   Completed in 1968, this formalist-style arena is the home base of the Vancouver Giants. Vancouver's junior hockey league team has only been around since 2000, but won Western and Canadian hockey league titles in 2006 and 2007. *100 N. Renfrew St.* ☎ *604/444-2687. www.vancouvergiants. com. Tickets C$17–C$19. Bus: 4. Map p 110.*●

Vancouver **Accommodations**

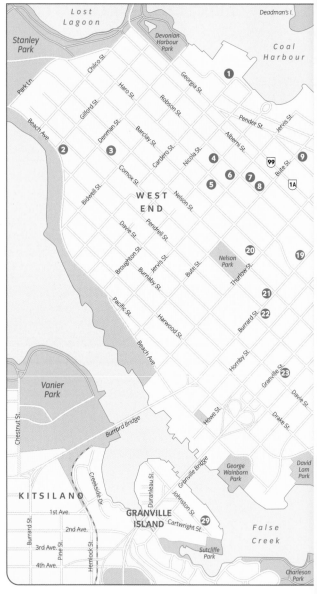

Previous page: The Victorian-style West End Guest House is the best B&B in Vancouver.

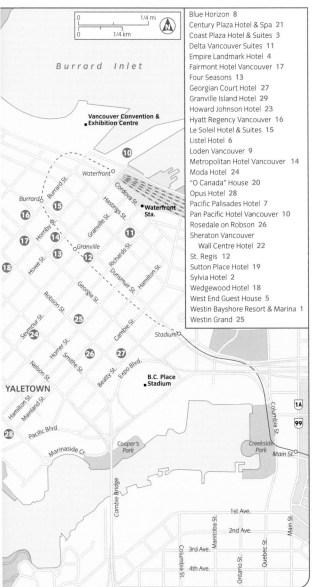

Blue Horizon 8
Century Plaza Hotel & Spa 21
Coast Plaza Hotel & Suites 3
Delta Vancouver Suites 11
Empire Landmark Hotel 4
Fairmont Hotel Vancouver 17
Four Seasons 13
Georgian Court Hotel 27
Granville Island Hotel 29
Howard Johnson Hotel 23
Hyatt Regency Vancouver 16
Le Soleil Hotel & Suites 15
Listel Hotel 6
Loden Vancouver 9
Metropolitan Hotel Vancouver 14
Moda Hotel 24
"O Canada" House 20
Opus Hotel 28
Pacific Palisades Hotel 7
Pan Pacific Hotel Vancouver 10
Rosedale on Robson 26
Sheraton Vancouver
  Wall Centre Hotel 22
St. Regis 12
Sutton Place Hotel 19
Sylvia Hotel 2
Wedgewood Hotel 18
West End Guest House 5
Westin Bayshore Resort & Marina 1
Westin Grand 25

Hotel Best Bets

Best **Grand Historic Hotel**
★★★ Fairmont Hotel Vancouver
$$$ *900 W. Georgia St. (p 126)*

Best Hotel **for Models and Trendsetters**
★★★ Opus Hotel $$$ *322 Davie St. (p 128)*

Best **for Old World Elegance**
★★★ Wedgewood Hotel $$$ *845 Hornby St. (p 130)*

Best **Family Hotel**
★ Rosedale on Robson $$ *838 Hamilton St. (p 129)*

Best **for Business Travelers**
★★★ Westin Grand $$$ *433 Robson St. (p 130)*

Best **Inexpensive Hipster Digs**
★ Moda Hotel $ *900 Seymour St. (p 127)*

The lobby of the Rosedale on Robson, a top spot for families visiting Vancouver.

Best **Discreet, Celebrity-Friendly Hotel**
★★★ Sutton Place Hotel $$$ *845 Burrard St. (p 129)*

Most **Romantic Hotel**
★★★ Wedgewood Hotel $$$ *845 Hornby St. (p 130)*

Best **B&B**
★ West End Guest House $ *1362 Haro St. (p 130)*

Best **Views**
★★★ Pan Pacific $$$$ *Canada Place (p 128)*; and ★ Coast Plaza $ *1763 Comox St. (p 125)*

Best **for Art Lovers**
★★ Listel Hotel $$$ *1300 Robson St. (p 127)*

Best **Cheap Hotel in an Idyllic Location**
★ Sylvia Hotel $ *1154 Gilford St. (p 130)*

Friendliest Staff
★ Blue Horizon $ *1225 Robson St. (p 125)*

Most **Stylin' Hotel Restaurant**
★★★ Yew at the Four Seasons $$$ *791 W. Georgia St. (p 98)*

Best **Revolving Rooftop Restaurant**
★ Empire Landmark Hotel $$ *1400 Robson St. (p 125)*

Best **Pool & Health Club**
★★★ Four Seasons $$$ *791 W. Georgia St. (p 126)*

Best **Feng Shui**
★★★ Metropolitan Hotel Vancouver $$$ *645 Howe St. (p 127)*

Best **Hotel Value**
★ Century Plaza $ *1015 Burrard St. (p 125)*; and ★ Blue Horizon $ *1225 Robson St. (p 125)*

Vancouver Hotels A to Z

A twin-bedded room at the Delta Vancouver Suites.

★ **Blue Horizon** WEST END   Low prices, a prime location, a super-friendly staff, and great views from the top 15 floors. Every room has a balcony, which offsets the only-average decor. *1225 Robson St. ☎ 800/663-1333 or 604/688-1411. www.bluehorizonhotel.com. 214 units. Doubles C$109–C$329. AE, DC, MC, V. Bus: 5. Map p 122.*

★ **Century Plaza Hotel & Spa** DOWNTOWN   This centrally located high-rise offers large rooms with full kitchens; a fun, modern lobby and restaurant; a well-regarded day spa; and a comedy club. Executive suites are enormous, and views are killer above the 12th floor. *1015 Burrard St. ☎ 800/663-1818 or 604/687-0575. www.century-plaza.com. 236 units. Studio suites C$85–$179. AE, DC, MC, V. Bus: 2, 22. Map p 122.*

★ **Coast Plaza Hotel & Suites** WEST END   High-rise with a great location, amazing views from most floors, plus a huge rooftop garden around its main tower. Decor is

unimaginative, but suites have full kitchens. *1763 Comox St. ☎ 800/716-6199 or 604/688-7711. www.coasthotels.com. 269 units. Doubles C$149–C$289. AE, DC, DISC, JCB, MC, V. Bus: 5. Map p 122.*

★★ **Delta Vancouver Suites** DOWNTOWN   All-suite high-rise close to Canada Place and Gastown. Suites' decor is comfortable business-hotel style, with lots of amenities but no kitchens. *550 West Hastings St. ☎ 888/890-3222 or 604/689-8188. www.deltahotels.com. 225 units. Suites C$159–C$299 AE, DC, DISC, MC, V. Bus: 5, 6. SkyTrain: Waterfront Station. Map p 122.*

★ **Empire Landmark Hotel** WEST END   Located on the edge of the Robson shopping district, this high-rise offers great views, comfortable if uninspired rooms, and the city's only revolving restaurant and lounge, Cloud Nine (p 106), on the 42nd floor. *1400 Robson St. ☎ 800/830-6144 or 604/687-0511.*

www.empirelandmarkhotel.com. 357 units. Doubles C$150–C$300. AE, DC, MC, V. Bus: 5. Map p 122.

★★★ Fairmont Hotel Vancouver DOWNTOWN

If you're looking for *the* classic old Vancouver hotel, this is it, with wonderful mid-20th-century room decor, a grand marble lobby with a classic lobby bar (p 105), and the overall ambience of a 1930s movie. Favorite touch? The resident dogs that greet guests in the lobby. *900 West Georgia St.* ☎ *866/540-4452 or 604/684-3131. www.fairmont.com/hotelvancouver. 556 units. Doubles C$289–C$429 AE, DISC, MC, V. Bus: 2, 22, 5. SkyTrain: Burrard Station. Map p 122.*

★★★ Four Seasons DOWNTOWN

Traditional luxury hotel with a perfect downtown location. Rooms are done in classic, comfortable style, and the heated pool is the most beautiful in town—half indoor and half out, on a garden terrace surrounded by skyscrapers. The lobby restaurant, Yew, is a stunner too

For luxe accommodations in Vancouver, it's hard to beat the Four Seasons.

(p 98). *791 W. Georgia St.* ☎ *800/819-5053 or 604/689-9333. www.fourseasons.com/vancouver. 372 units. Doubles C$240–C$380. AE, DC, DISC, JCB, MC, V. Bus: 2, 22. SkyTrain: Burrard Station. Map p 122.*

★ Georgian Court Hotel DOWNTOWN

Located at the less glamorous eastern edge of Downtown, the Georgian Court nevertheless offers comfortable rooms and suites, and proximity to many Downtown and Yaletown attractions. *773 Beatty St.* ☎ *800/663-1155 or 604/682-5555. www.georgiancourt.com. 178 units. Doubles C$169–C$350. AE, DC, DISC, MC, V. Bus: 15, 17. SkyTrain: Stadium Station. Map p 122.*

★★ Granville Island Hotel GRANVILLE ISLAND

The only hotel on Granville Island offers a quiet waterside location; comfortable if not eye-popping rooms; an on-site brewpub; and proximity to the island's theaters, shopping, restaurants, and bars. Only drawback? Expensive cab rides back from Downtown after dark. *1253 Johnston St.* ☎ *800/663-1840 or 604/683-7373. www.granvilleislandhotel.com. 82 units. Doubles C$150–C$240. AE, DC, DISC, JCB, MC, V. Bus: 50. Map p 122.*

★ Howard Johnson Hotel DOWNTOWN

Located amid Granville Street's bars-and-clubs strip, this HoJo occupies an older, renovated building, giving it more character than you'd expect. Rooms are very simply decorated and have very small windows, but antique radiators and photos of old Vancouver add a nice touch. *1176 Granville St.* ☎ *888/654-6336 or 604/688-8701. www.hojovancouver.com. 110 units. Doubles C$79–C$299. AE, DISC, MC, V. Bus: 50, 6. Map p 122.*

★★ Hyatt Regency Vancouver DOWNTOWN

Double-duty business/leisure hotel has a great location

A deluxe twin-bedded room at Le Soleil Hotel & Suites.

and spacious, comfortable rooms with crisp but not severe decor, and an outdoor heated pool. Only corner rooms have balconies, but others offer good views. *655 Burrard St.* ☎ *800/633-7313 or 604/683-1234. www.vancouver.hyatt.com. 644 units. Doubles C$170–C$450. AE, DC, DISC, JCB, MC, V. Bus: 2, 22. Sky-Train: Burrard Station. Map p 122.*

★★ **Le Soleil Hotel & Suites** DOWNTOWN   A luxe French country hotel in the heart of Downtown. Expect lots of rich fabrics, gold trim, and plush carpeting, plus wonderful service. *567 Hornby St.* ☎ *877/632-3030 or 604/632-3000. www.hotellesoleil.com. 119 units. Doubles C$175–C$500. AE, MC, V. Bus: 98B. SkyTrain: Burrard Station. Map p 122.*

★★ **Listel Hotel** WEST END   An environmentally friendly hotel for art lovers, the Listel has "Gallery Rooms" with artworks from the Buschlen Mowatt Gallery (p 28) and "Museum Rooms" featuring art and furnishings by First Nations artists. The decor is clean and minimal, the vibe is friendly and educated. *1300 Robson St.* ☎ *800/663-5491 or 604/684-8461. www.thelistelhotel.com. 129 units. Doubles C$139–C$299. AE, DC, DISC, JCB, MC, V. Bus: 5. Map p 122.*

★★★ **Loden Vancouver** WEST END   At the edge of Coal Harbour, this 14-story boutique hotel (built in 2008) is aimed at travelers with lots of style and even more cash. Room decor is immaculately modern, with razor-edge lines softened by plush beds and luxe linens. Bathrooms have heated floors, and a sliding wall lets in natural light from the bedroom. The street-level restaurant and lounge are ultrachic. *1177 Melville St.* ☎ *877/225-6336 or 604/669-5060. www.lodenvancouver.com. 77 units. Doubles C$199–C$399. AE, DC, DISC, MC, V. Bus: 19. Map p 122.*

★★★ **Metropolitan Hotel Vancouver** DOWNTOWN   Centrally located luxury hotel with great, free-flowing feng shui. Rooms are luxe-homey, with great beds and marble bathrooms. There's a heated indoor pool under a curving glass roof, and a great restaurant, Diva at the Met (p 95). *645 Howe St.* ☎ *800/667-2300 or 604/687-1122. www.metropolitan.com/vanc. 197 units. Doubles C$165–C$240. AE, MC, V. Bus: 2, 22. Map p 122.*

★ **Moda Hotel** DOWNTOWN   Built in 1908, this place was completely transformed 100 years later into a hip, modern Downtowner mixing original details with stylish modern touches. Rooms (all nearly identical) are done in a simple, youthful, minimalist style. Bathrooms mix antique floors with all-modern appointments. There's a hip, intimate wine bar off the lobby, and a restaurant to match. *900 Seymour St.* ☎ *604/683-4251. www. modahotel.ca. 57 units. Doubles C$99–C$399. AE, DC, DISC, MC, V. Bus: 6. SkyTrain: Granville Station. Map p 122.*

★★ "O Canada" House WEST END
An 1897 Victorian built by a composer of Canada's national anthem. Meticulously restored, with a cozy front parlor with fireplace; wraparound front porch; and rooms with period furnishings and private baths. *1114 Barclay St.* ☎ *877/ 688-1114 or 604/688-0555. www. ocanadahouse.com. 7 units. Doubles C$135–C$285. MC, V. Bus: 2, 22. Map p 122.*

★★★ Opus Hotel YALETOWN
Vancouver's most stylish hotel, the 7-story Opus exists on the border of fashion and fantasy—fashion from the lobby lounge (Vancouver's hottest, with guest international DJs) and overall vibe, fantasy from the design concept: Five imaginary guests (a rock star, fashion exec, doctor, actress, and food critic) were used to create the five different room types, designed to their tastes. Expect super-stylish decor and artwork, lots of natural light, a playful color scheme, and lots of amenities. *322 Davie St.* ☎ *866/642-6787 or 604/642-6787. www.opushotel.com. 96 units. Doubles C$240–C$430. AE, MC, V. Bus: C21, C23, 6. Map p 122.*

★★ Pacific Palisades Hotel
WEST END A fun, playfully designed, pet-friendly hotel with free evening wine and cheese, animal-print bathrobes, and a nice outdoor patio. Penthouse suites are totally mod, standard rooms plainer, many with kitchens or kitchenettes. *1277 Robson St.* ☎ *800/663-1815 or 604/688-0461. www.pacificpalisades hotel.com. 232 units. Doubles C$225– C$405. AE, DC, DISC, MC, V. Bus: 5. Map p 122.*

★★★ Pan Pacific Hotel Vancouver DOWNTOWN
Topping Canada Place, this 23-story hotel offers some of the city's best views from spacious, comfortable, comtemporary rooms. There's a heated outdoor pool with views of the North Shore mountains, and an excellent spa and health club.

The Penthouse Suite at the "O Canada" House.

The colorful lobby of the Pacific Palisades Hotel.

Canada Place, at north terminus of Burrard St. ☎ 800/663-1515 in Canada, 800/937-1515 from the U.S., or 604 662 8111. www.panpacific.com/Vancouver. 504 units. Doubles C$410–C$700. AE, DC, MC, V. Bus: 2, 22. SkyTrain: Waterfront Station. Map p 122.

★ **Rosedale on Robson** DOWNTOWN   Good value and location on Library Square, plus an indoor lap pool and a lovely roof garden. All rooms are one- and two-bedroom suites with kitchens, but average furnishings. 838 Hamilton St. ☎ 800/661-8870 or 604/689-8033. www.rosedaleonrobson.com. 225 units. Suites C$179–C$389. AE, DC, DISC, MC, V. Bus: 5. Map p 122.

★★ **Sheraton Vancouver Wall Centre Hotel** DOWNTOWN Looking like a futuristic corporate office park, the Sheraton caters to many business travelers and tour groups. Rooms are done in a contemporary, light-toned style, and there's a huge health club with an indoor pool. The complex's curved, black glass north tower is one of the more distinctive buildings on the city's skyline. 1088 Burrard St. ☎ 877/271-2018 or 604/331-1000. www.sheratonvancouver.com. 733 units. Doubles C$209–C$309. AE, DC, MC, V. Bus: 2, 22. Map p 122.

★ **St. Regis** DOWNTOWN   Built in 1913 (and designed by W. T. Whiteway, the architect responsible for the Sun Tower; p 57, ⑭), the 6-story St. Regis got a C$6.5-million renovation in 2008 that gave its rooms a contemporary kick, with clean lines and lovely bathrooms. It's centrally located and comes with a slew of nice amenities. 602 Dunsmuir St. ☎ 800/770-7929 or 604/681-1135. www.stregishotel.com. 65 units. Doubles $134–$179. AE, JCB, MC, V. Bus: 98B. SkyTrain: Granville Station. Map p 122.

★★★ **Sutton Place Hotel** DOWNTOWN   Discreet, traditionally luxurious, and popular with movie types. Rooms are done in tasteful European style, with surround-sound TV/stereos. There's a woody, old-world bar; a beautiful indoor pool and outdoor garden; and a restaurant that

serves high tea. *845 Burrard St.*
☎ *866/378-8866 or 604/682-5511.*
www.vancouver.suttonplace.com.
397 units. Doubles C$331–C$496. AE,
DC, DISC, JCB, MC, V. Bus: 22, 44, 98B.
SkyTrain: Burrard Station. Map p 122.

★ **Sylvia Hotel** WEST END   A sen-
timental favorite since 1912, popular for its English Bay location; its
old-fashioned, vine-covered character; and for Sylvia's Bar (p 105).
Rooms are dated, lack pizazz, and
have small windows, but you still
gotta love the place. Ask for a bay-
facing room in the hotel's old section. *1154 Gilford St.* ☎ *604/681-
9321. www.sylviahotel.com. 120
units. Doubles C$80–C$200. AE, DC,
MC, V. Bus: 5, 6. Map p 122.*

★★★ **Wedgewood Hotel** DOWN-
TOWN   If you're looking for ornate,
old-world elegance (think top-hatted
doormen and Oriental rugs), this is
your place. Located opposite Robson
Square, it offers a wide selection of
rooms and suites, some with his-and-
hers baths, some with Jacuzzis in the

*The Penthouse living room at the
stylish Opus Hotel (p 128).*

room. All rooms have balconies,
though those on the upper floors facing Hornby are best. *845 Hornby St.*
☎ *800/663-0666 or 604/689-7777.*
www.wedgewoodhotel.com. 83 units.
Doubles C$199–C$299. AE, DC, DISC,
*MC, V. Bus: 5. SkyTrain: Burrard Sta-
tion. Map p 122.*

★★ **West End Guest House**
WEST END   Just 1 block from Robson Street, this ornate (and pink!)
Victorian exudes the vibe of old Vancouver, full of polished woodwork,
palms, brocade wallpaper, and a mix
of period and modern furnishings.
Each room is different, some with a
fireplace, others with divan lounges
and skylights. Out back are a small
garden and terrace. *1362 Haro St.*
☎ *888/546-3327 or 604/681-2889.*
*www.westendguesthouse.com. 8
units. Doubles C$135–C$300. AE,
DISC, MC, V. Bus: 5. Map p 122.*

★★★ **Westin Bayshore Resort
& Marina** COAL HARBOUR
Located right on Coal Harbour, this
is the only Vancouver hotel you can
access by car, boat, or seaplane.
Rooms are cheerfully modern, with
large windows and elegant baths.
Niceties include indoor/outdoor
pools and proximity to Stanley Park.
1601 Bayshore Dr. ☎ *888/625-5144
or 604/682-3377. www.westinbay
shore.com. 511 units. Doubles
C$195–C$315. AE, DC, MC, V. Bus: 19.
Map p 122.*

★★★ **Westin Grand** DOWNTOWN
An understated, modern all-suite
hotel has a great location equidis-
tant from central Downtown and
Yaletown. Spacious, contemporary
rooms have lots of light, kitchens,
roomy bathrooms, and good business amenities. *433 Robson St.*
☎ *888/625-5144 or 604/602-1999.*
*www.westingrandvancouver.com. 207
units. Doubles C$179–C$479. AE, DC,
DISC, MC, V. Bus: 5, 6. Map p 122.* ●

The Sea to Sky Highway

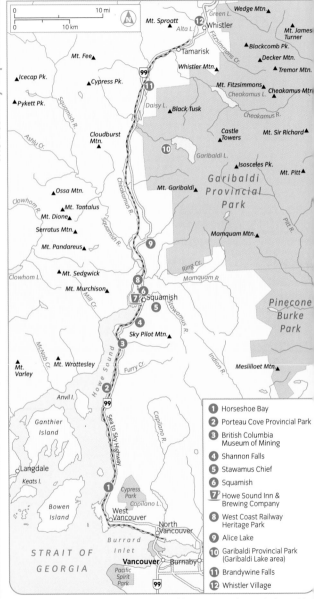

0   10 mi
0   10 km

Wedge Mtn.
Mt. Sproatt
Alta L.
Green R.
Whistler
Mt. James Turner
Blackcomb Pk.
Tamarisk
Decker Mtn.
Mt. Fee
Whistler Mtn.
Tremor Mtn.
99
Cypress Pk.
Mt. Fitzsimmons
Cheakamus L.
Cheakamus Mtn.
Icecap Pk.
Cheakamus R.
Pykett Pk.
Daisy L.
Black Tusk
Castle Towers
Mt. Sir Richard
Cloudburst Mtn.
Garibaldi L.
Isosceles Pk.
Mt. Pitt
10
Garibaldi
Provincial
Park
Mt. Garibaldi
Ossa Mtn.
Mt. Tantalus
Mt. Dione
Serratus Mtn.
Mamquam Mtn.
Mt. Pandareus
Ring Cr.
Mamquam R.
Mt. Sedgwick
Mt. Murchison
Squamish
Pinecone
Burke
Park
Mt. Varley
Mt. Wrottesley
Sky Pilot Mtn.
Meslilloet Mtn.
Furry Cr.
Indian R.
Anvil I.
99
Ganthier
Island
Capilano R.
Langdale
Keats I.
Bowen
Island
Cypress Park
Capilano L.
West Vancouver
North Vancouver
STRAIT OF GEORGIA
Burrard Inlet
Vancouver
Burnaby
Pacific Spirit Park
99

1 Horseshoe Bay
2 Porteau Cove Provincial Park
3 British Columbia Museum of Mining
4 Shannon Falls
5 Stawamus Chief
6 Squamish
7 Howe Sound Inn & Brewing Company
8 West Coast Railway Heritage Park
9 Alice Lake
10 Garibaldi Provincial Park (Garibaldi Lake area)
11 Brandywine Falls
12 Whistler Village

Previous page: The Sea to Sky Highway is one of the most scenic byways in the world.

The driving route between Vancouver and Whistler is an attraction all in itself, a gorgeous 105km (65-mile) road trip that starts at West Vancouver's Horseshoe Bay, slaloms along the edge of steep, rainforest-lined Howe Sound (North America's southernmost fjord), then zigzags into the mountains en route to skiing paradise. BC gave the route C$600 million in improvements in preparation for the Vancouver 2010 Olympic and Paralympic Winter Games, and what it's lost in two-lane charm, it's gained in safety and drivability. The whole trip takes about 2 hours without traffic, but there's enough to see along the way to make it a full-day excursion.

START: **From Downtown Vancouver, take W. Georgia St. (aka Hwy. 99) north through Stanley Park and across the Lions Gate Bridge into West Vancouver, then follow the signs until 99 turns into the Sea to Sky.**

① ★ Horseshoe Bay. The official starting point of the Sea to Sky is also one of Vancouver's main ferry hubs. It's a very picturesque spot, with a lovely marina and a town full of little shops and restaurants. ⏱ *30–45 min. Located at mile 0, where Hwy. 99 turns sharply north. www.horseshoebaybc.ca.*

② ★ Porteau Cove Provincial Park. Located on the shores of glacier-carved Howe Sound, Porteau Cove offers stunning water and mountain views, a rocky beach, and waterside picnic areas, and is a great spot for kayaking and for scuba diving among several large vessels that were sunk to create a manmade reef. ⏱ *30 min., more for activities. Located about 24km (15 miles) north of Horseshoe Bay. www.env.gov.bc.ca/bcparks/explore/parkpgs/porteau. C$1/hr or C$3/day parking fee.*

③ ★ kids British Columbia Museum of Mining. It would be easy to drive past the little town of Britannia Beach were it not for the unbelievably enormous ore truck and the weird building that steps up the hillside behind it. That's the BC Museum of Mining, a former copper

A ferry to Vancouver Island crosses Horseshoe Bay.

mine that operated from 1904 to 1974. Inside, visitors can tour the mill, don hardhats and headlamps for a guided tour through the mine tunnels, see demos on mining and fossils, and do a little goldpanning. The town has little else of note, but there is a food shop and a store selling First Nations art. ⏱ *1½-2 hr. Located 33km (21 miles) north of Horseshoe*

An ore truck welcomes visitors to the British Columbia Museum of Mining.

Bay. ☎ 800/896-4044 or 604/896-2233. www.bcmuseumofmining.org. Adults C$17, seniors and students C$14, kids 6–12 C$12. Winter rate C$7.50 all ages (gold panning not included). Open Tues–Sun 9am–4:30pm in summer, Mon–Fri 9am–4:30pm mid-Oct to spring.

④ ★ **Shannon Falls.** BC's third-highest waterfall cascades 335m (about 1,000 ft.) down a series of cliffs, looking like a whitewater river tilted on its side. An easy 350m (¼ mile) trail leads to the viewpoint. The falls were once owned by the Carling O'Keefe Brewery, which used their water to make beer. ⏲ 30 min. Located about 42km (26 miles) north of Horseshoe Bay. www.env.gov.bc.ca/bcparks/explore/parkpgs/shannon. C$1/hr or C$3/day parking fee.

⑤ ★★ **Stawamus Chief.** They say "The Chief" is the second-largest granite monolith in the world, which makes you expect something big, but still manageable. Then you arrive in the town of Squamish, look up, and see its 700m (2,300-ft.) vertical cliff face completely blocking out the surrounding landscape. This monolith is a mountain. It's also a major destination for rock-climbers, and for hikers who want a super-steep hike to one of its three peaks. ⏲ 5 min. to view, about 4 hr. to hike round-trip. Located about 44km (27 miles) north of Horseshoe Bay. www.env.gov.bc.ca/bc parks/explore/parkpgs/stawamus. C$1/hr or C$3/day parking fee.

⑥ **Squamish.** The main town between Vancouver and Whistler, Squamish is something between a base camp for outdoor activities and a pit-stop for road trippers. Many outfitters have their operations here, and the town offers many restaurants and shops, with chain establishments clustered near the highway and local joints lining the more interesting town center, just a few blocks west. From November through February, the town is invaded by thousands of bald eagles, who come to feed on salmon in the Squamish and Cheakamus rivers. ⏲ 30 min. to see the town, longer to eat. Located about 46km (29 miles) north of Horseshoe Bay. www.squamish.ca/visitors.

Set near the end of Squamish's main drag, the ⑦ **Howe Sound Inn & Brewing Company** is a friendly, high-ceilinged brewpub/restaurant serving excellent homebrew and a big menu of sandwiches, pizza, pasta, mains, etc. Big windows and a patio look out on the Stawamus Chief. 37801 Cleveland Ave., Squamish. ☎ 604/892-2603. www.howesound.com. $.

⑧ ★ kids **West Coast Railway Heritage Park.** Established in 1994 by the nonprofit West Coast Railway Association, this 5-hectare (12-acre) railyard museum is home to more than 70 locomotives and cars (some fully restored, some undergoing restoration) dating as far back as 1890, plus rail artifacts, railway stations, and a miniature railroad for

The immense granite monolith that is the Stawamus Chief.

Picturesque Garibaldi Provincial Park is a great place for outdoor recreation.

kids. Rail fans would give this place 3 stars, but there's enough here to keep the interest of casual visitors too. 🕑 *1–2 hr. 39645 Government Rd., Squamish.* ☎ *604/898-9336. www.wcra.org/heritage. Adults C$10, seniors and students C$8.50. Open 10am–5pm daily.*

9 ★ **Alice Lake.** Surrounded by mountains and grassy areas, pretty little Alice Lake is ideal for picnicking, swimming at its two sandy beaches, canoeing, and hiking, with 10 different trails winding back into the forest. 🕑 *30 min to 3 hr. Off Hwy. 99, 13km (8 miles) north of Squamish. www.env.gov.bc. ca/bcparks/explore/ parkpgs/alice_lk. C$1/hr or C$3/day parking fee.*

10 ★★ **Garibaldi Provincial Park.** Covering about 1,950 sq. km (753 sq. miles), this enormous wilderness park stretches from Squamish to Whistler, just east of the Sea to Sky Highway. Hikers get 90km (59 miles)

of hiking trails, but anyone with eyes can take in its snow-capped mountains (including 2,678m/8,786-ft. Mount Garibaldi), clear lakes, and abundant wildlife. The scenic area around Garibaldi Lake, midway to Whistler, is the park's scenic heart. 🕑 *At least 2 hrs. for hiking, though you could also spend a week. To access the Garibaldi Lake area, take the turnoff from Hwy. 99 just past the Rubble Creek Bridge, 37km (23 miles) north of Squamish, then drive the 2.5km (1½-mile) paved road to the Garibaldi Lake parking lot. www.env. gov.bc.ca/bcparks/explore/parkpgs/ garibaldi. C$1/hr or C$3/day parking fee.*

11 ★ **Brandywine Falls.** While Shannon Falls **4** cascades down an angled mountain face, Brandywine shoots directly out from a cliff, falling 70m (230 ft.) into Daisy Lake at the bottom of a steep-walled canyon. It's like something out of an *Indiana Jones* movie. The main viewing area is a 10-minute walk from the parking lot, along a trail that crosses the Canadian National Rail line. If you're there at the right time, you can wave to the Whistler Mountaineer (p 190) as it chugs north. 🕑 *30–45 min. Located 10km (6 miles) south of Whistler off Hwy 99. www.env.gov.bc.ca/bc parks/explore/park pgs/brandywine_ falls. C$1/hr or C$3/ day parking fee.*

12 ★★★ **Whistler Village.** You're here. Go ski. Go mountain bike. Have fun. *See chapter 11 for more complete information on Whistler.*

Brandywine Falls is both dramatic and easily accessible, making it a favorite of shutterbugs.

Victoria

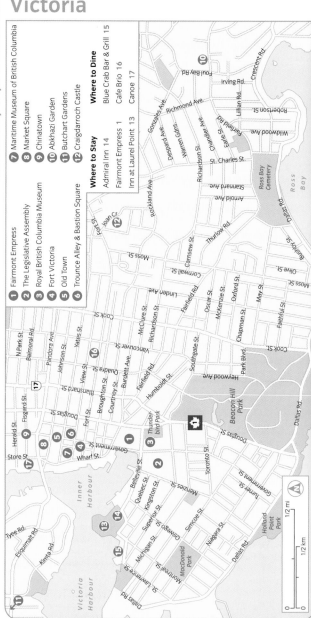

1 Fairmont Empress
2 The Legislative Assembly
3 Royal British Columbia Museum
4 Fort Victoria
5 Old Town
6 Trounce Alley & Bastion Square
7 Maritime Museum of British Columbia
8 Market Square
9 Chinatown
10 Abkhazi Garden
11 Butchart Gardens
12 Craigdarroch Castle

Where to Stay

Admiral Inn 14
Fairmont Empress 1
Inn at Laurel Point 13

Where to Dine

Blue Crab Bar & Grill 15
Cafe Brio 16
Canoe 17

While shiny new Vancouver generally lacks a historic feel, Victoria, the provincial capital, has the look of 19th-century Britain, but with a better climate. Tour the well-maintained Old Town and the Inner Harbour, surrounded by century-old British government buildings. Just outside town, gorgeous formal gardens add to the Anglo allure, while fleece-clad locals, snowcapped mountains, and whale-watching in Juan de Fuca Strait remind you that you really are in Pacific Canada after all. START: **Victoria is 183km (114 miles) southwest of Vancouver (the city) at the tip of Vancouver (the island). See "Getting to Victoria" on p 138 for travel info. Because of the distance, this is no day trip: To really see the place, plan on spending at least 2 nights.**

① ★★★ The Fairmont Empress. Built in 1908, this ivy-covered Edwardian beauty was designed by Francis Rattenbury (architect of the Vancouver Art Gallery; p 11, **⑥**) to provide a visual complement to the Legislative Assembly buildings he designed nearby. Talk about effective: The two have been the very symbol of Victoria ever since. The hotel embodies the feel of its era, from its Gothic dormers and steep slate roof to its ornate Colonial lobby, with its potted palms, ornate woodwork, and overstuffed furniture. For visitors, High Tea is the big draw. If you want to go and plan on arriving in the afternoon, call a week or two ahead for reservations and dress nice: no torn jeans, short-shorts, beachwear, jogging pants, or tank tops. ⏱ *30 min.; more for tea. 721 Government St.* ☎ *250/389-2727 for tea reservations. www.fairmont.com/empress. Tea served beginning at noon, priced from C$49–C$60 per person.*

② ★★ The Legislative Assembly. Surrounded by wide lawns and fountains, the home of British Columbia's provincial legislature exudes the appropriate gravitas, all heavy stone and multiple copper domes. A regal statue of Queen Victoria (who ruled when the buildings were completed in 1898) stands at the head of the grounds, gazing out at the Inner Harbour, the lovely cove around which the whole city grew. Visitors can tour public areas on their own to see the beautiful marble, mosaic, and stained-glass details. When the assembly is in session, visitors can watch the proceedings from the upper galleries. There are also free guided tours that explain the legislative processes and the history, art, and architecture of the buildings (and are worth it if you're looking for detailed insight). ⏱ *30 min.–1 hr. 501 Belleville St.* ☎ *250/387-3046. www. leg.bc.ca. Free admission. Buildings open 9am–5pm Mon–Thurs, 9am–7pm Fri–Sun (mid-May to Aug), 8:30am–5pm Mon–Fri (Sept to mid-May). Tours depart several times per hour, but schedule may vary based*

The Legislative Assembly, a neo-Baroque success designed by Francis Rattenbury in 1893.

Getting to Victoria

Daily service between Vancouver and Victoria is provided by Pacific Coach Lines (☎ 604/662-8074; www.pacificcoach.com), with departures between 5:45am and 7:45pm (later in summer). Buses transport passengers from **Pacific Central Station** (1150 Station St.) or Canada Place to Tsawwassen (about 45 min. drive south of Downtown), where you board the ferry for Swartz Bay, then take another bus for the 20-minute drive into Victoria. The whole trip takes about 4 hours one-way, and costs C$95 round-trip. Pacific Coach also offers various packages, including a 2-day/1-night deal that bundles transportation with a Victoria hotel stay and attractions discounts (priced from C$150–C$300, depending on the hotel you choose). Other ferry services depart from Horseshoe Bay, in West Vancouver. Both services take cars if you want to explore Vancouver Island that way (**BC Ferries,** ☎ 888/223-3779; www.bcferries.com). Regular passenger car fee is C$45, plus a C$13 per passenger fare.

on interest. Off-season, a guaranteed tour is offered at 4pm.

③ ★★★ The Royal British Columbia Museum. This museum focuses on BC's land and people. Towering totem poles at the entrance and the large First Peoples Gallery inside explore the art and culture of BC's Northwest First Nations people; the Natural History Gallery looks at geology, plants, and animals

Totem poles in Thunderbird Park.

from the province's 80-million-year history; and the Modern History gallery looks back at the last 200 years, with re-creations of early Victoria street scenes. There's also an IMAX movie theater. Adjacent to the museum is Thunderbird Park, a gorgeous spot displaying First Nations totem poles and a ceremonial house. ⏱ *2 hr. 675 Belleville St.* ☎ *250/356-7226. www.royalbcmuseum.bc.ca. Adults C$15, seniors and kids 6–18 C$9.50. Open 9am–5pm daily.*

④ Fort Victoria. Hey, look: no fort. At least not anymore. In 1848—just 50 years before the very civilized Legislative Assembly buildings went up—the Hudson's Bay Company built the kind of defensible headquarters you'd expect on the frontier: a 91×101m (300×330-ft.) quadrangle with tall cedar-log walls, corner bastions armed with cannons, and the usual assembly of houses, trade shops, and storage buildings inside. The fort was torn down during the 1860s Gold Rush, but today you can see its outline demarcated by a double row of bricks, each engraved with

Market square is a favored spot for shopping and dining in Victoria.

the name of one of Victoria's original settlers. ⏱ *10 min. Most of the memorial bricks are located on the west side of Government St. from Bastion Square/View St. south toward Broughton St. www.victoria.ca/archives/archives_refbrk.shtml.*

⑤ ★★ Old Town. Victoria's Old Town grew up around Fort Victoria during the 19th century, and it's been the city's commercial and tourist focal point ever since, its streets filled with heritage buildings that once functioned as warehouses, factories, gambling dens, and chandleries, but now house shops and restaurants. Government St., running north-south through its center, is tourist central, lined with cheap souvenir shops. ⏱ *1 hr., with time for shopping. Old Town extends from Fort St. north to Pandora Ave. and from Wharf St. east to Douglas St. The city's downtown area encircles Old Town.*

⑥ ★★ Trounce Alley & Bastion Square. Pedestrian-only Trounce Alley is cute as a button, lit by century-old gaslights, and lined with boutiques and flower baskets. Bastion Square, west of Government, offers more shopping, restaurants, craft vendors, and great views of the Inner Harbour. ⏱ *1 hr., as part of your overview of Old Town. Trounce runs east from Government St., Bastion Sq. is west of Government.*

⑦ ★ Maritime Museum of British Columbia. In the old Provincial Courthouse on Bastion Square, this museum offers two floors of exhibits on early exploration, whaling, shipbuilding, piracy, and other aspects of Victoria's seafaring past. The building's third floor holds the old courtroom, which served as both the Supreme Court of BC and the Vice-Admiralty Court for maritime

The Gate of Harmonious Interest in Victoria's Chinatown.

Victoria Whale-Watching

The waters around Victoria are known for their spectacular whale-watching, with boats plying Juan de Fuca Strait, Haro Strait, and the Strait of Georgia in search of the semi-resident Orca (killer whales) and migratory Gray, Humpback, and Minke whales. Orca are common from April through October, but summer months are best. Humpbacks are commonly sighted between August and October, and Grays swim off Vancouver Island from March to mid-May, during their northward migration. Dozens of boats depart hourly from the harbor, some of them (such as **Orca Spirit Adventures,** ☎ 888/672-6722 or 250/383-8411; www.orcaspirit.com) large leisure craft and others (such as **Prince of Whales,** ☎ 888/383-4884 or 250/383-4884; www.princeof whales.com) using fast, inflatable Zodiac boats. Whichever you choose, be sure your outfitter bills itself as a "Responsible Whale Watcher," following practices that minimize disturbing the whales. Three-hour tours cost about C$95 for adults, C$60 to C$75 for kids.

litigation. ⏱ *45 min. 28 Bastion Sq.* ☎ *250/382-2869. www.mmbc.bc.ca. Adults C$10, seniors and student C$8, kids 6–11 C$5. Open 9:30am–4:30pm daily ('til 5pm in summer).*

8 ★ **Market Square.** This former complex of shipping offices and supply stores is now a restored, self-contained shopping, dining, and

The world-renowned Butchart Gardens are spectacular year-round.

entertainment area, with 35-plus shops. ⏱ *At least 45 min. 560 Johnson St. (at Wharf/Shore sts.).* ☎ *250/386-2441. www.marketsquare.ca.*

9 ★ **Chinatown.** North America's second-oldest Chinese community was established in 1858. Its 12m (38-ft.) "Gate of Harmonious Interest" features hand-carved stone lions from Suzhou, China. Nearby, Fan Tan Alley is promoted as "the world's narrowest street," a former warren of opium, gambling, and prostitution houses that now sticks primarily to the souvenir trade. You can enter the Chinatown Trading Company through its back-alley door, which lets on to several interconnected shops and museum displays of Chinatown's past. ⏱ *1 hr. Chinatown is centered on Fisgard St. between Store & Douglas sts. The Gate of Harmonious Interest stands at the corner of Government & Fisgard sts. Chinatown Trading Co. is at 551 Fisgard St.*

10 ★★ **Abkhazi Garden.** Talk about a labor of love. In the 1920s, the young Peggy Pemberton-Carter first met exiled Prince Nicholas

Rhododendrons bloom in the magnificent Abkhazi Garden.

Abkhazi of Georgia and began a correspondence that would last 2 decades. Following World War II, during which both were interned in prisoner of war camps, the two reunited, decided to marry, and moved to Victoria. The .4-hectare (1-acre) jewelbox garden they created there was their passion for the next 40 years. Highlights include a rhododendron garden shaded by native Garry Oaks; a tiny summer-house looking out to a small pond; and the "Yangtse River," a band of green lawn winding the length of the property, lined by an edge of purple heather and rock outcrops. On afternoons, you can order lunch in the former sitting room of the Abkhazis' home. 🕐 *1 hr. 1964 Fairfield Rd. (near Foul Bay Rd.), Oak Bay. ☎ 250/598-8096; www.abkhazi.com. Adults C$10, seniors and students C$7.50, kids 12 and under free. Open daily 11am–5pm (Mar–Sept), 11am–3pm (Oct–Dec & Feb), closed Jan.*

⑪ ★★★ **Butchart Gardens.** Some 23km (14 miles) north of downtown Victoria on the Saanich Peninsula, the Butchart Gardens started life as a limestone quarry around 1905. Once owner Robert Butchart had exhausted the mine, his wife Jennie transformed it into a sumptuous Sunken Garden, with limestone

mounds that allow a 360-degree view. Other gardens and attractions were added over the years: English, Italian, and Japanese gardens inspired by their travels; the magnificent Ross Fountain in another exhausted quarry (this one turned into a lake); and a Rose Garden that Jennie laid out where their kitchen vegetable patch had been. Today, the 22-hectare (54-acre) gardens are comprised of some 1 million plants representing 700 varieties, and attract close to a million visitors every year. 🕐 *2–3 hr. 800 Benevenuto Ave., Brentwood Bay. ☎ 866/652-4422 or 250/652-4422. www.butchartgardens. com. Adults C$27, kids 13–17 C$13, kids 5–12 C$3. Open daily 9am–sundown.*

⑫ ★ **Craigdarroch Castle.** Built in the 1880s as the home of millionaire Scottish coal magnate Robert Dunsmuir, this Highlands-style castle is 4 stories high, 39 rooms strong, topped with stone turrets and furnished in opulent Victorian splendor: Persian rugs, stained-glass windows, fine woodwork, and paintings and sculpture throughout. 🕐 *1 hr. 1050 Joan Crescent, off Fort St. ☎ 250/ 592-5323. www.craigdarrochcastle. com. Adults C$12, seniors C$11, kids*

An antiques-furnished sitting room inside Craigdarroch Castle.

6–18 C$3.75. Open daily 10am–5pm Sept to mid-June, 10am–7:30pm mid-June through Labour Day. You can | walk from the Inner Harbor via Fort Street in 30–40 min., or take a taxi.

Where to **Stay & Dine**

Admiral Inn INNER HARBOUR This family-run, 3-story hotel offers reasonable rates and a great location on the Inner Harbour, though the rooms lack flair. Some rooms have balconies. *257 Belleville St.* ☎ *888/823-6472 or 250/388 6267. www.admiral.bc.ca. 29 units. Doubles C$99–C$199. AE, DISC, MC, V. Map p 136.*

★ **Blue Crab Bar & Grill** INNER HARBOUR *SEAFOOD* One of the city's best seafood restaurants, offering innovative recipes, an excellent wine list, and beautiful Inner Harbour views. Its ingredients are often organic, and its seafood is harvested using sustainable practices. *At the Coast Victoria Harbourside Hotel, 146 Kingston St.* ☎ *250/480-1999. www.bluecrab.ca. Entrees C$28–C$45. AE, DC, MC, V. Breakfast, lunch & dinner daily. Map p 136.*

★★★ **Cafe Brio** DOWNTOWN *REGIONAL/ITALIAN* This two-story, tile-roofed restaurant is a charmer, with a warm, woody interior, a 46-sq.-m (500-sq.-ft.) dining patio, and Tuscan-influenced regional cuisine, with an emphasis on fresh seafood. *944 Fort St.* ☎ *866/270-5461 or 250/383-0009. www.cafe-brio.com. Entrees C$26–C$45. AE, MC, V. Dinner daily. Map p 136.*

★ **Canoe** INNER HARBOUR *BREW-PUB/REGIONAL* Housed in a former generator building dating to 1894, Canoe makes the most of its brick-and-timber atmosphere, with three seating choices: a chandelier-hung loft, a cozy pub, and an outside deck for super sunset views. The menu

The Fairmont Empress Hotel is the most prestigious place to stay in Victoria.

ranges from pub food (burgers, pizza) to seafood, steaks, curry, and pasta. *450 Swift St.* ☎ *250/361-1940. www.canoebrewpub.com. Entrees C$12–C$26. AE, MC, V. Lunch & dinner daily Map p 136.*

★★★ **Fairmont Empress** INNER HARBOUR Victoria's most historic hotel (p 137, ❶) offers a classic experience, though standard rooms are smaller than you can get elsewhere. Only deluxe harbour-view rooms and suites face the Inner Harbour. *721 Government St.* ☎ *866/540-4429 or 250/384-8111. www.fairmont.com/empress. 477 units. Doubles C$169–C$569. AE, DC, DISC, MC, V. Map p 136.*

★★★ **Inn at Laurel Point** INNER HARBOUR More stylish resort than "Inn," Laurel Point offers a contemporary minimalist decor, a pond and Japanese garden (complementing the Asian artwork inside), and a promontory setting right on the Inner Harbour. *680 Montreal St.* ☎ *800/663-7667 or 250/386-8721. www.laurelpoint.com. 200 units. Doubles C$99–C$229. AE, DC, DISC, MC, V. Map p 136.* ●

Best of Whistler **in Winter**

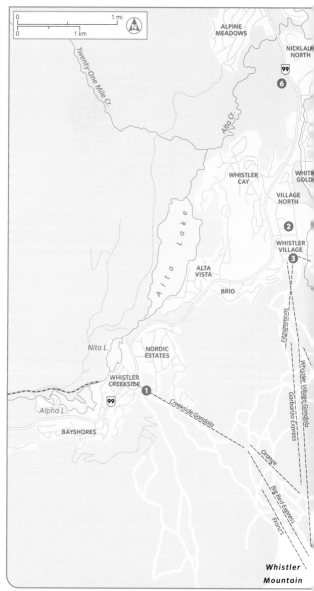

ALPINE
MEADOWS

NICKLAU
NORTH

99

6

WHISTLER
CAY

WHIT
GOLD

VILLAGE
NORTH

2

WHISTLER
VILLAGE

3

Twenty-One Mile Cr.

Alta Cr.

A l t a   L a k e

ALTA
VISTA

BRIO

Nita L.

NORDIC
ESTATES

WHISTLER
CREEKSIDE

1

99

Creekside Gondola

Fitzsimmons

Whistler Village Gondola

Garbanzo Express

Alpha L.

BAYSHORES

Orange

Big Red Express

Franz's

Whistler
Mountain

0 — 1 mi
0 — 1 km

Previous page: A skier zips down the slopes of Whistler Mountain.

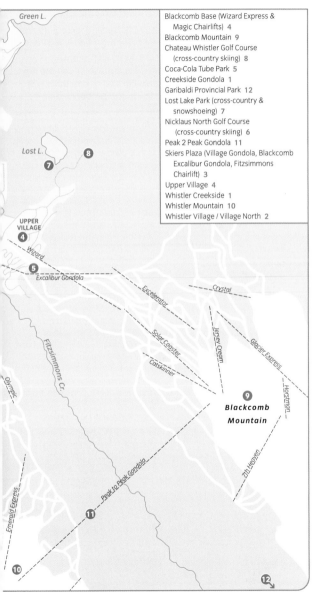

Blackcomb Base (Wizard Express & Magic Chairlifts) 4
Blackcomb Mountain 9
Chateau Whistler Golf Course (cross-country skiing) 8
Coca-Cola Tube Park 5
Creekside Gondola 1
Garibaldi Provincial Park 12
Lost Lake Park (cross-country & snowshoeing) 7
Nicklaus North Golf Course (cross-country skiing) 6
Peak 2 Peak Gondola 11
Skiers Plaza (Village Gondola, Blackcomb Excalibur Gondola, Fitzsimmons Chairlift) 3
Upper Village 4
Whistler Creekside 1
Whistler Mountain 10
Whistler Village / Village North 2

Green L.

Lost L.

UPPER VILLAGE

Wizard

Excalibur Gondola

Excelerator

Crystal

Solar Coaster

Jersey Cream

Glacier Express

Catskinner

Horstman

Fitzsimmons Cr.

Olympic

Blackcomb Mountain

7th Heaven

Peak to Peak Gondola

Emerald Express

Recipe for a great ski resort: Take two mountains with more than 1,500m (4,921 ft.) and 3,307 hectares (8,172 acres) of ski-able terrain. Add enough annual snowfall to bury a house, carve out about 200 individual trails, then add 38 lifts, great backcountry and cross-country skiing, and a killer mountain village with world-class après ski potential. Short story: For the adrenaline junkie on skis, Whistler is *it*: The biggest, the highest, the best. START: **You can drive to Whistler along the Sea to Sky Highway (p 132) or take the bus or the Whistler Mountaineer train from Vancouver (p 190).**

Skiing & Snowboarding

★★★ Downhill Skiing/Snow-boarding.

Whistler exists because of skiing. In 1960 a group of Vancouver businessmen began laying the groundwork for an alpine ski area on what was then called London Mountain (later Whistler, renamed for a local alpine marmot that makes a whistling sound). It opened in 1966, and skiing in North America has never been the same. Today the resort encompasses two mountains, each with more than 100 trails (the longest of which stretch some 11km/7 miles). Their high alpine skiing is unmatched in North America, with 12 massive alpine bowls, steep chutes, and three glaciers offering days' worth of opportunities for skiers and, increasingly, snowboarders. Originally two different resorts, Whistler and Blackcomb (the latter usually considered the more extreme mountain) merged in 1997, so one lift ticket covers everything. Primary access to Whistler is via the lifts and gondolas at Skiers Plaza in Whistler Village (plus the Creekside Gondola at Whistler Creekside). Blackcomb is primarily accessed from the Upper Village. See "Walkable Whistler" (p 158) for more info on the resort's layout. Individual and small-group ski and snowboard instruction is available on both mountains for every age and skill level. 🕐 *During ski season, the average stay in Whistler is 6 days, though 1- to 10-day lift tickets are available. Whistler Blackcomb* ☎ *888/403-4727. www.whistler blackcomb.com. 2-day lift tickets cost C$125–C$178 adults, C$106–C$152 seniors and teens, C$65–C$92 kids 7–12. Beginner ski or snowboard lessons from C$110. Private lessons from*

An extensive lift system makes getting from Whistler Village to the slopes easy.

Saving Money with Package Deals

Whistler is as efficient as a beehive, with everything working toward one goal: Lure the target market, show it a good time, and send it home happy. As so much of the resort is either controlled by Whistler Blackcomb itself (part of the giant Intrawest resort company) or has business relationships with it, you can essentially plan your whole trip on the resort's website, **www.whistler blackcomb.com**. Various packages are available that bundle hotel accommodations and lift tickets, often at heavily discounted rates. The site also lists deals on airfare, restaurants, and activities. Just remember to book early—no later than September for the peak winter months.

C$315 for a half-day. The season runs roughly from late Nov through mid-June. Lessons available Dec–Apr.

★★★ The Peak 2 Peak Gondola.

Newly opened at the end of 2008, the Peak 2 Peak stretches horizontally between Whistler and Blackcomb mountains at a high elevation (some 436m/1,427ft. above the valley floor), allowing skiers and snowboarders—as well as sightseers—to shuttle quickly from one mountain to the other, following the best alpine snow and weather conditions. The gondola system itself is 4.4km (2¾ miles) long, with an unsupported span of 3km (2 miles)—the longest in the world. ⏱ *11 min., end to end. Cabins depart every 49 seconds. Whistler Blackcomb.* ☎ *888/403-4727. www.whistlerblackcomb.com. Access to the gondola is included in regular lift ticket prices.*

★★★ Backcountry Skiing/Snowboarding.

Beyond the lift lines, various guided small-group tours bring skiers and snowboarders into the pristine bowls, glaciers, gladed runs, and oodles of powder surrounding Whistler Blackcomb, mostly within enormous Garibaldi Provincial Park (p 135, ❿). These tours are geared toward intermediate and advanced skiers, but no specific backcountry experience is needed. Some multi-day tours—such as the Spearhead Traverse, a long, U-shaped swing between Whistler and Blackcomb Mountains, crossing the Spearhead and Fitzsimmons Ranges and 13 glaciers over the course of 4 days—are for more experienced backcountry skiers. *Day and multiday tours and backcountry clinics are available through Whistler Blackcomb (*☎ *604/938-7669; www.whistlerblackcomb.com) and through the Whistler Alpine Guides Bureau, 4314 Main St.* ☎ *604/938-3228. www.whistlerguides.com. 1-day tours start at around C$215. Offered daily in season.*

Whistler is a snowboarder's paradise.

Lost Lake Park is a favorite with snow-shoers thanks to its many trails.

★ **Cross-Country Skiing.** Though Whistler's cross-country options don't hold a candle to its downhill skiing, the Resort Municipality of Whistler does maintain 28km (17 miles) of groomed, track-set cross-country trails spread among scenic Lost Lake Park, the Chateau Whistler Golf Course (full of hilly terrain), and the flatter Nicklaus North Golf Course. Different routes suit different levels of expertise. *Lost Lake Park is a short walk from anywhere in the Village. Information, tours, and lessons are available through Cross Country Connection, 7400 Fitzsimmons Rd.*

South. ☎ 604/905-0071. www.cross countryconnection.bc.ca. Day passes C$17 adults, C$10 teens, C$8.50 kids 6–12. The season normally lasts Nov–March.

Adventure Sports
★ **Ice Climbing.** The Whistler area offers great ice faces suitable for every level of climber, from absolute beginner to expert. You can hire a guide for an ice-climbing tour that visits various areas between Whistler and Lillooet, and is customized to your skill level. *Whistler Alpine Guides Bureau, 4314 Main St. ☎ 604/938-3228. www.whistler guides.com. Custom 1- or 2-person tours C$237–C$395 per person.*

Tubing
★★ kids **Coca-Cola Tube Park.** There's something very Adam Sandler about this attraction, and I mean that in a good way. Located in the Base 2 zone on Blackcomb (above the Upper Village), the tube park has eight individual lanes (rated by difficulty) that give both kids and adults the chance to ride inner tubes down the mountain, giggling like idiots. Lanes are about 305m (1,001 ft.) long and there's a lift to get you and your tube to the top. ⏱ *Tickets are sold in 1- and 2-hr. increments.*

Other Winter Whistler Tours & Activities

In addition to the options described in this section, Whistler and its various independent tour operators offer many other winter tours and activities, including **dogsled tours** led by professional mushers; **snowmobile tours** on Whistler and Blackcomb Mountains; **heli-skiing/boarding tours** in the backcountry; **snowcat sightseeing tours;** and **backcountry wildlife tours.** All are bookable through Whistler Blackcomb, either by phone at ☎ 888/403-4727, or online at www.whistlerblackcomb.com.

Taking a horse-drawn carriage ride is a fun way to experience Whistler.

Primary access to the tube park is via the Excalibur Gondola, from Skiers Plaza in Whistler Village. ☎ 888/403-4727. www.whistler blackcomb.com. 1-hr. tickets C$16 adults, C$12 seniors and teens, C$10 kids. Open Dec–Apr, noon–8pm Mon–Fri, 11am–8pm Sat–Sun.

A variety of excellent ice faces makes Whistler a prime destination for ice climbers.

Miscellaneous Winter Activities

★ **Snowshoeing.** Three trails rated for difficulty and length traverse Lost Lake Park, the shortest taking about 1 hour, the longest 3 hours, all passing through a landscape of forest, frozen lakes, and magnificent view-points. *Equipment rentals and guided or self-guided tours are available from Cross Country Connection, 7400 Fitzsimmons Rd. South.* ☎ *604/905-0071. www. crosscountryconnection.bc.ca. Self-guided 2-hr. tour (including equipment and trail pass) C$25 adults, C$20 teens, C$16 kids.*

★ **Horse-Drawn Sleigh Rides.** The Whistler equivalent of taking a horse-drawn carriage around Central Park in New York—hokey but fun. Each evening in season, sleighs depart from different locations around Whistler for short dashes through the snow, in two-horse open sleighs that can carry up to 15 people apiece. Warm blankets and warm beverages are included. 🕐 *30–50 min. Tours bookable through Whistler Blackcomb.* ☎ *888/403-4727. www.whistler blackcomb.com. Tours C$29–C$59 per person.*

Best of Whistler **in Summer**

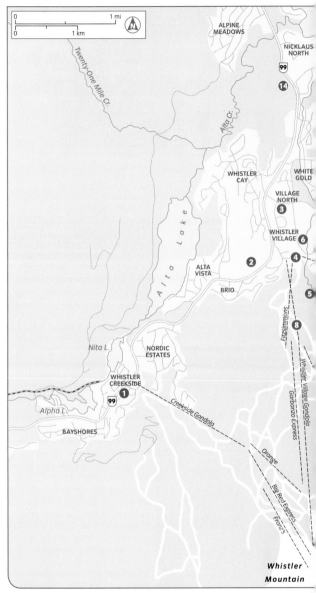

ALPINE
MEADOWS

NICKLAUS
NORTH

99

14

Twenty-One Mile Cr.

Alta Cr.

WHISTLER
CAY

WHITE
GOLD

VILLAGE
NORTH

3

A l t a   L a k e

WHISTLER
VILLAGE

6

2

4

ALTA
VISTA

BRIO

5

8

Nita L.

NORDIC
ESTATES

WHISTLER
CREEKSIDE

1

99

Creekside Gondola

Alpha L.

BAYSHORES

Fitzsimmons

Whistler Village Gondola

Garbanzo Express

Orange

Big Red Express

Franz's

Whistler
Mountain

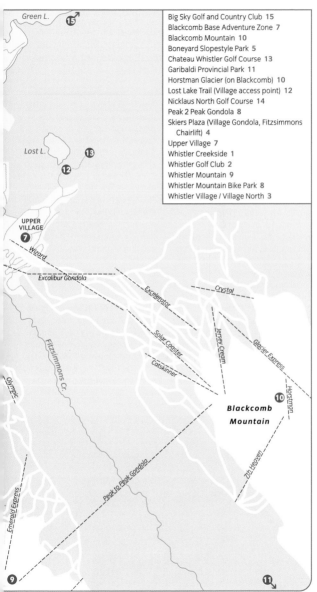

Big Sky Golf and Country Club 15
Blackcomb Base Adventure Zone 7
Blackcomb Mountain 10
Boneyard Slopestyle Park 5
Chateau Whistler Golf Course 13
Garibaldi Provincial Park 11
Horstman Glacier (on Blackcomb) 10
Lost Lake Trail (Village access point) 12
Nicklaus North Golf Course 14
Peak 2 Peak Gondola 8
Skiers Plaza (Village Gondola, Fitzsimmons Chairlift) 4
Upper Village 7
Whistler Creekside 1
Whistler Golf Club 2
Whistler Mountain 9
Whistler Mountain Bike Park 8
Whistler Village / Village North 3

I n summer, Whistler takes on a different character. Flowers bloom on the high alpine slopes, while mountain bikers take over trails and runs that were covered in snow just weeks before. Down in the valley, golf courses grow lush in the warm air, and restaurant patios serve international cuisine with a side of Canadian mountain sunshine. And you can even do a little skiing—as long as you're willing to go high enough.

Mountain Biking
★★★ Whistler Mountain Bike Park.

Once upon a time Whistler was all about skiing, and summers were quiet. Then somebody invented the mountain bike, and Whistler said, "Heyyyy, we have hills and trails here. . . . " And thus, in 1998, was born what is almost inarguably the world's finest mountain bike park, with about 200km (125 miles) of trails and a total vertical descent of 1,100m (3,608 ft.). Riders head up the mountain from Skiers Plaza in Whistler Village via the Fitzsimmons Chairlift and the Village Gondola, ascending to the Olympic Station area at 1,019m (3,343 ft.). From there, you can choose to ride down the trails of the lower park (aka the Fitzsimmons Zone) or keep going on the Garbanzo Chair to ride the upper and more difficult Garbanzo Zone, which tops out at 1,662m (5,453 ft.). Chairlifts within the park are reengineered in summer so that every other chair is a rack able to hold four bikes, so your ride stays with you (or close to you) at all times. Toward the bottom of the Fitzsimmons Zone, in plain sight of Skiers Plaza, the Boneyard Slopestyle Park was designed by professional mountain biker John Cowan, and is loaded with wooden ramp jumps, manmade dirt jumps, and drops for high-intermediate and advanced riders. 🕐 *Lift tickets are sold in 1-, 2-, and 3-day packages.* ☎ *866/218-9690 or 604/904-8134. www.whistlerbike.com. 1-day lift tickets are C$49 adults, C$43 teens, and C$27 kids 10–12. Heavy-duty bike rentals are available from the park itself or from dozens of other operators for about C$65 half-day, C$100 full-day. The season runs from mid-May to mid-Oct.*

Whistler Mountain Bike Park is arguably the world's finest.

☎ 888/403-4727, www.whistler blackcomb.com. Daily greens fees (excluding late-afternoon and twilight play) C$87–C$177, depending on the season.

★★★ Chateau Whistler Golf Club.
Set at the base of Blackcomb Mountain on the northern edge of the Upper Village, the club offers a 6,635-yard, par-72 course with over 122m (400 ft.) in elevation change. Designed by Robert Trent Jones, Jr., it takes full advantage of its dramatic mountain setting. *Tee times can be booked through Whistler Blackcomb,* ☎ *888/403-4727, www. whistlerblackcomb.com. Daily greens fees (excluding late-afternoon and twilight play) C$125–C$195, depending on the season.*

★★★ Nicklaus North.
Five minutes north of Whistler, this 6,908-yard, par-71 course was designed by the legendary Jack Nicklaus among mountain peaks, glacier-fed lakes, and forests. *8080 Nicklaus North Blvd., off the Sea to Sky Hwy. Tee times can be booked through Whistler Blackcomb,* ☎ *888/403-4727, www. whistlerblackcomb.com. Daily greens fees (excluding late-afternoon and twilight play C$125–C$189, depending on the season.*

You'll find good slope conditions in Whistler even in summer thanks to the Horstman Glacier.

Mountain bikers will find trails in Whistler that cater to every ability level.

Skiing
★★★ Summer Glacier Skiing/ Snowboarding.
In summer, when the bikers have taken over Whistler Mountain, the high Horstman Glacier on Blackcomb still provides skiing and riding opportunities, serviced by two chairlifts. In addition to day skiing/riding, there's also a variety of multi-day ski camps on the glacier, where you can work on specific skills with world-class athletes. *Whistler Blackcomb.* ☎ *888/403-4727 or 604/ 904-7060. www.whistlerblackcomb. com. 1-day glacier ski tickets C$52 adults, C$45 seniors and teens, C$27 kids 7–12. Camp charges vary by program. Season June–July.*

Golf
★★★ Big Sky Golf and Country Club.
Thirty minutes north of Whistler, this 7,001-yard, par-72 course was designed by Robert Cupp in the shadow of Mt. Currie, with great views and a subtle layout, plus one of the top golf academies in Canada. *1690 Airport Rd., Pemberton. Tee times can be booked through Whistler Blackcomb,*

The Chateau Whistler Golf Club takes advantage of its scenic location.

Whistler Golf Club. On the western edge of Whistler Village, this 6,676-yard, par-72 course was the first in Canada designed by Arnold Palmer, who melded the area's natural contours with manmade lakes and a redirected creek to create a challenging, enjoyable course. It also offers a driving range tucked just across Whistler Way from the Hilton. *Tee times can be booked through Whistler Blackcomb,* ☎ *888/403-4727, www.whistler blackcomb.com. Daily greens fees*

(excluding late-afternoon and twilight play) C$79–C$119, depending on the season.

Hiking
★★★ **Hiking.** The Whistler area offers dozens of hiking options, from easy trails that take off from the Village to mountaintop trails reachable by gondola. Close in, the 30km (19-mile) **Lost Lake Trail** starts at the day skier parking lots between the Village and Upper Village, winding through beautiful country. The **Valley Trail System** is an easy, paved trail that connects many parts of Whistler. Up on the mountain, accessible via the Whistler Village Gondola and a chairlift ride, you can access more than a dozen trails, from easy loops like the .6km (⅓-mile) Paleface Trail, which accesses views, Alpine flowers, and old-growth forest; to the 21km (13-mile) Musical Bumps and Singing Pass trails, which start at Whistler peak and wind down through Garibaldi Provincial Park, ending back at the village 3 to 5 hours later. There are also free 2-hour round-trip hiking tours that depart daily at 11:30am from the top of the Whistler Village Gondola. By riding the Peak 2 Peak gondola

If you prefer wheels to skis, ATV tours are a great way to explore Whistler.

There are dozens of hiking trail options in Whistler, almost all of them incredibly scenic.

(p 147), hikers can also access trails on Blackcomb. *Whistler Blackcomb,* ☎ *888/403-4727, www.whistler blackcomb.com. 1-day gondola passes cost C$32 adults, C$26 teens, and C$13 kids 7–12. Gondolas accommodate hikers from late June to mid-Sept.*

Fun for Kids

★ kids **Blackcomb Base Adventure Zone.** A sort of mini-Whistler for kids, the Adventure Zone offers 10 different "adventures" that range from a 315m (1,000-ft.) luge run and an 80m (250-ft.) zipline to bungee trampolines that help you jump up to 8m (25 ft.) in the air. Other activities include miniature golf, NASA-style human gyroscopes, and an 8m (25-ft.) web that kids can crawl around on like Spiderman. *In the Upper Village, at the base of Blackcomb Mountain. 5-, 10-, and 15-adventure passes are available, for C$41, C$74, and C$99 respectively (all ages). The Zone's season runs mid-June to early Sept.*

Other Warm-Weather Whistler Tours & Activities

In addition to the activities described in this section, Whistler and its independent tour operators offer many other summer tours and activities, including **river-rafting tours** on the nearby Green, Birkenhead, and Elaho-Squamish Rivers; guided **horseback trail riding;** guided **fishing trips** to the area's eight major rivers and many Alpine lakes (fishing was Whistler's original claim to fame, before skiing); and **ATV** and **4X4** tours to the peak of Whistler Mountain, among others. All are bookable through Whistler Blackcomb by calling ☎ 888/403-4727 or online at www.whistler blackcomb.com.

Best of **All-Weather Whistler**

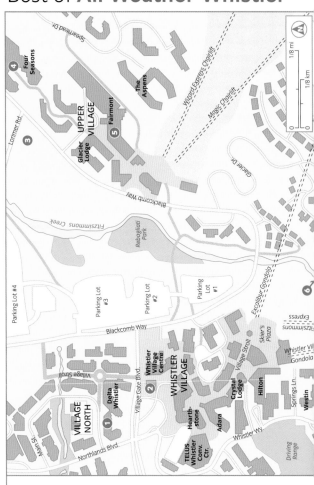

Solarice Wellness Spa
(Delta Whistler location) 1

Solarice Wellness Spa
(Gateway Drive location) 2

Spa at Four Seasons Resort 4

Squamish Lil'wat
Cultural Centre 3

Vida Wellness Spa at
the Fairmont 5

Ziptrek Ecotours zone 6

Though Whistler does a complete seasonal chameleon routine between summer and winter, some things never change. In addition to the cultural, adventure, and sybaritic options below, you can also ride the Peak 2 Peak gondola (p 147) between the mountains year-round, or hike the paved, 35km (22 mile) Valley Trail (p 154), which winds between the Village and surrounding lakes, parks, and residential communities.

Adventure Sports

★★ **Ziptrek Ecotours.** Ziplining—in which you're strapped into a harness and sent gliding along a wire from platform to platform, far above the ground—is big news at resorts today, and Whistler has one of the longest tree-to-tree versions in the world, located in the valley between Whistler and Blackcomb Mountains. You can sign up for two options: the "Bear Tour," with five ziplines joined by a network of suspension bridges, boardwalks, and trails; or the "Eagle Tour," with five different lines including a 701m (2,300-ft.) stretch that drops you 20 stories at speeds of up to 80kmph (60mph). 🕐 *Tours last about 3 hr. Guest services desk is located in the Carleton Lodge, across from the Whistler Village Gondolas. A shuttle takes you to the zipline base.* ☎ *866/935-0001 or 604/935-0001. www.ziptrek.com. Tours C$99–C$119 adults, C$79 seniors and kids 6–14. Tours available daily, year-round.*

The Peak 2 Peak gondola enables visitors to transfer easily between Whistler and Blackcomb year-round.

demonstrations of traditional crafts. The center's lovely 3-story, Douglas-fir-and-glass building is a modern reinterpretation of a Squamish Longhouse and Lil'wat Istken, or underground pit dwelling. 🕐 *1–2 hr. 4584 Blackcomb Way.* ☎ *866/441-7522. www.slcc.ca. Admission C$18 adults, C$14 seniors, C$11 teens, C$8 kids 6–12. Open daily 9:30am–5pm.*

Museums

★ **Squamish Lil'wat Cultural Centre.** One of Whistler's few museums, this new center (opened in 2008) showcases BC's neighboring Squamish and Lil'wat First Nations peoples through exhibitions of carvings, regalia, canoes, baskets, and other artifacts, as well as films, performances of music and dance, and

Day Spas

★★ **Solarice Wellness Spa.** The Solarice blends traditional Eastern and western with a menu of massage, bodywork, Chinese medicine, acupuncture, facials, body wraps, nutritional counseling, and personal

Neither rain nor snow nor sunshine stops the ziplines from running over Whistler.

Walkable Whistler

The Whistler Blackcomb resort is laid out as a large but easily navigable pedestrian village, with a spider-web of roads linking the Sea to Sky Highway to a myriad of underground parking garages and outdoor lots. Once you arrive, you can pretty much forget your car until it's time to leave.

Whistler Village is the main hub of restaurants, nightlife, shopping, and hotels. It's quite a trick, but the vast majority of vacationers here tend to be younger than the Village's 30-year-old chalet-style buildings—thus the area's youthful, energetic vibe. The Village Stroll is the main walking avenue, winding like Venice's Grand Canal through the Village center and into **Village North,** which—due to its greater distance to the slopes—is slightly downscale, with a grocery and fast-food outlets at its far northern end. The gondolas up onto Whistler (and one to Blackcomb) board at Skiers Plaza at the southernmost end of Whistler Village.

The **Upper Village,** located a few minutes' walk east of the Village/Village North, just across Fitzsimmons Creek, is the base for the Blackcomb chairlifts, and offers a much quieter, generally more upscale vibe than either the main or north village. It's home to the Four Seasons. 'Nuff said.

Whistler Creekside, about 5km (3 miles) southwest of Whistler Village on the Sea to Sky Highway, was the area's original resort development. Today it offers gondola access to Whistler Mountain for people (including many families) who want a calmer vacation experience, well clear of the young buzz of Whistler Village.

training, plus drop-in yoga, tai chi, Pilates, and meditation classes. *4230 Gateway Dr., above the Whistler Info Centre.* ☎ *604/935-1222; www.solarice.com. Most treatments C$75–C$215. AE, MC, V. Open daily 8am–10pm. There's a second location at the Delta Whistler Village Suites.*

★★★ **Spa at Four Seasons Resort.** Whistler's best hotel spa, this immaculately designed facility offers nearly 50 treatments and services, including a "Personal Steam Tent Infusion" partially inspired by First Nations sweat lodges. *4591 Blackcomb Way.* ☎ *888/935-2460 or 604/935-3400.*

The Vida Wellness Spa is one of the top spas in the Whistler area and a great place to relax after a long day of hiking or skiing.

Whistler Village is the social center of the Whistler-Blackcomb area and has a youthful vibe.

www.fourseasons.com/whistler. *Most treatments C$145–C$310. AE, DC, MC, V. Open daily 8am–10pm.*

★★★ Vida Wellness Spa.

Located at the Fairmont Chateau Whistler (p 174), the Vida bases many of its treatments on the Indian Ayurvedic system, which stresses balance. Eight Ayurvedic treatments are on tap, along with a range of massages, body wraps, facials, and a one-on-one restorative yoga session. *4599 Chateau Blvd. ☎ 604/938 2086. www.fairmont.com/whistler. Most treatments C$125–C$370. AE, DC, DISC, MC, V. Open daily 8am–10pm.*

Outdoor Tours

★★★ Helicopter Flightseeing, Hiking & Glacier Tours. West-

ern Canada's coastal mountains are in one of the world's most heavily glaciated regions, and the best way to see them and appreciate their sheer enormity is by helicopter tour. It's literally like getting a glimpse back into the ice age. Options change depending on the season. A range of short tours (all under an

hour) are available year-round, including the **"Whistler Explorer"** flight (an overview of the area's highlights, including the village, Garibaldi Provincial Park, and the peaks and glaciers of the coastal range) and the **"Alpine Adventure with Glacier Landing"** (which touches down on one of the area's glaciers for a quick walkabout). In summer (June–Sept), things get more interesting, with the best option of all being a naturalist-led heli-glacier walking tour that takes you up onto the ice for a full day. Another option is the heli-hiking tour, which takes in the breadth of the alpine terrain, from coastal forest to mountain meadows and glacial ice fields. There's also a **"Glacier Picnic"** tour that's exactly what it says: a gourmet meal up among the snowy peaks. ⏱ *30 min.–7 hr. Whistler Blackcomb. ☎ 888/403-4727. www.whistlerblackcomb.com. Whistler Explorer C$189, Alpine with Glacier Landing C$329, full-day glacier walking tour C$715, glacier picnics C$515. Tours include pick-up and drop-off in Whistler Village.*

Shopping in Whistler

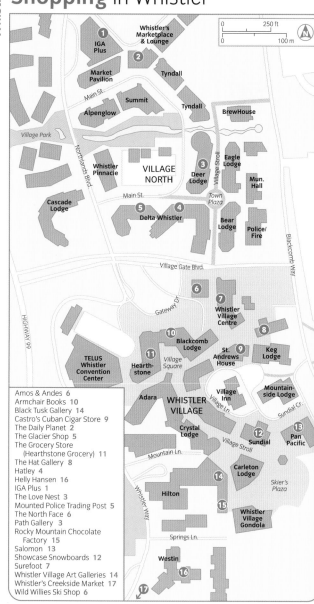

Shopping Best Bets

Best **Ski Shop**
★★★ Wild Willies Ski Shop, *4320 Sundial Crescent (p 165)*

Best **Sex Shop**
★ The Love Nest, *4338 Main St. (p 162)*

Best **Snowboard Shop**
★★ Showcase Snowboards, *4340 Sundial Crescent (p 165)*

Best **for Ski Boots**
★★★ Surefoot, *4295 Blackcomb Way (p 165)*

Best **Bookstore**
★★ Armchair Books, *4205 Village Sq. (p 162)*

Best **Candied Apples**
★★ Rocky Mountain Chocolate Factory, *4190 Springs Lane (p 163)*

Cutest **Kids' Clothes**
★★ Hatley, *4308 Main St. (p 163)*

Best **Art Gallery**
★★ Black Tusk Gallery, *4293 Mountain Sq. (p 162)*

Best **for Groceries & Beer**
★★ The Grocery Store & BC Liquor, *4211 Village Sq. (p 164)*

Best **Canadian Kitsch**
★ Mounted Police Trading Post, *4308 Main St. (p 162)*

Shop Until You Drop

Whistler has so much shopping that folks on bus tours from Vancouver often do nothing but shop—which is the idea, I guess. The streets of the Village and Village North (and to a lesser extent the Upper Village) are lined with ski stores, boutiques, souvenir shops, and innumerable national chain clothing and lifestyle shops such as Roots, Nike, Eddie Bauer, Quicksilver, Lululemon, L'Occitane, Chlorophylle, and Merrill.

Armchair Books is the best place in Whistler to pick up the latest bestseller.

Whistler Shopping A to Z

"Adult Accessories"
★ **The Love Nest** VILLAGE NORTH
Every ski resort needs a good sex—
er, "romantic accessories"—shop.
Look here for sexy lingerie, toys,
oils, and novelties. *4338 Main St.*
☎ *604/932-6906. AE, MC, V.*
Map p 160.

Art Galleries
★★ **Black Tusk Gallery** WHISTLER
VILLAGE   One of Whistler's best First
Nations galleries, selling fine sculp-
ture, totem poles, paintings, prints,
masks, and jewelry. *4293 Mountain
Sq. (on Art Gallery Row).* ☎ *604/
905-5540. www.blacktusk.ca. MC, V.
Map p 160.*

★★ **Path Gallery** VILLAGE NORTH
More Northwest Coast First Nations
art, including both large- and small-
scale works. *4338 Main St.* ☎ *604/
932-7570. www.pathgallery.com.
MC, V. Map p 160.*

★★ **Whistler Village Art
Gallery** WHISTLER VILLAGE   Fine
contemporary art by Canadian and
international artists, including
paintings of dome-shaped polar

bears by Jimmy Wright—seemingly
ubiquitous around Whistler on my
last visit, and deservedly so. *4293
Mountain Sq.* ☎ *604/938-3001.
www.whistlerart.com. AE, MC, V.
Map p 160.*

Books
★★ **Armchair Books** WHISTLER
VILLAGE   A well-stocked, well-
arranged, welcoming little bookstore right in the center of the
Village, selling hard-cover and
paperback fiction, nonfiction,
children's books, magazines,
and regional titles. *4205 Village Sq.*
☎ *604/932-5557. MC, V. Map p 160.*

Canadian Kitsch
★ **Mounted Police Trading
Post at Whistler** VILLAGE NORTH
The real Royal Canadian Mounted
Police are there to *"Maintiens le
droit"* (maintain the law). This shop
is here to maintain a cute, corny
stock of RCMP clothing, books, uni-
formed teddy bears, etc. *4308 Main
St.* ☎ *604/938-6204. AE, MC, V.
Map p 160.*

For large- and small-scale First Nations works, the Path Gallery is a good choice.

If you're hankering for a Cohiba, Castro's Cuban Cigar Store is the place to shop.

Cigars & Tobacco

★ Castro's Cuban Cigar Store WHISTLER VILLAGE The woody interior and wooden Indian evoke an early-20th-century cigar shop, as, for Americans, does their stock of Cohibas and other fine Cubans—a reminder of pre- (and, eventually) post–Cold War good times. *4433 Sundial Pl.* ☎ *604/905-4440. www.getcubans.com. AE, MC, V. Map p 160.*

Chocolate

★ Rocky Mountain Chocolate Factory WHISTLER VILLAGE Fresh-made chocolates by the ounce or the package, plus candied apples, homemade gelato, etc. Their "peak cookies" are deadly, in a good way. *4190 Springs Lane.* ☎ *604/298-2462. www.rockychoc.com. No credit cards. Map p 160.*

Clothing, Shoes & Accessories

★ Amos & Andes WHISTLER VILLAGE This cute little shop is all about colorful, casual sweaters for

women—the kind you wear after skiing, while curled up by a fire with hot chocolate. *4321 Village Gate Blvd.* ☎ *604/932-7202. AE, MC, V. Map p 160.*

★ The Hat Gallery WHISTLER VILLAGE Head cold? This place stocks hundreds of ways to keep it warm and stylish. *4295 Blackcomb Way.* ☎ *604/938-6695. AE, MC, V. Map p 160.*

★★ Hatley VILLAGE NORTH This place is just too cute, selling cartoon-animal and nature-themed clothing for kids and grown-up kids, plus housewares, such as oven mitts and cocktail napkins. *4308 Main St.* ☎ *514/272-8444. www.hatleystore. com. MC, V. Map p 160.*

Gifts, Housewares & Knickknacks

★ The Daily Planet VILLAGE NORTH An eclectic selection of home knickknacks, gift items, antiques, and furnishings, with a ski-cabin meets country condo in the world marketplace kind of vibe. *4340 Lorimer Rd.* ☎ *604/905-4044. MC, V. Map p 160.*

The Hat Gallery is a good bet for stylish head coverings.

Need a cute après-ski sweater? Amos and Andes is where you'll find it.

Groceries, Beer & Wine
★★ The Grocery Store (Hearthstone Grocery)

WHISTLER VILLAGE   With so many Whistler hotel rooms offering kitchens and kitchenettes, you need somewhere centrally located to buy groceries. This is it, right in the Village Square. There's a good selection of pre-cooked meals, plus produce, packaged goods, and a large attached liquor store. *4211 Village Sq.* ☎ *604/932-3628. www.whistler grocery.com. AE, MC, V. Map p 160.*

★ IGA Plus VILLAGE NORTH

Another grocery option, farther out from the village center that's more convenient for those staying in the Village North. *4330 Northlands Blvd.* ☎ *604/938-2850. www.market placeiga.com. AE, MC, V. Map p 160.*

★★ Whistler's Creekside Market CREEKSIDE   A more upscale choice near the Creekside lifts, with fine meats and seafood, fresh produce, artisan bread, and a large deli counter. *2071 Lake Placid Rd.* ☎ *604/938-9301. www.creekside market.com. AE, MC, V. Map p 160.*

Outdoor, Ski & Sporting Gear
★★ The Glacier Shop VILLAGE

NORTH   Whistler's largest ski shop carries all that you need to hit the slopes: skis, boots, clothing, and après-ski wear. *4314 Main St.* ☎ *604/938-7432. AE, MC, V. Map p 160.*

★★ Helly Hansen WHISTLER

VILLAGE   One of the many famous-name outdoor-clothing brands that have their own stores in the Village. This one's known best for its parkas and foul-weather gear.

Whistler Village Art Gallery (p 162) has a great selection of pieces by Canadian and international artists.

If you're in the market for a snowboard, you'll find a large selection of them at Showcase Snowboards.

4295 Blackcomb Way. ☎ 604/932-0143. www.hellyhansen.com. AE, MC, V. Map p 160.

★ **The North Face** WHISTLER VILLAGE   Famous-name outdoor and casual clothing for men and women. *4230 Gateway Dr.* ☎ 604/932-4193. www.thenorthface.com. AE, MC, V. Map p 160.

★★ **Salomon** WHISTLER VILLAGE Performance ski and snowboard gear and clothing from the famous manufacturer, plus sunglasses, accessories, etc. *4320 Sundial Crescent (in the Pan Pacific).* ☎ 604/905-2295. www.salomonsports.com. AE, DC, MC, V. Map p 160.

★★ **Showcase Snowboards** WHISTLER VILLAGE   Whistler's oldest snowboard shop, with a stock of boards, boots, gear, clothing, and accessories. *4340 Sundial Crescent.* ☎ 604/905-2246. www.showcase snowboards.com. AE, MC, V. Map p 160.

★★★ **Surefoot** WHISTLER VILLAGE Specializing in perfectly fitting ski boots, with orthotic and alignment services available. *4295 Blackcomb Way.* ☎ 604/938-1663. www.sure foot.com. AE, MC, V. Map p 160.

★★★ **Wild Willies Ski Shop** WHISTLER VILLAGE   Perennially named Whistler's best ski shop, Wild Willies' keeps a large stock of gear and accessories, and is especially known for boot fitting. *4320 Sundial Crescent.* ☎ 604/938-8036. www.wildwillies.com. AE, MC, V. Map p 160.

Helly Hansen sells great parkas and other winter-weather gear.

Dining in Whistler

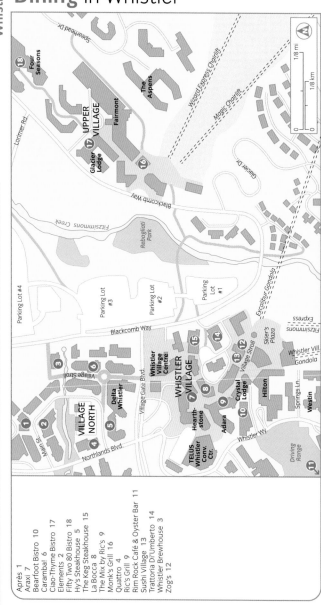

Après 1
Araxi 7
Bearfoot Bistro 10
Carambal 6
Ciao-Thyme Bistro 17
Elements 2
Fifty Two 80 Bistro 18
Hy's Steakhouse 5
The Keg Steakhouse 15
La Bocca 8
The Mix by Ric's 9
Monk's Grill 16
Quattro 4
Ric's Grill 9
Rim Rock Café & Oyster Bar 11
Sushi Village 13
Trattoria Di'Umberto 14
Whistler Brewhouse 3
Zog's 12

Dining Best Bets

For award-winning regional cuisine and a superb wine list, you can't do better than Araxi.

Best **BC Regional Cuisine**
★★★ Araxi $$$ *4222 Village Sq.*
(p 168)

Best **Seafood**
★★★ RimRock Café & Oyster Bar
$$$$ *2117 Whistler Rd. (p 170)*

Best **Steakhouse**
★★★ Hy's Steakhouse $$$ *4308
Main St. (p 169)*

Best **Family Restaurants**
★ Caramba! $$ *4314 Main St.*
(p 168); and Whistler Brewhouse
$$ *4355 Blackcomb Way (p 171)*

Best **Quick, Hip Meals**
★ The Mix by Ric's $$ *4237 Village
Stroll (p 169)*

Best **Italian**
★★ Quattro $$$ *4319 Main St.*
(p 170)

Best **Sushi**
★ Sushi Village $–$$ *4272 Mountain Sq. (p 171)*

Best **Poutine**
★ Zog's $ *4340 Sundial Crescent*
(p 171)

Best **Brewpub**
Whistler Brewhouse $$ *4355 Blackcomb Way (p 171)*

Best **Pub Menu**
★★ Dubh Linn Gate Irish Pub $$
4320 Sundial Crescent (p 180)

Best **Tuscan**
★★ Trattoria D'Umberto $$$ *4417
Sundial Pl. (p 171)*

Best **Value**
★ Zog's $ *4340 Sundial Crescent*
(p 171)

Best **for Wine Lovers**
★★★ Araxi $$$ *4222 Village Sq.*
(p 168)

Whistler Dining A to Z

★★ Après VILLAGE NORTH *MOD-ERN EUROPEAN* An intimate, 50-seat spot with a modern, high-design look and regionally sourced, slow-cooked nouveau-Euro cuisine. Menus change seasonally, with highlights such as Dungeness crab, Quebec foie gras, and regional meats. Wines are sourced from the Pacific Coast. *4338 Main St.* ☎ *604/935-0200. www.apresrestaurant.com. Entrees C$24–C$35. AE, DC, MC, V. Dinner daily. Map p 166.*

★★★ Araxi WHISTLER VILLAGE *BC REGIONAL* A perennial "best restaurant in Whistler" award-winner, Araxi serves a menu of West Coast regional cuisine incorporating Pacific seafood and local farm produce and meats. The wine list is superb (and huge, with 800 different labels), the decor is contemporary Mediterranean, and there's a great heated patio for good weather dining. *4222 Village Square.* ☎ *604/932-4540. www.araxi.com. Entrees C$28–C$40. AE, DC, MC, V. Dinner daily. Map p 166.*

★★★ Bearfoot Bistro WHISTLER VILLAGE *BC REGIONAL* The Bearfoot serves custom and prix-fixe three- and five-course tasting menus featuring regional, seasonal, innovative concoctions, from the wild Arctic caribou chop to the "King Crab Trio," with coconut chili soup, croquette, and soy pop rocks. High-back leather chairs, low lighting, an open kitchen, and a spiral stair to the wine cellar highlight the dining room, while the stylish Champagne Bar features an ice-rail to cool your drink, and a simpler bar menu. *4121 Village Green.* ☎ *604/932-3433. www.bearfootbistro.com. 3-course tasting menu C$48. AE, DC, DISC, MC, V. Dinner daily. Map p 166.*

★ kids Caramba! VILLAGE NORTH *MEDITERRANEAN* Not a Mexican restaurant, despite the name, Caramba serves fresh, flavorful pasta, wood-oven pizza, rotisserie meats, and seafood in a fun, casual, family-oriented environment. *4314 Main St.* ☎ *604/938-1879. www. caramba-restaurante.com. Entrees C$13–C$21. AE, MC, V. Lunch & dinner daily. Map p 166.*

★★ Ciao-Thyme Bistro UPPER VILLAGE *BC REGIONAL* A casual cafe whose menu of fresh, seasonal dishes betrays a vaguely French influence. Inside, there's a packed little room with an open kitchen. Outside (in good weather), the patio is surrounded by an herb and vegetable garden. *4573 Chateau Blvd.* ☎ *604/932-7051. www.chef bernards.ca/restaurant. Entrees C$19–C$26. AE, MC, V. Breakfast, lunch & dinner daily. Map p 166.*

★ Elements VILLAGE NORTH *TAPAS* A fun, hip tapas joint with a view kitchen, a softly lit woody interior, and a burbling waterfall and copper accents for ambience. Plates emphasize Mediterranean and regional tastes, with nods eastward

Innovative cuisine and an elegant setting make Bearfoot Bistro a winner.

The mildly French-influenced cafe cuisine at Ciao-Thyme Bistro packs in the crowds.

to Asia. *4359 Main St. (at the Summit Lodge).* ☎ *604/932-5569. www.
wildwoodrestaurants.ca/htm/pbistro.
html. Small plates C$5–C$15. MC, V.
Breakfast, lunch & dinner daily. Map
p 166.*

★★★ **Fifty Two 80 Bistro** UPPER
VILLAGE *BC REGIONAL* Named for
Blackcomb's skiable vertical feet, the
Four Seasons' casual but *très* mod
restaurant is centered on a tiled circular fireplace, with backlit onyx
accents inside and a large heated
patio out. The regional menu concentrates on seafood, with a raw bar
and entrees such as Nova Scotia
lobster and seared ahi tuna minute
steak. There's also a "wellness tasting menu" with wine pairings. *4591
Blackcomb Way (in the Four Seasons).* ☎ *604/935-3400. www.four
seasons.com/whistler/dining.html.
Entrees C$22–C$43. AE, DISC, MC, V.
Breakfast, lunch & dinner daily. Map
p 166.*

★★★ **Hy's Steakhouse** VILLAGE
NORTH *STEAK* Whistler's top steakhouse, Hy's is a classic, cozy, wood-paneled room serving a menu of
aged AAA Alberta beef steaks,
seafood, oysters, hearty soups (think
baked French onion), classic salads
(think prepared at the table), etc.,
with a good wine list to wash it all
down. *4308 Main St.* ☎ *604/905-
5555. www.hyssteakhouse.com/hys-
whistler.html. Entrees C$30–C$50. AE,
MC, V. Dinner daily. Map p 166.*

The Keg Steakhouse WHISTLER
VILLAGE *STEAK* A big, fun, casual
chain steakhouse and bar with reasonable prices, The Keg is pretty
much what they mean by "family
steakhouse." The ground floor
house's Brandy's Bar (p 180) while the
second and third floors are for dining.
4229 Sundial Place. ☎ *604/932-5151.
www.kegsteakhouse.com/whistler.
Entrees C$20–C$45. AE, MC, V. Dinner
daily. Map p 166.*

★ **La Bocca** WHISTLER VILLAGE
FUSION This funky little pseudo-bistro has an interior of beam-and-stucco ceilings, antiqued red walls,
and cozy booths, and a perfectly
located outdoor patio. The menu
blends east and west with seafood,
pastas, wok dishes, steaks, schnitzel,
and fondue. *4232 Whistler Village Sq.*
☎ *604/932-2112. www.labocca.
moonfruit.com. Entrees C$16–C$39.
AE, MC, V. Breakfast, lunch & dinner
daily. Map p 166.*

★ **The Mix by Ric's** WHISTLER
VILLAGE *FUSION* A stylish little
spot with a chic interior and a patio
along the Village Stroll. The menu
offers tapas and such standout main
courses as seafood chowder, organic
beef sliders (minihamburgers), and
dinner steaks. Drinks trend toward
fresh-fruit martinis. *4237 Village
Stroll.* ☎ *604/932-6499. www.rics
grill.com. Entrees C$15–C$29. AE, MC,
V. Breakfast, lunch & dinner daily.
Map p 166.*

A menu of tapas, pizza, and burgers makes Garibaldi Lift Co. Bar & Grill a popular spot for a casual meal (p 181).

★ **Monk's Grill** UPPER VILLAGE *ECLECTIC* Located right next to the Upper Village lifts, Monk's is part après ski bar, part fine dining restaurant with a menu of steaks/chops, seafood, and small plates. The interior is moody and stylish yet laid back, the views are great, and there are two heated outdoor patios. *4555 Blackcomb Way.* ☎ *604 /932-9677. www.monksgrill.com. Entrees C$19–C$28. AE, DC, MC, V. Lunch and dinner daily (winter & summer), dinner Wed–Sun & lunch Fri–Sun (spring & fall). Map p 166.*

★★ **Quattro** VILLAGE NORTH *ITALIAN* Classic romantic Italian with

low lights, gleaming wood, fireplaces, and attentive service. The large menu includes more than 18 appetizers (from classic minestrone soup to Alaska king crab), plus a dozen different pastas and almost as many meat and seafood entrees. *4319 Main St. (in the Pinnacle Hotel).* ☎ *604/905-4844. www.quattrorestaurants.com/windex.html. Entrees C$22–C$47. AE, MC, V. Dinner Tues–Sat. Map p 166.*

★★ **Ric's Grill** WHISTLER VILLAGE *ECLECTIC* A modern, stylish room with a chic ambience, Ric's serves a menu of steaks, seafood, and miscellaneous specialties that incorporate Italian, Asian, and "other" influences—think Thai coconut green curry chicken, or organic roasted chicken in a mushroom Madeira sauce. *4237 Village Stroll (in the Crystal Lodge).* ☎ *604/932-7427. www.ricsgrill.com. Entrees C$19–C$42. AE, DC, MC, V. Dinner daily. Map p 166.*

★★★ **RimRock Café & Oyster Bar** CREEKSIDE *SEAFOOD* This cozy and casual spot serves some of the best seafood in town. Patrons dine at antique wooden tables under a high, peaked ceiling, amid rustic beams and with two stone fireplaces to keep them warm in winter. Oysters, served six different ways, are a good starter. Seafood and game entrees (including caribou and venison) rotate with the

The Mix by Ric's is a good choice for a low-key but stylish meal.

The Whistler Brewhouse serves up informal family meals and a good array of beers and ales.

seasons. *2117 Whistler Rd.* ☎ *877/932-5589 or 604/932-5565. www.rimrockwhistler.com. Entrees C$37–C$47. AE, DC, MC, V. Dinner daily. Map p 166.*

★ **Sushi Village** WHISTLER VILLAGE *SUSHI* Located close to the lifts, this busy, casual spot has been a Whistler institution for more than a quarter century, serving a large menu of fresh sushi, sashimi, and teriyaki dishes. *4272 Mountain Square.* ☎ *604/932-3330. www.sushivillage.com. Sushi rolls C$4–C$12. AE, MC, V. Dinner daily, lunch Fri–Sun. Map p 166.*

★★ **Trattoria Di'Umberto** WHISTLER VILLAGE *ITALIAN* Two wonderfully warm, rustic dining rooms are the setting for classic Tuscan meals. The kitchen is open, the service is friendly, and the pastas and risottos are delicious. *4417 Sundial Pl.* ☎ *604/932-5858. www.hotelvilladelia.com/restaurant_trattoria.cfm. Entrees C$20–C$40. AE, MC, V. Lunch & dinner daily. Map p 166.*

Just one of many delectable Tuscan-inspired dishes at Trattoria Di'Umberto.

kids **Whistler Brewhouse** VILLAGE NORTH *BREWPUB* A chunky, woody interior has the usual family-oriented mountain brewpub amenities: fermenting tanks, fireplaces, TVs in the bar area, an open kitchen, and a menu of pizzas, pasta, burgers, soups, salads, and homebrewed beers and ales. A model train circles a track up near the ceiling. *4355 Blackcomb Way.* ☎ *604/905-2739. www.markjamesgroup.com/whistler.html. Entrees C$14–C$36. AE, MC, V. Lunch & dinner daily. Map p 166.*

★ **Zog's** WHISTLER VILLAGE *STREET FOOD* An open-air restaurant right in Skier's Plaza, Zog's is famous for its poutine, a French-Canadian combination of fries, gravy, cheese curds, and options such as meat sauce and chili. Heart-healthy it's not, but yum. There's also burgers, hot dogs, veggie dogs, and fried "beavertail" pastries. Heaters keep the outdoor seats warmish. *4340 Sundial Crescent.* ☎ *604/938-6644. All items under $10. Cash only. Open 8am–2:30am daily. Map p 166.*

Hotels in Whistler

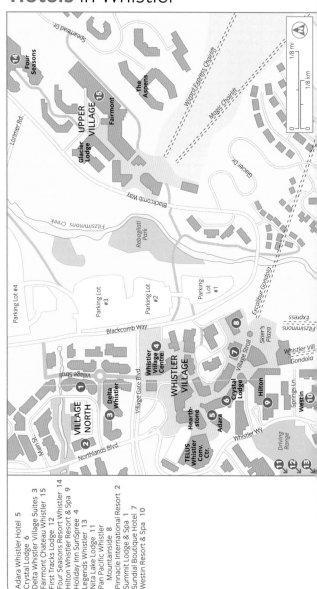

Adara Whistler Hotel 5
Crystal Lodge 6
Delta Whistler Village Suites 3
Fairmont Chateau Whistler 15
First Tracks Lodge 12
Four Seasons Resort Whistler 14
Hilton Whistler Resort & Spa 9
Holiday Inn SunSpree 4
Legends Whistler 13
Nita Lake Lodge 11
Pan Pacific Whistler
  Mountainside 8
Pinnacle International Resort 2
Summit Lodge & Spa 1
Sundial Boutique Hotel 7
Westin Resort & Spa 10

Hotel Best Bets

Best Location
★★ Pan Pacific Whistler Mountain-
side $$$ *4320 Sundial Crescent*
(p 176)

Most Unbelievably Luxurious
★★★ Four Seasons Resort
Whistler $$$ *4591 Blackcomb Way*
(p 173)

Best Hipster Digs
★★ Adara Whistler Hotel $$
4122 Village Green (p 174)

Best Boutique Hotel (in the Village)
★★ Sundial Boutique Hotel $$
4340 Sundial Crescent (p 177)

Best Boutique Hotel (Outside the Village)
★★★ Nita Lake Lodge $$ *2131
Lake Placid Rd. (p 176)*

Best Hotel Spa
★★★ Four Seasons Resort
Whistler $$$ *4591 Blackcomb Way*
(p 175); and ★★ Fairmont Chateau
Whistler $$$ *4599 Chateau Blvd.*
(p 174)

Best Budget Hotel
Holiday Inn SunSpree $ *4295 Black-
comb Way (p 176)*

Best Hot Tub
★★ Pan Pacific Whistler Mountain-
side $$$ *4320 Sundial Crescent*
(p 176)

Home away from Home

If you're on a budget, are traveling with a large group, or want a little more privacy and quiet than you'd get at a major resort, Whistler has a large supply of private townhouses or condominiums that you can rent for the duration of your stay. Quality (and amenities and decor) varies according to the individual owner, but generally speaking, most lodgings are renovated often and are kept in good shape. Amenities range from hot tubs and fireplaces to private porches and modern full kitchens.

You can book a condo or townhouse through the official reservations service for **Tourism Whistler** (☎ 800/WHISTLER; www.whistler.com). Another great online booking service, **Allura Direct** (☎ 866/425-5872; www.alluradirect.com), lets you rent condos (ranging from studios to six-bedroom units) directly from their owners. It showcases numerous available properties in Whistler and offers photos, details, and instant reservations capability. Deals vary according to the season, but going the condo route will often net you a bargain in very pricey Whistler.

Whistler Hotels A to Z

★★ Adara Whistler Hotel

WHISTLER VILLAGE   A sister-property to Vancouver's super-stylish Opus Hotel (p 128), the Adara has a youthful, internationalist vibe, its chic contemporary decor including wry takes on traditional lodge styling. Check out artist Erich Ginder's series of glossy red "Ghost Antlers" in the lobby. *4122 Village Green. ☎ 866/502 2372 or 604/905-4009. www.adarahotel.com. 41 units. Doubles C$149–C$600. AE, MC, V. Map p 172.*

★ Crystal Lodge

WHISTLER VILLAGE   Crystal Lodge was one of the first hotels in Whistler, and has the location to prove it: right on Mountain Square, about 100m (328 ft.) from the lifts. Standard rooms aren't the village's most inspiring, but the suites are a big improvement. There's a heated pool outside, and the rec-room style Crystal Lounge attracts a young, snowboard crowd. *4154 Village Green. ☎ 800/667-3363 or 604/932-2221. www.crystal-lodge.bc.ca. 159 units. Doubles C$101–C$324. AE, DISC, MC, V. Map p 172.*

★ Delta Whistler Village Suites

VILLAGE NORTH   A solid, unpretentious hotel located a few minutes' walk from the lifts. The majority of rooms are one- and two-bedroom suites, all with full kitchen, fireplace, and washer/dryer. There's a heated outdoor pool and hot tubs inside and out. *4308 Main St. ☎ 888/299-3987 or 604/905-3987. www.deltahotels.com. 205 units. Doubles C$109–C$699. AE, DC, DISC, MC, V. Map p 172.*

★★ Fairmont Chateau Whistler

UPPER VILLAGE   They're not kidding about the "chateau" part: The lobby goes for a Swiss mountain lodge feel, though the majority of the public areas and the spacious, comfortable rooms stick to contemporary decor. The hotel's location at the base of Blackcomb Mountain makes skiing easy, and there's a spa and an 18-hole, par-72 Robert Trent Jones, Jr. golf course on site. *4599 Chateau Blvd. ☎ 866/540-4424 or 604/938-8000. www.fairmont.com/whistler. 550 units. Doubles C$199–C$949. AE, DC, DISC, MC, V. Map p 172.*

★★ First Tracks Lodge

CREEKSIDE   Set at the base of the mountain in Whistler Creekside, First Tracks offers 1-, 2-, 3-, and 4-bedroom suites, each with a balcony or patio, gas fireplace, full kitchen, and

A regular guest room at the Pan Pacific Whistler Mountainside (p 176).

The lobby of the Fairmont Chateau Whistler.

washer/dryer. Its location is great for people wanting a quieter experience than you get in the Village. *2202 Gondola Way.* ☎ *866/385-0614 or 604/990-6610. www.firsttracks lodge.com. 84 units. 1-bedroom suite C$129–C$450. AE, MC, V. Map p 172.*

★★★ Four Seasons Resort Whistler UPPER VILLAGE

Whistler's most refined, luxurious hotel, a huge but surprisingly intimate place snuggled into the quiet Upper Village. Public areas exude a millionaire-rustic vibe, while rooms and suites are done in sober dark woods, leather, and rich fabrics. Everything looks like it will last for generations. All rooms have a fireplace, balcony, and bathroom with separate tub and extra-large shower. A separate wing has two- to four-bedroom suites for longer stays. The gorgeous spa includes First Nations–inspired treatments, and the outdoor courtyard has a large heated pool and three hot tubs. *4591 Blackcomb Way.* ☎ *888/935-2460 or 604/935-3400. www.fourseasons.com/whistler. 310 units. Doubles C$255–C$495. AE, DC, MC, V. Map p 172.*

★★ Hilton Whistler Resort & Spa WHISTLER VILLAGE Located

close to the lifts, the Hilton offers a vibe that's part resort, part convention hotel. Rooms and suites are very spacious, with thick beds plus deep soaker tubs in the bathrooms. Premiere Rooms have galley kitchenettes. Suites offer a variety of additional perks, such as full kitchens, fireplaces, balconies, and private steam rooms. There's a heated outdoor pool, indoor and outdoor hot tubs, outdoor patio fireplace, and the Cinnamon Bear Bar, a popular sports bar (p 180). *4050 Whistler Way.* ☎ *800/515-4050 or 604/932-1982. www.whistlerresort.hilton.com. 289 units. Doubles C$149–C$599. AE, DC, DISC, MC, V. Map p 172.*

A one-bedroom suite at the Crystal Lodge.

The lobby of the Pinnacle International Resort.

Holiday Inn SunSpree

WHISTLER VILLAGE   Located a short walk from the Village lifts, the Holiday Inn offers good value for the price. All rooms have fireplaces and kitchen facilities. Deluxe studio rooms have full kitchens, a Murphy bed for additional guests, and large bathrooms with soaker tubs. Some rooms have balconies. *4295 Blackcomb Way.* ☎ *800/229-3188 or 604/938-0878. www.whistlerhi.com. 115 units. Doubles C$109–C$359. AE, DC, DISC, MC, V. Map p 172.*

★ kids Legends Whistler CREEKSIDE

A sister-property to First Tracks Lodge, this family-friendly hotel is right next to the Creekside Gondola. All accommodations are one- to three-bedroom suites done in a comfy home style, each with a gas fireplace, full kitchen, washer/dryer, sofa bed, bathtub/shower combo, and a balcony, patio, or terrace.

The lobby of the Fours Seasons Resort Whistler.

There's a heated outdoor pool and hot tub. *2036 London La.* ☎ *866/385-0611 or 604/990-6610. www.legendswhistler.com. 121 units. 1-bedroom suites C$109–C$360. AE, MC, V. Map p 172.*

★★★ Nita Lake Lodge CREEKSIDE

A gorgeous boutique hotel in a quiet residential neighborhood near Creekside, on the shore of Nita Lake. Interiors are high-design rustic, all dark woods, leather upholstery, and stone floors. All rooms have fireplaces, wonderful king beds, galley kitchens, and enormous bathrooms with a separate large shower and soaker tubs. Most rooms have balconies. There's a fantastic lobby lounge, rooftop hot tubs and herb garden, and small outdoor pool. The Whistler Mountaineer's Whistler station is part of the hotel, and the Valley Trail to the Village is right outside. *2131 Lake Placid Rd.* ☎ *888/755-6482 or 604/966-5700. www.nitalakelodge.com. 70 units. Studio suites C$159–C$423. AE, MC, V. Map p 172.*

★★ Pan Pacific Whistler Mountainside

WHISTLER VILLAGE   The closest hotel to the Whistler and Blackcomb gondolas, the Pan Pacific offers studios and one- and two-bedroom suites, all with full kitchens, gas fireplaces, oversize bathtubs, and views of the mountain or valley from balconies or floor-to-ceiling windows. Decor is pleasantly contemporary. The roof deck is home to Whistler's best pool-and-Jacuzzi setup, with great views of the slopes. *4320*

Sundial Crescent. ☎ 888/905-9995 or 604/905-2999. www.panpacific.com/en/WhistlerMountainside/Overview.html. 121 units. Suites C$260–C$1079. AE, MC, V. Map p 172.

★ Pinnacle International Resort

VILLAGE NORTH   In Village North's Marketplace area, about 10 minutes' walk from the lifts, the Pinnacle offers good value for the money. All rooms are studios, and come with gas fireplaces, full kitchens, and Jacuzzi tubs in the main room. There's a heated outdoor pool and hot tub, and an Italian restaurant, Quattro (p 170), on the ground floor. 4319 Main St. ☎ 888/999-8986 or 604/938-3218. www.whistlerpinnacle.com. 84 units. C$160–C$459. AE, MC, V. Map p 172.

★ Summit Lodge & Spa

VILLAGE NORTH   Located near the Pinnacle (above), about 10 minutes' walk from the lifts, the Summit's studios and 1-bedroom suites are smallish and lack distinctive decor, but are reasonably priced and outfitted with kitchenettes, gas fireplaces, large tubs, and balconies. There's an outdoor pool and hot tub, and an "east meets west" spa on site. 4359 Main St. ☎ 888/913-8811 or 604/932-2778. www.summitlodge.com. 81 units. C$119–C$425. AE, MC, V. Map p 172.

★★ Sundial Boutique Hotel

WHISTLER VILLAGE   Sharing "best location" honors with the Pan Pacific Mountainside and the Westin, the Sundial offers beautifully appointed boutique accommodations just steps from the Whistler and Blackcomb gondolas. The feel is homey, low-key, and quietly hands-off, as if you're a long-term resident. All rooms are one- and two-bedroom suites with living rooms, full kitchens, gas fireplaces, contemporary West Coast mountain styling, and windows all around for views. Some suites have deep-soaker Jacuzzi tubs in the bedroom; eight have decks with hot tubs looking toward mountain or village views. There's a single public rooftop hot tub (but no views if you're in the water) and a spa on site. 4340 Sundial Crescent. ☎ 800/661-2321 or 604/932-2321. www.sundialhotel.com. 49 units. 1-bedroom suites C$149–C$409. AE, MC, V. Map p 172.

★★ Westin Resort & Spa

WHISTLER VILLAGE   With a great location right by the lifts, the huge Westin offers junior and one- and two-bedroom suites, some with loft bedrooms. All have full kitchens, gas fireplaces, soaker tubs, slate-lined showers, and a decor scheme that's comfortable and homey if not overly stylish. There's an indoor/outdoor pool (separated by glass doors, with a swim-through channel in between) and hot tubs, an on-site spa, and a fitness club. 4090 Whistler Way. ☎ 888/634-5577 or 604/905-5000. www.westinwhistler.com. 419 units. Junior suites C$189–C$849. AE, DC, MC, V. Map p 172.

A suite at the Sundial Boutique Hotel.

Nightlife & Entertainment
in Whistler

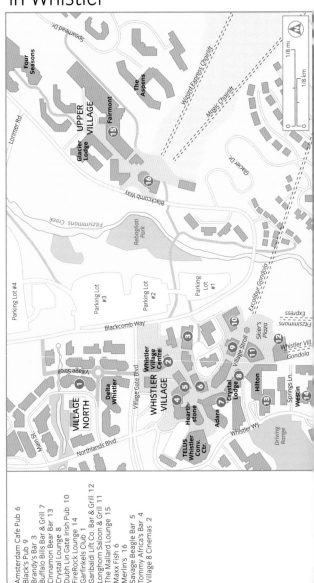

Amsterdam Cafe Pub 6
Black's Pub 9
Brandy's Bar 3
Buffalo Bills Bar & Grill 7
Cinnamon Bear Bar 13
Crystal Lounge 8
Dubh Lin Gate Irish Pub 10
FireRock Lounge 14
Garfinkels Club 1
Garibaldi Lift Co. Bar & Grill 12
Longhorn Saloon & Grill 11
The Mallard Lounge 15
Maxx Fish 6
Merlin's 16
Savage Beagle Bar 5
Tommy Africa's Bar 4
Village 8 Cinemas 2

Nightlife & Entertainment
Best Bets

You can hoist an authentic pint of Guinness indoors or out at the Dubh Linn Gate Irish Pub.

Best **Dance Club**
★★ Garfinkels Club, *4308 Main St.* *(p 182)*

Best **Funky Little Bar**
★ Amsterdam Cafe Pub, *4232 Village Stroll (p 180)*

Best **for Billiards**
★★ Cinnamon Bear Bar, *4050 Village Way (p 180)*

Best **Snowboarder's Lounge**
Crystal Lounge, *4154 Village Green (p 180)*

Best **Irish Pub**
★★ Dubh Linn Gate Irish Pub, *4320 Sundial Crescent (p 180)*

Best **Country Club Atmosphere**
★ The Mallard Lounge, *4599 Chateau Blvd. (p 181)*

Best **Movie Theater**
Village 8 Cinemas, *4295 Blackcomb Way (p 182)*

Best **Location**
★★ Garibaldi Lift Co. Bar and Grill, *at the base of the Whistler Gondola (p 181)*

Best **Roadhouse Party Atmosphere**
★ Longhorn Saloon & Grill, *4280 Mountain Sq. (p 181)*

Most Original **DJ Booth**
★ Merlin's, *4545 Blackcomb Way (p 182)*

Best Place **to Drink Beer While Minding Your Kids**
Whistler Brewhouse, *4355 Blackcomb Way (p 171)*

Whistler **Nightlife & Entertainment**

Après Ski Bars & Lounges

★ Amsterdam Cafe Pub

WHISTLER VILLAGE   A warm, woody, posters-on-the-wall, big-TV kind of bar centrally located on the Village Square and catering to a mostly young crowd. There's an outdoor patio, and a menu of pub food in case beer isn't enough. *4232 Village Stroll.* ☎ *604/932-8334. www. amsterdampub.moonfruit.com. Map p 178.*

★ Black's Pub WHISTLER VILLAGE

A real Canadian pub with a large beer and whiskey menu. It's located at the base of Whistler and Blackcomb gondolas, and there's a patio overlooking the slopes. *4270 Mountain Sq.* ☎ *604/932-6945. www. whistlerpubrestaurant.com. Map p 178.*

Brandy's Bar WHISTLER VILLAGE

On the main floor of The Keg steakhouse, Brandy's is a casual, woody place to catch a drink and some pub food while watching sports on multiple TVs. *4429 Sundial Pl.*

☎ *604/932-5151. www.kegsteak house.com/whistler. Map p 178.*

★★ Cinnamon Bear Bar

WHISTLER VILLAGE   One of Whistler's favorite après ski joints, the Cinnamon Bear has a high-ceilinged central area with a stone fireplace, leather armchairs, built-in backgammon and chess boards, and two great pool tables. It's frequently named Whistler's best pool-playing bar. *4050 Whistler Way (in the Hilton).* ☎ *604/932-1982. www. hiltonwhistler.com. Map p 178.*

Crystal Lounge WHISTLER VILLAGE   Located underground in the Crystal Lodge, this lounge looks like a big rec room and attracts a young, snowboarding crowd. There's live music sometimes, TV sports on others, and drunk young folks often. *4154 Village Green.* ☎ *604/938-1081. Map p 178.*

★★ Dubh Linn Gate Irish Pub

WHISTLER VILLAGE   Located in rock-throwing distance from Blackcomb's

The Crystal Lounge is sort of a giant rec room for the young and active set—with lots of beer.

For a casual but not rowdy nightlife atmosphere, the FireRock Lounge is a good place to get a drink.

Excalibur Gondola, this Irish pub has an authentic, wood-filled interior (brought piece-by-piece from Dublin) full of memorabilia and cozy touches. The Guinness is well-poured, the pub menu is fantastic, there's a large beer and whiskey menu, frequent live music, and TVs for sports. *4320 Sundial Crescent (in the Pan Pacific Lodge).* ☎ *604/905-4047. www. dubhlinngate.com. Map p 178.*

★ **FireRock Lounge** WHISTLER VILLAGE Casual but elegant, this adult-oriented space is more ski-and-golf than snowboard-and-mountain-bike. Its interior is smooth-jazz meets rustic—the latter provided by river rocks, timbers, and a large stone fireplace. *4090 Whistler Way (at the Westin).* ☎ *604/905-5000. www.westinwhistler.com. Map p 178.*

★★ **Garibaldi Lift Co. Bar and Grill** WHISTLER VILLAGE You can't get any closer to the slopes than this: The Garibaldi is perched right at the lower edge of the slopes, between the Fitzsimmons Chairlift and the Whistler Express Gondola. Big and fun, it's got a large slopeside patio; a big fireplace; windows all around; reggae and dance music in the evenings; and a menu of tapas, pizza, and burgers. *Skiers Plaza, at the base of the Whistler Gondola.* ☎ *604/905-2220.*

www.whistlerblackcomb.com/todo/apresnightlife/glc.htm. Map p 178.

★ **Longhorn Saloon & Grill** WHISTLER VILLAGE Big, loud, and very young, the Longhorn is located close to the Garibaldi but has more of a wings-and-nachos vibe, with TVs, pool tables, and video games to distract you if the beer and snowboard babes don't. *4280 Mountain Sq.* ☎ *604/932-5999. www.longhorn saloon.ca. Map p 178.*

★ **The Mallard Lounge** UPPER VILLAGE This very grown-up room is country club all the way, with a big fireplace, sofas and club chairs, and a menu of classic cocktails, Scotch, wine, "alpine warmers" (including flaming coffee), and fine cigars. Outside, three fire pits keep things warm on the Mallard Terrace, nestled beside Blackcomb's slopes. *4599 Chateau Blvd. (at the Fairmont Chateau).* ☎ *604/938-8000. www. fairmont.com/whistler. Map p 178.*

Dance Clubs & Live Music
★★ **Buffalo Bills Bar & Grill** WHISTLER VILLAGE A total party spot, dance club, live music venue, and après-snowboard bar rolled into one. Many nights are themed—some focus on sports, some on DJs, some on variations of "Party!" Weekend

The immense Longhorn Saloon & Grill is where the young and rowdy like to get their beer and their pool cue time.

nights are a madhouse. *4122 Village Green.* ☎ *604/932-6613. www. buffalobills.ca. Map p 178.*

★★ Garfinkels Club VILLAGE NORTH   Another hot Whistler nightspot, Garfinkels focuses on DJ dance nights, plus occasional live bands. It's all about the drinking. I mean the dancing. I mean . . . *4308 Main St.* ☎ *604/932-2323. www.garfswhistler.com. Map p 178.*

★ Maxx Fish WHISTLER VILLAGE A particularly young crowd packs this space for DJ-spun house and hip-hop, dancing or lounging like wannabe VIPs in the booths. *4232 Village Stroll.* ☎ *604/932-1904. www.maxxfish.moonfruit.com. Map p 178.*

★ Merlin's UPPER VILLAGE   Sort of a Longhorn's of the Upper Village, Merlin's is part party bar and part club, with its DJ booth lodged in a retired gondola car. It's family-friendly at lunch and dinner, but things change after 9pm or so.

4545 Blackcomb Way. ☎ *604/938-7700. Map p 178.*

★ Savage Beagle Bar WHISTLER VILLAGE   Mo' dance. This two-level space offers rooms to chill out (loudly) up top and a happening dance space below. *4222 Village Sq.* ☎ *604/938-3337. www.savage beagle.ca. Map p 178.*

★★ Tommy Africa's Bar WHISTLER VILLAGE   In business for more than 20 years, this dance club has various themed party nights, guest DJs, and special events. *4216 Gateway Dr.* ☎ *604/932-6090. www.tommyafricas.com. Map p 178.*

Movie Theaters

Village 8 Cinemas WHISTLER VILLAGE   Current Hollywood fare on eight screens, with a cafe on-site. *4295 Blackcomb Way.* ☎ *604/932-5833. www.village8.ca. Map p 178.* ●

The
Savvy Traveler

Before You Go

Tourist Office

The **Canadian Tourism Commission** (☎ 604/638-8300; www. canada.travel); **British Columbia Tourism,** 200 Burrard St., Plaza level (☎ **800/435-5622** or 604/683-2000; www.hellobc.com); and **Tourism Vancouver,** 200 Burrard St., Ste. 210 (☎ **604/682-2222**; www.tourism vancouver.com), are all useful sources of information, but their websites sometimes lack the kind of perspicacity we might prefer in our travel guidance. For example, the restaurant search on Vancouver's site turns up three McDonald's and a Red Robin among its seven "Family Restaurants." Thankfully, its "Things to Do" listings and, in particular, its practical travel advice (for instance, for travelers with disabilities) are much more useful.

The website of **Tourism Whistler,** 4010 Whistler Way (☎ **888/869-2777**; www.tourism whistler.com), is a pretty good source of information on the resort, but it's not as good as the resort's own site, **www.whistler blackcomb.com**.

The Best Time to Go

Vancouver's prime tourist months are May to September, when the weather is fine, the city's major festivals are in full swing, and Canada Place fills up with cruise ships and their passengers, bound for or returning from Alaska. Hotel rooms are at their priciest during these months. Travelers who don't mind a chill in the air and the possibility of rain can get some great deals during the shoulder months of October and November and March and April, which have their own charm. From late March through April, for example, the city's 36,000 Japanese ornamental cherry trees are in bloom, along with many flowers.

In Whistler, the ski season stretches from December until June, with glacier skiing extending through July. From mid-May to mid-October, the resort transforms into the world's premier mountain bike park. Great deals are to be had in the shoulder seasons (May to early June and Oct into early Nov), when you practically have the resort to yourself, even if ski and/or bike conditions may not be optimal.

Festivals & Special Events

JAN The **New Year's Polar Bear Swim** (☎ **604/665-3418;** www. city.vancouver.bc.ca) draws thousands of thick-skinned bathers to the frigid waters of English Bay on Jan. 1.

JAN Make your reservations! **Dine Out Vancouver** (Tourism Vancouver; ☎ **604/683-2000;** www.tourism vancouver.com), held during the last 2 weeks of the month, offers foodies the chance to enjoy three-course dinners at more than 180 of Vancouver's best restaurants for between C$15 and C$35.

JAN The Punjabi musical style Bhangra is at the heart of the **City of Bhangra Festival** (☎ **604/ 628-6406;** www.vibc.org), which features 10 days of live music, dance, workshops, art, and competitions at various downtown venues.

JAN–FEB **The PuSh International Performing Arts Festival** (☎ **604/ 605-8284;** www.pushfestival.ca) offers more than 100 original, boundary-pushing theater, dance, music, and hybrid performances over 20 days at various venues.

Previous page: Seabus ferries are a convenient way to get around Vancouver's harbor.

JAN–FEB Expect firecrackers, dragon parades, and other festivities during **Chinese New Year** (information at Dr. Sun Yat-Sen Garden; ☎ **604/662 3207;** www.vancouverchinese garden.com). Celebrations take place throughout Vancouver's Chinatown and the nearby, heavily Chinese city of Richmond over the course of 2 weeks.

MAR Stretching over 5 days at mid-month, **CelticFest** (www.celticfest vancouver.com) offers more than 40 music, dance, and other Celtic cultural events at dozens of venues and three Downtown stages.

MAR–APR The major wine event in Canada, the **Vancouver Playhouse International Wine Festival** (☎ **604/873-3311;** www.playhouse winefest.com) is a weeklong festival featuring more than 1,600 wines from nearly 200 international wineries. It takes place at the Vancouver Convention and Exhibition Centre in late March, sometimes running into early April.

MAR–APR The **Vancouver Cherry Blossom Festival** (www.vcbf.ca) celebrates the flowering of Vancouver's 36,000 Japanese cherry trees with haiku and photo competitions, a concert, walking, bike, and trolley tours, and more. It begins in the last few days of March and runs through April.

APR Canada's biggest 10K footrace, the **Vancouver Sun Run** (☎ **604/ 689-9441;** www.sunrun.com), hosts more than 50,000 participants every year. It's usually held on the *third Sunday* in April, and the finish line is at BC Place Stadium.

APR The 10-day **TELUS World Ski & Snowboard Festival** (☎ **604/ 938-3399;** www.wssf.com), held in Whistler, is the largest snow-sport and music event in North America, with pro ski and snowboard competitions, free daily concerts, free ski and snowboard demos, a dog parade, and more.

MAY On the first Sunday in May, the **Vancouver International Marathon** (☎ **604/872-2928;** www.bmovanmarathon.ca), the largest marathon in Canada, attracts more than 12,000 participants.

MAY Featuring activities, plays, music, storytelling, puppetry, circus arts, and crafts, the **International Children's Festival** (☎ **604/708-5655;** www.childrensfestival.ca) offers a bit of everything. It's held over 1 mid-month week in Vanier Park.

JUNE North America's largest dragon boat festival, the **Rio Tinto Alcan Dragon Boat Festival** (☎ **604/ 683-4707;** www.adbf.com) draws more than 180 local and international teams to False Creek for 2 mid-month days of races, music, dance, and Chinese acrobatics to provide atmosphere.

JUNE–JULY A massive, 10-day event that presents more than 1,800 international jazz and blues players at 400 concerts around the city, the **Vancouver International Jazz Festival** (Jazz Hot Line; ☎ **604/ 872-5200;** www.coastaljazz.ca) is a must-see.

JUNE–SEPT **Bard on the Beach** (☎ **604/739-0559;** www.bardon thebeach.org) is one of Vancouver's most beloved festivals, presenting Shakespeare's plays throughout the summer in big tents in Vanier Park. For more info, see p 113.

JULY Held on July 1, **Canada Day** commemorates the anniversary of Britain's "North America Act," which created the united country of Canada. Canada Place (www.canada place.ca/canadaday) has a free all-day celebration with music, dance, cultural events, and fireworks. There are also celebrations at Granville Island (p 60), Grouse Mountain (p 82), and other Vancouver locations. In Whistler, the celebration includes a parade through the village.

JULY A 10-day festival of modern and classical dance, **Dancing on the Edge** (☎ 604/689-0926; www.dancingontheedge.org) is held at the Firehall Arts Centre and other venues.

JULY Featuring 3 days of international folk music, the **Vancouver Folk Music Festival** (☎ 604/602-9798; www.thefestival.bc.ca) is held at Jericho Beach Park (on the West Side) over the second or third weekend in July.

JULY Held over the third or fourth weekend in July, the **Caribbean Days Festival** (☎ 604/515-2400; www.caribbeandays.ca) presents 2 days of Caribbean food, arts, music, and crafts, plus a parade. It's held in North Vancouver's Waterfront Park, adjacent to the SeaBus terminal.

JULY **The Whistler Children's Art Festival** (☎ 604/938 9221; www.whistlerartscouncil.com) is a mid-month weekend event in which professional and emerging artists, artisans, and performers come to Whistler to do their thing for kids in workshops, performances, and free activities.

JULY A major 3-day music event, the **Pemberton Festival** (tickets at ☎ 800/594-8499; www.pembertonfestival.com) brings dozens of major acts (Tom Petty, Jay-Z, Nine Inch Nails, and others in its most recent years) to this town just north of Whistler.

JULY–AUG Held over the course of 10 days late in the month, the **HSBC Celebration of Light** (☎ 604/641-1293; www.celebration-of-light.com) sees internationally known fireworks designers putting on their best displays over English Bay, set to music simulcast over radio station ROCK 101 (101.1 FM).

JULY–AUG **Artwalk** (☎ 604/938-9221; www.whistlerartscouncil.com) brings artists from up and down the Sea to Sky corridor,

setting up exhibits of their work in galleries, restaurants, cafes, hotels, and stores around Whistler Village between July 1 and Aug 31. Self-guided tour maps are available.

AUG An annual 2-day festival of Japanese culture, the **Powell Street Festival** (☎ 604/739-9388; www.powellstreetfestival.com) features dance, music, film, visual arts, martial arts demonstrations, amateur sumo wrestling, craft vendors, and food. It's held the first weekend of the month.

AUG Held on the first Sunday in August, at the culmination of Gay Pride Week, during which many gay and lesbian nightclubs around the city hold their own celebrations, the **Gay Pride Parade** (☎ 604/687-0955; www.vancouverpride.ca) is one of the largest gay pride events in North America.

AUG **Festival Vancouver** (☎ 604/688-1152; www.festivalvancouver.bc.ca) is a 2-week, multi-venue celebration of orchestral, choral, opera, chamber music, world music, and jazz.

AUG Held over a weekend early in the month, in Whistler, the **Canadian National BBQ Championship** (www.whistlerblackcomb.com/todo/events) is a major regional barbecue cook-off. It functions as a qualifying event for the American Royal World Championships in Kansas City and the Jack Daniel's World Championship BBQ event in Lynchburg, Tennessee.

AUG **Kokanee Crankworx** (www.crankworx.com) is Whistler's biggest mountain bike fest, with 9 days of free-ride competitions and demonstrations, plus music and entertainment.

AUG–SEPT In addition to a great wooden roller coaster, the **Pacific National Exhibition** (☎ 604/253-2311; www.pne.bc.ca), held on the Pacific National carnival grounds in East Vancouver, offers livestock demonstrations, logger competitions, fashion shows, and a carnival midway. It takes place between mid-August and Labour Day (the first Mon in Sept).

SEPT Held over the first 2 weeks of September the **Vancouver Fringe Festival** (☎ 604/257-0350; www. vancouverfringe.com) presents more than 500 edgy shows by Canadian and international theater groups, in venues around the city.

SEPT The **Vancouver Global ComedyFest** (www.comedyfest.com) brings comedians from Canada and the U.S. for almost 10 days of performances at venues around town.

SEPT Featuring storytelling, music, and a lantern festival, the **Mid-Autumn Moon Festival** is held at the Dr. Sun Yat-Sen Garden (☎ 604/662-3207; www.vancouverchinese garden.com) in early to mid-Sept.

SEPT The **Cheakamus Challenge** (www.cheakamuschallenge.ca) cross-country mountain bike race starts in Squamish and finishes 70km (43 miles) later in Whistler. It's held on the third Saturday of the month.

SEPT–OCT Presenting new films from around the world over the course of 2 weeks the **Vancouver International Film Festival** (☎ 604/683-3456; www.viff.org) is one of the city's major cultural events,

NOV Held early in the month, the **Whistler Cornucopia** (www.whistler cornucopia.com) is a 5-day celebration of food and wine, featuring seminars, tastings, winemaker dinners, chef-led farm trips, and after-parties.

DEC Held nightly throughout Dec, the **Carol Ship Parade of Lights Festival** (☎ 604/878-8999; www. carolships.org) is a chance for boat owners to decorate their craft with Christmas lights (some 150,000 of

them recently, on more than 80 boats) and sail past Vancouver's different waterfront communities, while their passengers sing carols.

DEC The **Whistler Film Festival** (☎ 877/838-3456; www.whistler filmfestival.com) offers 4 days of screenings in early December, showing more than 100 new films.

DEC Every night in December, enjoy the **Festival of Lights and Christmas Craft and Gift Market** (☎ 604/878-9274; www.vandusen garden.org) at VanDusen Botanical Garden. You'll be treated to great light displays, plus Santa and some Scandinavian Christmas elves.

DEC **Bright Nights in Stanley Park** (☎ 604/257-8531; http://vancouver. ca/parks/events/brightnights/index. htm) decorates the middle of Stanley Park (the Children's Farmyard, train line, and surrounding forest) with more than a million holiday lights. Get tickets for the Stanley Park holiday train for the full experience.

The Weather

Like the U.S. Pacific Northwest, **Vancouver** is blessed with near idyllic summers followed by overcast, rainy winters, with fall and spring acting more like foyers than full-fledged seasons. The city receives some 47 inches of rain annually, most of it between Nov and March. Due to the generally mild temperatures, spring comes early, with some buds beginning to show as early as late February. By late March, the cherry trees begin to bloom.

Winter temperatures on the slopes in **Whistler** average –5°C (22°F). Average temperatures in the Whistler Valley May through October range from 16°C to 27°C (60°F–80°F). Temperatures in **Victoria** are roughly comparable to those in Vancouver, though it gets only half as much rain and overcast.

The Savvy Traveler

AVERAGE MONTHLY TEMPERATURES & RAINFALL

	JAN	FEB	MAR	APR	MAY	JUNE
High °F/°C	42/5	44/7	50/10	57/14	64/18	70/21
Low °F/°C	38/4	38/3	41/5	44/7	50/10	55/13
Rain in./cm	5/13	4.5/11.5	4/10.5	3/7.5	2.5/6	2/4.5

	JULY	AUG	SEPT	OCT	NOV	DEC
High °F/°C	73/23	73/23	64/18	57/14	48/9	43/6
Low °F/°C	58/15	59/15	54/12	47/8	42/5	40/4
Rain in./cm	1.5/3.5	1.5/4	2.5/6.5	4.5/11.5	6.5/16.5	6.5/16

Useful Websites

In addition to the "Information" websites at the top of this chapter, check out the following:

- **www.translink.bc.ca**: Information on Vancouver's public transportation system.

- **www.canada.com/vancouver sun**: Website of the *Vancouver Sun*, the city's major daily.

- **http://vancouver.ca/parks**: Information on all the city's parks.

- **http://vancouver.ca/commsvcs/ planning/heritage/walks/index. htm**: Official city walking tours of various neighborhoods.

- **http://vancouver.ca/engsvcs/ transport/cycling**: A guide to cycling in Vancouver, with maps and tips.

- **http://vancouver.ca/publicart_ wac/publicart.exe/city_map**: A registry of all the city's public art.

- **http://vancouverchinatown.ca**: Great historical and practical information on Chinatown.

Cellphones

Vancouver, Whistler, and Victoria have excellent cellular phone coverage. Phones using CDMA network technology—currently the most common type in use in both Canada and the U.S.—will work in Canada. GSM/GPRS phones—the dominant standard pretty much everywhere else—also work here, thanks to roaming agreements. Check with your provider to see if you'll be hit with any international usage fees.

Car Rentals

Vancouver's walkable enough (and its public transportation extensive enough) that you can get around using taxis, buses, and your own two feet if you so choose. But it's pretty much essential if you want to get to outlying attractions or get out of town with any sort of expediency.

In addition to rental agencies at the airport, all the major car rental agencies have multiple offices around town. For a list of agencies that operate in the area, see p 200.

Getting **There**

By Plane

Visitors arriving by plane touch down at **Vancouver International Airport** (YVR; ☎ **604/207-7077;** www. yvr.ca), located 13km (8 miles) south of downtown Vancouver, across the Fraser River from the neighboring city of Richmond. It's the largest airport on Canada's west coast and is the air hub for both Vancouver and

Whistler. All the major car-rental firms have operations here.

Beginning in late 2009, the new **Canada Line** rail service (www.canadaline.ca) will link Vancouver International directly with downtown Vancouver, cutting your travel time to under 30 minutes and your cost to about C$7 (final pricing not determined at press time). Its Downtown terminus is at Waterfront Station, near Canada Place and Gastown. Other options include taxis (whose average fare to downtown is C$23–C$26) and the **YVR Airporter** bus service (☎ 800/668-3141 or 604/946-8866; www.yvrairporter.com), which drops off and picks up at the major downtown hotels and the cruise ship terminal. It leaves from Level 2 of the Main Terminal every 15 minutes daily from 6:30am until midnight and takes about 30 minutes. Adult fares are C$14 one-way or C$22 round-trip, with lower rates for children, seniors, and families.

By Car
From the U.S., you'll probably take U.S. **Interstate 5** from Seattle, which becomes Hwy. 99 once you cross the Canadian border. (Remember, you'll need your passport.) The 210km (130-mile) drive from Seattle takes about 2½ hours. After you cross the Oak Street Bridge the highway becomes Oak Street. Turn left at any major street and continue until you reach Granville Street. Turn right onto Granville and continue across the Granville Street Bridge into Downtown.

Travelers coming from other parts of Canada or the eastern U.S. states may take **Trans-Canada Hwy. 1.** From the east, exit at Cassiar St. and turn left at the first light onto Hastings St. (Hwy. 7A), which is adjacent to Exhibition Park. Follow Hastings 6.4km (4 miles) into Downtown. When coming to Vancouver from parts north, take exit 13/Taylor Way

and cross the Lions Gate Bridge into Vancouver's West End.

U.S. driver's licenses are valid in Canada. Visitors from other countries must acquire an International Driving Permit before renting or driving a car in Canada.

By Train
Amtrak (☎ 800/872-7245; www.amtrak.com) offers daily service from Seattle, either via train (morning only) or an Amtrak bus. Tickets cost C$30–C$35. Trains arrive at **Pacific Central Station,** 1150 Station St. (☎ 800/872-7245), located just south of Chinatown at Main St. and Terminal Ave. You can take the SkyTrain from Main St. Station (1 block from Pacific Central) into Downtown, or grab a taxi.

By Bus
Greyhound Bus Lines (☎ 800/231-2222 or 604/482-8747; www.greyhound.ca) offers daily bus service between Vancouver and Seattle and all major Canadian cities. When traveling across the U.S./Canada border, passengers must debark and trundle their bags through Customs. Buses terminate at Pacific Central Station (see "By Train," above for more information).

Getting to Whistler
Travelers with cars can make the 105km (65-mile), 2-hour drive along the **Sea to Sky Highway** from Vancouver to Whistler (p 132), but there are alternatives.

On the cheap end, **Greyhound** (☎ 800/661-8747; www.greyhound.ca) runs regular limited-stop service between Pacific Central Station (1150 Station St.) and Whistler Village at frequent intervals throughout the day, year-round. The trip takes between 2 and 2¾ hours, and round-trip tickets cost C$46 adults, C$24 kids 5–11.

More expensively, **Limojet Gold Express** (☎ **800/278-8742** or 604/273-1331; www.limojetgold. com) offers private limo service from Vancouver to Whistler for 3–6 passengers. The one-way full-vehicle rate is C$295.

In summer (approx. May–Oct), the **Whistler Mountaineer** (☎ **888/687-7245** or 604/606-8460; www.whistlermountaineer.com) offers a classic 3-hour rail journey, complete with an observation car dating to 1914. The round-trip fare starts from C$199 adults, C$109 kids 2–11. The train departs from North Vancouver Station, at the corner of Philip Ave. and W. 1st St. in North Vancouver. In Whistler, the terminus is at Nita Lake, near Whistler Creekside. Shuttles transport passengers from Downtown Vancouver to the station, and from Nita Lake to Whistler Village.

Getting **Around**

By Car

You probably won't need or want a car in either Vancouver or Whistler. True, driving isn't difficult here—British Columbian drivers are very polite—but the city is so walkable that it would be a crime not to explore it on foot. If you arrived by car, park it for the duration and use public transportation to get to your day's starting point unless (a) you're heading out to Vancouver's University of British Columbia for its Museum of Anthropology (p 16, ❻) and other attractions, or (b) doing my Multicultural Vancouver tour (p 40), or (c) planning on doing my Sea to Sky Highway tour (p 132). In Whistler, you can walk or take public transportation pretty much everywhere. The vast majority of hotels in Vancouver and Whistler offer guest parking, either complementary or for a fee.

In Vancouver's Downtown and the West End, parking on major streets is metered, costing between C75¢ and C$2.50 per hour, depending on the area. Unmetered parking on side streets sometimes requires a residency sticker. Public parking lots are scattered around the city, including at Robson Square and the Pacific Centre mall. Prices range from C$1 to C$3 per half-hour, with a daily maximum. The two biggest parking lot companies have online lot locators: For **EasyPark** go to www.easyparkvancouver.com and for **Impark** go to https://impark. myparkingworld.com.

On Foot

Central Vancouver is exceptionally walkable, and if you plan your travel to concentrate on certain neighborhoods on certain days, there's no reason you'll need transportation at all except maybe to get there from your hotel. Downtown, the West End, Coal Harbour, Granville Island, Chinatown, Commercial Drive, and portions of Kitsilano and Stanley Park are all places where you'd be doing yourself a disservice if you didn't walk. Up north, Whistler Village was designed to be walked, not driven.

By Public Transportation

Vancouver's **TransLink** system (☎ **604/521-0400;** www. translink.bc.ca) offers excellent service to all sectors of the city via buses, light rail, and ferry. There are also private ferry services that crisscross False Creek and are a must-do travel experience. Fares for TransLink are based on a zone system and are the same for buses, SeaBus (the

Must-Know Bus Routes

There are so many bus routes around the city that maps and schedules can be very difficult to make sense of at first, so keep the key routes listed below in mind.

Buses 2 and 22: run the entire length of Burrard St. through Downtown

Bus 5: runs along Robson St. from Richards, then turns south toward English Bay on Denman St.

Bus 6: runs the length of Davie St., from Yaletown to Denman

Bus 7: runs from Downtown to East Vancouver

Bus 8: runs from Hastings St. through Downtown and then follows Granville St. all the way south through the West Side

Bus 19: is the bus to Stanley Park, via W. Pender and W. Georgia Sts.

Bus 98B: is an express that runs north-south from Downtown and along Granville St. all the way through the West Side

Bus 99B: is the east-west express between Downtown and the University of British Columbia campus on the West Side

public ferry system), and SkyTrain: A 1-zone fare is C$2.50, 2-zone is C$3.75, and 3-zone is C$5. You can also get a 1-day all-zone pass for C$9. Children 4 years and younger ride free for free when accompanied by an adult.

TransLink buses are the most ubiquitous option, offering regular service as well as express routes to more distant destinations like the University of British Columbia. Bus stops are well marked. Note that bus drivers won't make change. For more information, see the "Must-Know Bus Routes" box below.

SkyTrain provides faster transportation, with two lines (the Millennium Line and Expo Line) covering a total of 28km (17 miles) on their way to Vancouver's suburbs. They provide an excellent way to get from Downtown to Chinatown and Commercial Drive. Their north terminus is at Waterfront Station. From late 2009 on, they'll be joined by the Canada Line, running from Waterfront Station south to Richmond and Vancouver International Airport.

SeaBus is a ferry service that runs between Waterfront Station and North Vancouver's Lonsdale Quay. It's not particularly scenic (there are few windows), but it's fast.

SeaBus and SkyTrain are fully **wheelchair accessible,** and most buses have either low-floor access or are lift-equipped.

In **Whistler,** the WAVE (Whistler and Valley Express) buses (www. bctransit.com/regions/whi) connect all areas of town, running almost 24 hours. Fares are C$2, and kids under 5 ride free. Exact change is required. All buses have ski and bike racks.

By Taxi

Taxis in Vancouver operate mostly on a radio-call system: Give a call to any of the major companies, tell them where you are, and a cab will show up to get you—usually quite quickly.

Options include **Black Top & Checker Cabs** (☎ 604/731-1111; http://blacktopcheckercabs.super sites.ca), **Yellow Cab** (☎ 604/681-1111; www.yellowcabonline.com), and **MacLure's** (☎ 604/683-6666; www.maclurescabs.ca). Cab fares start at C$2.70 (which covers the first 1/13th of a kilometer).

Each additional kilometer is C$1.58 more, with a maximum of C$28.20 per hour. Those fares cover 1 to 4 passengers.

The **Vancouver Taxi Fare Finder** (http://vancouver.taxiwiz.com) calculates approximate fares between addresses and major landmarks.

Fast **Facts**

ADDRESSES One quirk in BC addresses is the fact that suite numbers are often listed as part of the street number: For instance, 33-4344 Example St. actually means the building is at 4344, and the business is in suite 33.

ATMS Automated teller machines are at least as ubiquitous in Vancouver as in most major U.S. and European cities, if not more so, and work exactly the same way—though they spit out Canadian dollars and offer French as one of your language options. (Thanks, Quebec.) Machines generally operate on the worldwide **Cirrus** (☎ 800/424-7787; www.mastercard.com), **PLUS** (☎ 800/843-7587; www.visa.com), and **Interac** (☎ 416/362-8550; www.interac.ca) networks, as do most debit cards. Be sure you know your personal identification number (PIN) before you leave home, and be sure your daily withdrawal limit will cover the amount of cash you'll need. Note that ATM fees can be higher for international transactions than for domestic.

BANKING HOURS Banks are generally open Mon–Fri 9:30am to 4:30pm, though some branches have hours on weekends as well.

BIKE RENTALS Vancouver and Whistler are lousy with bike rental shops—the former for riding around town and Stanley Park, the latter for

trail riding. Near Stanley Park, the most popular outlet is **Spokes,** 1798 W. Georgia St., at Denman (☎ 604/688-5141; www.vancouverbikerental.com), where bikes go for about C$9.50/hr or C$26 for a half-day. The city has a website offering information and maps of great **bike routes:** http://vancouver.ca/engsvcs/transport/cycling/routes.htm. The **Vancouver Area Cycling Coalition** (☎ 604/878-8222; www.vacc.bc.ca) is a great resource for advice on routes, local tips, and other info. **TransLink** has a page of information on taking bikes on public transportation, using bike lockers, routes, etc., at www.translink.bc.ca/Transportation_Services/Bikes.

Mountain bikes in Whistler are much pricier, with heavy-duty bikes available from the **Whistler Mountain Bike Park** itself (☎ 604/904-8134; www.whistlerbike.com), from **Summit Sports** at the Hilton (☎ 604/932-6225; www.summitsport.com), and from dozens of other operators for about C$65 half-day, C$100 full-day.

BUSINESS HOURS Hours vary by shop, but as a general rule most open daily around 10am and stay open until at least 6pm. Shops in central sections of Vancouver (along Robson St.) and in malls usually stay open later. Citywide, most are open daily, though some close on Sunday.

CONSULATES & EMBASSIES The **U.S. Consulate** is at 1075 W. Pender St. (☎ 604/685-4311). The **British Consulate** is at 1111 Melville St., Ste. 800 (☎ **604/683-4421**). The **Irish Consulate** is at 100 W. Pender St., 10th Floor (☎ 604/683-9233). The **Australian Consulate** is at 888 Dunsmuir St., Ste. 1225 (☎ **604/684-1177**). The consulate of **New Zealand** is at 888 Dunsmuir St., Ste. 1200 (☎ **604/684-7388**).

CURRENCY EXHANGE Currency exchange counters can be found at the airport and at prominent tourist locations, but you'll get a better rate just using ATMs (p 192) or going to Vancouver Currency Exchange, 800 W. Pender St. (☎ **604/682-7921**; www.vbce.ca). Be sure to check current exchange rates before your trip via www.xe.com or any of the other major currency trackers.

CUSTOMS U.S. residents will pass through **Canada Border Services** (☎ **800/461-9999** or 204/983-3500; www.cbsa-asfc.gc.ca) upon arrival. If you're concerned about items you intend to bring into the country, check the website's "Information for Visitors" section. You'll pass through **U.S. Customs** (☎ **877/CBP-5511**; www.cbp.gov) on departure from Canada. The standard personal duty-free allowance for U.S. citizens returning from Canada is US$800. There are also limits on the amount of alcoholic beverages (usually 1 liter), cigarettes (1 carton), cigars (100 total, and no Cubans), and other tobacco products you may include in your personal duty-free exemption. **Joint Customs declarations** are possible for family members traveling together. For instance, for a husband and wife with two children, the total duty-free exemption would be US$3,200. Note that most meat or meat products, fruit, plants, vegetables, or plant-derived products will be seized by U.S. Customs agents unless they're accompanied by an import license from a U.S. government agency. For more specifics, visit the **U.S. Customs Service** website (www.customs.gov).

U.K. citizens should visit the **U.K. Customs and Excise** site (www.hmce.gov.uk); Australians should go to the **Australia Customs Service** (www.customs.gov.au), Kiwis should check the **New Zealand Customs Service** (www.customs.govt.nz), and citizens of Ireland should check the **Irish Revenue** site (www.revenue.ie).

DENTISTS Most major hotels have a dentist on call. **Vancouver Centre Dental Clinic,** Vancouver Centre Mall, 11-650 W. Georgia St. (☎ **604/682-1601**), is another option. You must make an appointment. The clinic is open Monday and Friday 9am to 6pm, Tuesday and Wednesday 8:30am to 6pm, and Thursday 8:30am to 5pm.

DINING Dining is a hot topic in Vancouver, so reservations are recommended for most of the city's restaurants, and are essential at the top-rated spots. Reservation policies vary by restaurant. You'll also want to make reservations for Whistler restaurants during peak seasons.

DOCTORS Hotels usually have a doctor on call. **Vancouver Medic Centre,** Bentall Centre, 1055 Dunsmuir St. (☎ **604/683-8138**), is a drop-in clinic open Monday through Friday 8am to 5pm.

ELECTRICITY Outlets and voltage (110 volts AC) are the same in Canada as in the United States, so laptops, chargers, hairdryers, and other small appliances from the U.S. will work just fine. Appliances from other countries will require an adapter and/or converter.

EMERGENCIES   For emergencies in Vancouver, Whistler, and Victoria, dial ☎ 911.

EVENT LISTINGS   The free weekly newspaper **Georgia Strait** (www.straight.com) publishes each Thursday and is the best source for entertainment listings. The **Tourism Vancouver** website has listings and an interactive calendar of events at www.tourismvancouver.com/visitors/events.

FAMILY TRAVEL   Vancouver and Whistler are both fantastically kid-friendly. **Tourism Vancouver** offers family-travel tips at www.tourismvancouver.com/visitors/things_to_do/family_and_kids/family_and_kids.

GAY & LESBIAN TRAVELERS   Vancouver has western Canada's largest gay and lesbian community, and gay marriage has been legal in BC since 2003. The West End is the epicenter of gay and lesbian life in the city, with many nightlife choices along Davie St.

Clubs, bars, and other social scenes are listed in the biweekly gay/lesbian newspaper *Xtra! West*, available at bars, cafes, and businesses throughout the West End. They're also online at www.xtra.ca/public/Vancouver.aspx.

The **Gay Lesbian Transgendered Bisexual Community Centre,** 1170 Bute St. (☎ 604/684-6869; www.lgtbcentrevancouver.com), is also a great resource, as are the **Vancouver Pride Society** (www.vancouverpride.ca) and the website **www.gayvan.com**.

For Whistler, check the website www.gaywhistler.com.

HOLIDAYS   British Columbia has 12 public holidays throughout the year, when banks, government offices, schools, and some shops are closed: New Year's Day (Jan 1), Easter (Sun following the first full moon after the vernal equinox), Good Friday (the Fri before Easter), Easter Monday (the day after), Victoria Day (the Mon before May 25), Canada Day (July 1), British Columbia Day (first Mon in Aug), Labour Day (first Mon in Sept), Thanksgiving (second Mon in Oct), Remembrance Day (Nov 11), Christmas (Dec 25), and Boxing Day (Dec 26).

INSURANCE   The cost of travel insurance varies widely, depending on the destination, the cost and length of your trip, your age and health, and the type of trip you're taking. You can get estimates from various providers through **InsureMyTrip.com.** Enter your trip cost and dates, your age, and other information, for prices from more than a dozen companies.

Medical Insurance: Most U.S. health plans do not provide coverage outside of the U.S., and the ones that do often require you to pay for services upfront and reimburse you only after you return home. As a safety net, you may want to buy travel medical insurance from providers like **MEDEX Assistance** (☎ 410/453-6300; www.medexassist.com) or **Travel Assistance International** (☎ 800/821-2828; www.travelassistance.com).

Trip-Cancellation Insurance: Trip-cancellation insurance typically covers you if you have to back out of a trip (due to illness, and so forth), if your travel supplier goes bankrupt, if there's a natural disaster, or if the State Department advises against travel to your destination—which isn't much of a worry for Vancouver. Some plans cover cancellations for any reason. **TravelSafe** (☎ 888/885-7233; www.travelsafe.com) offers both types of coverage. **Expedia** (www.expedia.com) also offers any-reason cancellation coverage for its air-hotel packages. Other recommended insurers include **Access America** (☎ 866/807-3982; www.accessamerica.com), **Travel Guard International** (☎ 800/826-4919; www.travelguard.com), **Travel Insured International** (☎ 800/243-3174; www.travelinsured.com), and **Travelex Insurance Services** (☎ 888/457-4602; www.travelex-insurance.com).

Lost-Luggage Insurance: If your luggage is lost, immediately file a lost-luggage claim at the airport, detailing the luggage contents. Most airlines require that you report delayed, damaged, or lost baggage within 4 hours of arrival. On international flights, baggage coverage is limited to approximately US$9.07 per pound, up to approximately US$635 per checked bag. If you plan to check items more valuable than what's covered by the standard liability, see if your homeowner's policy covers your valuables, or get baggage insurance as part of your comprehensive travel-insurance package.

INTERNET ACCESS   Almost all hotels in Vancouver, Whistler, and Victoria now provide some kind of Internet access, either wireless, wired, or via a business center. There are also free Wi-Fi hot spots in many, many locations around town, many of them coffee shops. The website http://vancouver.wifimug.org breaks them down by neighborhood. If you don't have a laptop with you, you can find Internet cafes by searching www.cybercaptive.com and www.cybercafe.com.

LIQUOR LAWS   The legal drinking age is 19. Bars, lounges, and restaurants that serve alcohol all close between midnight and 2am, depending on when they got their liquor license. Government-operated liquor stores have a near monopoly on the sale of hard liquor, and also stock beer and wine. Privately owned specialty wine stores (see p 78 for some of the best) mostly stick to the grape, but usually also carry a small selection of beer and spirits.

LOST PROPERTY   For property lost on city buses, SkyTrain, or SeaBus, contact the **TransLink Lost Property Office** at the Stadium SkyTrain Station, 590 Beatty St. (☎ 604/682-7887), open Monday through Friday 8:30am to 5pm. For baggage lost at **Vancouver International Airport,** contact the Customer Service Counter in the International Terminal, Departures Level 3 (☎ 604/276-6104). It's open 9am to 5:30pm daily. If your luggage is lost in transit, check in with your airline's baggage agent immediately.

If you lose your passport, contact your country's embassy or consulate immediately (see "Consulates & Embassies," above).

MAIL & POSTAGE   Mailing a letter within Canada costs C52¢. To the U.S., it's C96¢. To all other international destinations, it's C$1.60. The main **Vancouver post office** is at 49 W. Georgia St. (☎ 604/662-5723; www.canadapost.ca), across from the Public Library at Homer and Hamilton streets. You can also buy stamps at many drugstores and convenience stores. In **Whistler Village,** there's a post office at 4360 Lorimer Rd. (☎ 604/932-5012).

MONEY   Canada's money is denominated the same as U.S. dollars, except its C$1 and C$2 denominations are coins rather than bills. The C$1 coin is known as a "loonie" as it has the image of a common loon on one side. The C$2 coin is known as a "toonie," for obvious comedic reasons. For exchange rates, see "Currency Exchange," p 193.

NEWSPAPERS & MAGAZINES   The major newspapers in BC are the

Vancouver Sun (www.vancouver sun.com), which publishes Monday through Saturday; the *Vancouver Province* (www.theprovince.com), which publishes Sunday through Friday; and the daily *Victoria Times Colonist* (www.timescolonist.com). The *Georgia Straight* (www. straight.com) is Vancouver's major source for entertainment, arts, and lifestyle news. It publishes every Thursday and is distributed free around the city.

PARKING   See "Getting Around: By Car," p 190.

PASSES   The **See Vancouver Card** (☎ **877/295-1157;** www.see vancouvercard.com) covers admission to more than 50 attractions in Vancouver and around BC. Adult prices range from C$119 for a 2-day pass to C$219 for a 5-day. Kids prices go from C$79 to C$149.

The C$25 **Explore Canada–Whistler Pass** (☎ **866/648-5873;** www.viator.com) offers savings of up to 50% on sleigh rides, dog sledding, rafting trips, ziplining, equipment rentals, and more.

PASSPORTS   U.S. citizens traveling to Canada by any means—air, sea, car, bus, train, or on foot—will need a passport but no visa. Ditto for citizens of Great Britain, Australia, Ireland, and New Zealand. If you're a citizen of another country, check the **Canada Border Services Agency** website, www.cbsa-asfc. gc.ca/travel-voyage, for specific requirements.

For safety, make two photocopies of your passport before leaving home. Take one set with you as a backup (keeping it separate from the original) and leave one at home.

PET-FRIENDLY TRAVEL   Tourism Vancouver has a great listing of pet-friendly accommodations and other tips for bringing your pet to the city, at www.tourismvancouver.com/ visitors/travel_tips/pet_friendly.

PHARMACIES   Well-known chains in Vancouver include Rexall, Guardian, IDA, and Pharmasave. One centrally located **Rexall** is at 1055 W. Georgia St., at Burrard (☎ **604/684-8204**). There's a **store locator** at http:// storelocator.rexall.ca.

POLICE   Call 911 for emergencies.

SAFETY   British Columbia is a terribly civil place, so you have little to fear. That said, don't be foolish. Don't leave valuables in your car or unattended in public places, and be alert for sketchy neighborhoods—for instance, the notoriously awful, drug-infested area around West Hastings St. in Vancouver, between Gastown and Chinatown. The Canadian Government website (**www. safecanada.ca**) shares a list of safety tips in case you need something to worry about.

SENIOR TRAVELERS   Shops, hotels, attractions, and services throughout BC often offer discounts for people over 65, with proof of age. Ditto for TransLink, which takes between C75¢ and C$2 off by-zone and day-pass ticket prices for seniors.

SMOKING   Smoking is prohibited in all public places in British Columbia, including bars, clubs, and restaurants.

TAXES   Most goods and services in BC (aside from food, restaurant meals, and children's clothing) are subject to 5% federal goods and services tax and a 7% provincial sales tax. Hotel rooms are subject to a 10% local lodging tax.

TELEPHONES   **Dialing within British Columbia** requires you to use full 10-digit phone numbers, including the area code, of which there are three in BC: 604, 250, and 778. **Phoning between the US and Canada** requires no special trick: Just dial 1 plus the area code and local number, as you would between states in the US. **To dial**

other countries direct from BC, dial the international access code (011) followed by the relevant country code (61 for Australia, 353 for Ireland, 64 for New Zealand, and 44 for the UK) and the local number with area code, if applicable. For information on cellphones, see "Cellphones," p 188.

To call BC from outside North America, dial the international access code (00 from the UK, Ireland, or New Zealand, or 0011 from Australia), the country code (1), and then the local number with area code.

For information on cellphone service, see "Cellphones" above.

TIME ZONE   British Columbia is located in the Pacific time zone, 8 hours behind Greenwich Mean Time. The province observes daylight savings time from the second Sunday in March to the first Sunday in November.

TIPPING   Customary tipping amounts are the same in Vancouver, Whistler, and Victoria as in major U.S. cities, with a target of 15% in restaurants and taxis. (Though many people round that up to 20%.) If porters help with your bags at hotels or airports, the usual tip is C$1 per bag (or C$2 if it's heavy).

TOILETS   As in many major North American cities, public toilets (known here mainly as washrooms) are often hard to find in Vancouver, though major tower complexes, shopping malls, popular tourist attractions, department stores, and fast food outlets have them if you look hard enough. The city has also begun installing a number of free, self-cleaning, space-age toilets around downtown. Some were already in place at press time; others were yet to be installed. There's a **map** of the locations at http://vancouver.ca/ENGSVCS/streets/furniture/map.htm.

TOURIST OFFICES   The following on-the-ground tourist centers can help with information, maps, suggestions, and booking accommodations: **Vancouver Tourist Info Centre,** 200 Burrard St. near Canada Place ☎ **604/683-2000;** www.tourismvancouver.com); **Whistler Activity and Information Centre,** 4010 Whistler Way, at the Village Bus Loop (☎ **877/991-9988 or 604/935-3357;** www.tourismwhistler.com); and **Tourism Victoria Visitor Centre,** 812 Wharf St., near Government St. (☎ **800/663-3883** or 250/953-2033; www.tourismvictoria.com).

TOURS   **Vancouver Trolley Company,** 875 Terminal Ave. (☎ **888/451-5581** or 604/801-5515; www.vancouvertrolley.com), offers several different city tours on buses designed to look like vintage San Francisco–style trolleys. Their hop-on, hop-off City Attractions Tour loops through Downtown, Stanley Park, Chinatown, Gastown, and Granville Island. You can get on and off at your leisure at any of 24 stops. Tickets are C$35 adults, C$19 kids (kids under 4 ride free), and are available on the trolley. City tours run daily 9am to about 5pm. Another company, the **Big Bus** (☎ **877/299-0701;** www.bigbus.ca), offers a similar (and similarly priced) tour via their big red buses with the Union Jack on the side. They run daily 9am to about 5pm.

The Big Bus also offers tours in **Victoria,** as does **Gray Line West,** 4196 Glanford Ave. (☎ **800/663-8390** or 250/744-3566; www.graylinewest.com). Their narrated 90-minute city tour costs C$27 adults, C$16 kids 2–11, and runs several times per day.

In Vancouver, **Harbour Cruises** (☎ **604/688-7246;** www.boatcruises.com) offers 1-hour boat tours of Burrard Inlet April through October, concentrating on the working port and areas around Stanley Park. Ferries depart from a dock in Coal Harbor, near the foot of Denman St. Tickets are C$25 adults, C$21 seniors and teens, C$10 kids 5–11. It runs two to four times per day, April through October.

TRAVELERS WITH DISABILITIES Vancouver is known as a particularly accessible city, with accommodations for wheelchairs built into most public transportation, as well as at attractions and other recreational sites. **SkyTrain, SeaBus,** and B-Line express **buses** are fully wheelchair accessible. Most other Vancouver-area buses have either low floor access or are equipped with lifts. For more information, see www.translink.bc.ca/Transportation_

Services/Accessibility. If you'd prefer a taxi, **Yellow Cab** (☎ 604/681-1111; www.yellowcabonline.com) will send a wheelchair-accessible cab by request.

Tourism Vancouver's **Accessible Vancouver** page, www.tourism vancouver.com/visitors/travel_tips/accessibility, has information on transportation, resources, and other tips.

WEIGHTS & MEASURES Canada uses the metric system, just like pretty much everybody in the world besides the U.S. Just remember: 1km=.62 miles, 1 liter=.26 gallons, 1 kilogram = 2.2 pounds, and Celsius temperatures are based on 0 being the freezing point (in Fahrenheit measurement, it's 32).

A Brief **History**

16,000–11,000 B.C.   The ancestors of the Coast Salish people arrive from Asia and like what they see, establishing a presence on English Bay.

1592–1774   Juan de Fuca finds Vancouver during his second voyage of exploration in search of the Northwest Passage. Spain subsequently claims the whole west coast of North America.

1778   Captain James Cook arrives during his third voyage of exploration to the Pacific.

1792   Englishman Captain George Vancouver arrives aboard the HMS *Discover,* sailing right into the Burrard Inlet.

1808   Explorer and fur trader Simon Fraser arrives from Eastern Canada via the river that now bears his name.

1827   The Hudson's Bay Company builds a trading post on the

Fraser River, marking the first permanent, non-native settlement in the Vancouver area.

1858   Some 25,000 prospectors begin arriving after a gold strike is reported on the banks of the Fraser.

1867   Barkeep "Gassy Jack" Deighton opens a saloon on the shore of Burrard Inlet, catering to the area's loggers and trappers. The area around the bar comes to be called Gastown.

1884   The Canadian Pacific Railway moves its terminal from the head of Burrard Inlet to the Granville area.

1886   Granville is re-incorporated as the City of Vancouver. On June 13, a fire burns the new city to the ground in less than 30 minutes. Soon after, the city incorporates its first fire department.

1887   The first transcontinental Canadian-Pacific train arrives in Vancouver. It's pulled by Engine 374, which is today displayed at The Roundhouse in Yaletown (p 59, **18**).

1889   The first Granville Street bridge is completed.

1890   The first lighthouse is built at Brockton Point, in what is today Stanley Park. Electric streetcars also begin operating in town.

1898   The Nine o'clock Gun is placed at Brockton point, functioning first as a signal cannon to alert fishermen and later as a 9pm signal by which Vancouverites and sailors could set their watches. Some still do.

1900   Vancouver surpasses BC capital Victoria in size.

1909   Vancouver's first skyscraper, the beautiful Dominion Building (p 57, **15**), opens at Hastings and Cambie streets.

1915   The University of British Columbia opens.

1938   The Lions Gate Bridge is completed, connecting the Downtown peninsula with North Vancouver.

1939   The landmark Hotel Vancouver—now the Fairmont Hotel Vancouver (p 126)—is completed.

1953   Vancouver's first TV station, CBUT, makes its debut.

1963   The Port of Vancouver ships more tonnage than any other Canadian port.

1970   The Vancouver Canucks play their first game in the National Hockey League, losing to the Los Angeles Kings.

1971   The pedestrian seawall at Stanley Park opens, and the Provincial Government names Gastown and Chinatown historic districts.

1983   BC Place Stadium opens with the world's largest air-supported dome as a roof, with 60,000 seats underneath.

1985   SkyTrain makes its first rounds.

1986   The 6-month Expo 86 marks Vancouver's centennial. It's the largest World's Fair ever staged in North America.

1990S–2000S   Vancouver becomes a major hub of Hollywood film production, working as a stand-in for other North American cities. It eventually earns the nickname "Hollywood North."

2002   The *Economist* magazine's Intelligence Unit names Vancouver one of the world's best cities to live in, tied with Melbourne for No. 1.

2003   Mercer Human Resource Consulting rates Vancouver as North America's most livable city. On July 1, the city is selected to host the 2010 Olympic and Paralympic Winter Games.

Toll-Free Numbers & Websites

Airlines

AIR CANADA
☎ 888/247-2262
www.aircanada.ca

ALASKA AIRLINES
☎ 800/252-7522
www.alaskaair.com

AIR NEW ZEALAND
☎ 800/262-1234 or -2468
☎ 0800/737-000
in New Zealand
www.airnewzealand.com

AMERICAN AIRLINES
☎ 800/433-7300
www.aa.com

BRITISH AIRWAYS
☎ 800/247-9297
☎ 0870/850-9-850
in the U.K.
www.british-airways.com

CONTINENTAL AIRLINES
☎ 800/525-0280
www.continental.com

DELTA AIR LINES
☎ 800/221-1212
www.delta.com

FRONTIER AIRLINES
☎ 800/432-1359
www.frontierairlines.com

NORTHWEST AIRLINES
☎ 800/225-2525
www.nwa.com

QANTAS
☎ 800/227-4500
☎ 612/131313 in Australia
www.qantas.com

UNITED AIRLINES
☎ 800/241-6522
www.united.com

US AIRWAYS
☎ 800/428-4322
www.usairways.com

Car Rental Agencies

ALAMO
☎ 800/327-9633
www.goalamo.com

AVIS
☎ 800/331-1212 in the
continental U.S.
☎ 800/TRY-AVIS
in Canada
www.avis.com

BUDGET
☎ 800/527-0700
www.budget.com

DOLLAR
☎ 800/800-4000
www.dollar.com

ENTERPRISE
☎ 800/325-8007
www.enterprise.com

HERTZ
☎ 800/654-3131
www.hertz.com

NATIONAL
☎ 800/CAR-RENT
www.nationalcar.com

THRIFTY
☎ 800/367-2277
www.thrifty.com

Major Hotel & Motel Chains

BEST WESTERN INTERNATIONAL
☎ 800/528-1234
www.bestwestern.com

COMFORT INNS
☎ 800/228-5150
www.hotelchoice.com

DELTA HOTELS & RESORTS
☎ 877/814-7706
www.deltahotels.com

DAYS INN
☎ 800/325-2525
www.daysinn.com

FAIRMONT HOTELS
☎ 800/257-7544
www.fairmont.com

FOUR SEASONS
☎ 800/819-5053
www.fourseasons.com

HILTON HOTELS
☎ 800/HILTONS
www.hilton.com

HOLIDAY INN
☎ 800/HOLIDAY
www.ichotelsgroup.com

HOWARD JOHNSON
☎ 800/654-2000
www.hojo.com

HYATT HOTELS & RESORTS
☎ 800/228-9000
www.hyatt.com

MARRIOTT HOTELS
☎ 800/228-9290
www.marriott.com

RADISSON HOTELS INTERNATIONAL
☎ 800/333-3333
www.radisson.com

RITZ-CARLTON
☎ 800/241-3333
www.ritzcarlton.com

SHERATON HOTELS & RESORTS
☎ 800/325-3535
www.sheraton.com

WESTIN HOTELS & RESORTS
☎ 800/937-8461
www.westin.com

Index

Photo **Credits**

lepper.com; p 69, top: © Ulana Switucha/Alamy; p 70, bottom: © Derek Lepper/www.derek lepper.com; p 71, top: © Derek Lepper/www.dereklepper.com; p 72, top: © Derek Lepper/ www.dereklepper.com; p 72, bottom: © Derek Lepper/www.dereklepper.com; p 73, top: © Derek Lepper/www.dereklepper.com; p 75, bottom: © Derek Lepper/www.dereklepper.com; p 76, bottom: © Derek Lepper/www.dereklepper.com; p 77, top: © Derek Lepper/www.derek lepper.com; p 78, bottom: © Derek Lepper/www.dereklepper.com; p 79: © romain bayle/ Alamy; p 81, middle: © JTB Photo Communications, Inc./Alamy; p 81, bottom: Michael Wheat-ley ©AllCanadaPhotos.com; p 82, top: © Dennis Frates/Alamy; p 83, top: © Danita Delimont/ Alamy; p 83, bottom: © Dennis Frates/Alamy; p 85, bottom: © David Smith/www.interface images.com; p 86, top: Chris Cheadle ©AllCanadaPhotos.com; p 86, bottom: © David R. Frazier Photolibrary, Inc./Alamy; p 87, top: © David South/Alamy; p 88, top: © Gunter Marx/ Alamy; p 88, bottom: © WorldFoto/Alamy; p 89: Courtesy Blue Water Café & Raw Bar, Vancouver; p 92, bottom: © Derek Lepper/www.dereklepper.com; p 93, top: Courtesy CinCin, Vancouver; p 94, bottom: © Derek Lepper/www.dereklepper.com; p 95, middle: Photos by Hamid Attie Photography; p 96, top: © Derek Lepper/www.dereklepper.com; p 96, bottom: © Derek Lepper/www.dereklepper.com; p 97, top: © Derek Lepper/www.dereklepper.com; p 97, bottom: © Derek Lepper/www.dereklepper.com; p 98, bottom: Courtesy West Restaurant, Van-couver; p 99: © Chris Mason Stearns; p 102, bottom: © Derek Lepper/www.dereklepper.com; p 103, top: © Derek Lepper/www.dereklepper.com; p 104, top: © Derek Lepper/www.derek lepper.com; p 104, bottom: © Derek Lepper/www.dereklepper.com; p 105, bottom: © Derek Lepper/www.dereklepper.com; p 106, top: © Derek Lepper/www.dereklepper.com; p 106, bot-tom: Courtesy Four Seasons Hotel, Vancouver; p 107, top: © Derek Lepper/www.dereklepper. com; p 107, bottom: © Yvette Cardozo/Alamy; p 108, bottom: Courtesy Donnelly Nightclubs; p 109: Photo by Tim Matheson; p 112, bottom: Courtesy Arts Club Theatre Company, Vancou-ver. Photo by David Cooper; p 113, top: Photo by David Cooper of Playhouse Theatre Company 2007/08 production The Wars; p 114, top: © Derek Lepper/www.dereklepper.com; p 114, bottom: Courtesy of Theatre Under the Stars, Vancouver. Photo by Tim Matheson; p 115, top: Image courtesy of Vancouver International Film Festival; p 116, top: Image courtesy of Vancou-ver International Film Festival; p 117, top: © Derek Lepper/www.dereklepper.com; p 117, bottom: Image provided by the VSO; p 118, top: © Derek Lepper/www.dereklepper.com; p 119, bottom: Courtesy Dancing on the Edge Festival, Vancouver; p 120, bottom: © UPI/drr. net; p 121: © Derek Lepper/www.dereklepper.com; p 124, bottom: © Derek Lepper/www.derek lepper.com; p 125, top: Courtesy Delta Vancouver Suites; p 126, bottom: Courtesy Four Seasons Hotel, Vancouver; p 127, top: Courtesy of Hotel Le Soleil, Vancouver; p 128, bottom: © Derek Lepper/www.dereklepper.com; p 129, top: Courtesy Kimpton Hotels & Restaurants; p 130, bottom: Courtesy Opus Hotel; p 131: © Gunter Marx/Alamy; p 133, middle: © Arco Images GmbH/Alamy; p 133, bottom: © Chris Cheadle/Alamy; p 134, bottom: © All Canada Photos/Alamy; p 135, top: © Rich Wheeler/All Canada Photos/Alamy Images; p 135, bottom: © Sensi Images/Alamy; p 137, bottom: © Dennis MacDonald/Alamy; p 138, bottom: Chris Cheadle ©AllCanadaPhotos.com; p 139, top: © David L. Moore - Canada/Alamy; p 139, bot-tom: Chris Cheadle ©AllCanadaPhotos.com; p 140, bottom: Barrett & MacKay ©AllCanada Photos.com; p 141, top: © Donald Enright/Alamy; p 141, bottom: © Wendy White/Alamy; p 142, middle: Courtesy of The Fairmont Empress Hotel, Victoria; p 143: © Alec Pytlowany/ Alamy; p 146, bottom: © Bonny Makarewicz photography; p 147, bottom: Randy Lincks © AllCanadaPhotos.com; p 148, top: Randy Lincks ©AllCanadaPhotos.com; p 149, top: © Randy Lincks/Alamy; p 149, bottom: © Bonny Makarewicz photography; p 152, bottom: © Gunter Marx/Alamy; p 153, top: © Steve Li/Whistler Blackcomb; p 153, bottom: © Paul Morri-son/Whistler Blackcomb; p 154, top: Chris Cheadle ©AllCanadaPhotos.com; p 154, bottom: © Gunter Marx/Alamy; p 155, top: Chris Cheadle ©AllCanadaPhotos.com; p 157, middle: © Bonny Makarewicz photography; p 157, bottom: © Randy Lincks/Alamy; p 158, bottom: Courtesy of The Fairmont Chateau, Whistler; p 159, top: © Peter Chigmaroff/Alamy; p 161, bottom: © Bonny Makarewicz photography; p 162, bottom: © Bonny Makarewicz photogra-phy; p 163, top: © Bonny Makarewicz photography; p 163, bottom: © Bonny Makarewicz photography; p 164, top: © Bonny Makarewicz photography; p 164, bottom: © Bonny Makarewicz photography; p 165, top: © Bonny Makarewicz photography; p 165, bottom: © Bonny Makarewicz photography; p 167, top: Courtesy of Araxi, Whistler; p 168, bottom: © Bonny Makarewicz photography; p 169, top: © Bonny Makarewicz photography; p 170, top: Randy Lincks ©AllCanadaPhotos.com; p 170, bottom: © Bonny Makarewicz photography; p 171, top: © Bonny Makarewicz photography; p 171, bottom: © Bonny Makarewicz photogra-phy; p 174, bottom: Courtesy Pan Pacific Whistler Mountainside.; p 175, top: Courtesy of The Fairmont Chateau, Whistler; p 175, bottom: Courtesy of The Crystal Lodge, Whistler; p 176, top: © Bonny Makarewicz photography; p 176, bottom: Courtesy Four Seasons Resort, Whistler; p 177, bottom: Courtesy of The Sundial Boutique Hotel, Whistler; p 179, top: © PCL/Alamy; p 180, bottom: © Bonny Makarewicz photography; p 181, top: © Bonny Makarewicz photography; p 182, top: © Bonny Makarewicz photography; p 183: © Chris Cheadle/Alamy; p 209: © Gunter Marx/Alamy; p 213, top: Randy Lincks ©AllCanadaPhotos. com; p 214, top: © The British Columbia Collection/Alamy; p 216, bottom: © VANOC/COVAN; p 217, top: © JBP/Alamy; p 218, top: © VANOC/COVAN

Vancouver 2010 **Olympic Winter Games**

Vancouver Olympic Venues

BC Place 3
Canada Hockey Place / General Motors Place 2
Cypress Mountain 6
Olympic and Paralympic Village 4
Pacific Coliseum 1
Richmond Olympic Oval 8
UBC Thunderbird Arena 7
Vancouver Olympic / Paralympic Centre 5

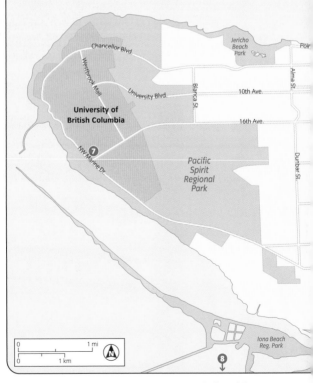

Previous page: A sign proclaiming Vancouver's status as the host of the Vancouver 2010 Winter Games.

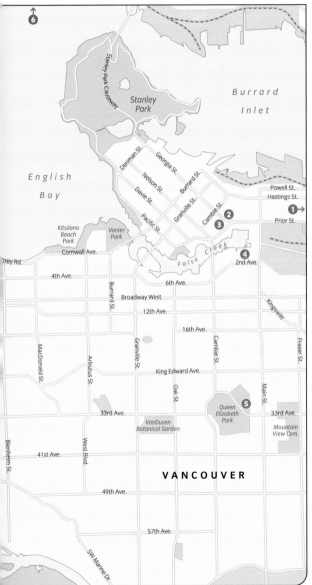

Whistler Olympic Venues

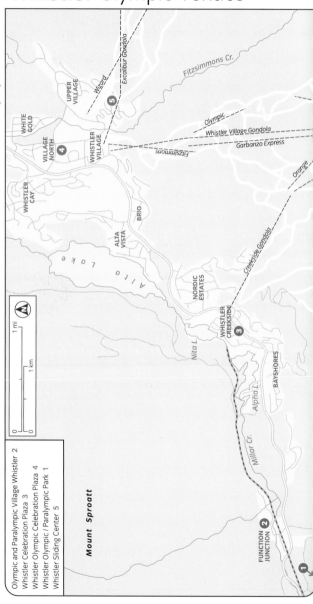

Olympic and Paralympic Village Whistler 2
Whistler Celebration Plaza 3
Whistler Olympic Celebration Plaza 4
Whistler Olympic / Paralympic Park 1
Whistler Sliding Center 5

Vancouver 2010 Winter & Paralympic Winter Games

The 2010 Winter Games will take place from February 12 to February 28, with competition sites stretching from Vancouver and neighboring Richmond about 105km (65 miles) north to the mountain resort of Whistler. The Paralympic Games will be held from March 12 to March 21 at many of the same venues. Nearly 7,000 athletes from more than 80 countries will participate in 86 Olympic and 64 Paralympic medal events. For Whistler, the games are a long-held dream: The whole resort was built in hopes of luring the 1968 Winter Games. Better 42 years late than never.

British Columbia has been preparing to host the games since 2003, investing heavily in building new venues, improving existing sports facilities, and creating forward-thinking transportation solutions and sustainable infrastructure. Vancouver's new Canada Line Sky Train (opening Nov 2009), for instance, links Downtown directly to Vancouver International Airport. And across False Creek from Downtown, the Vancouver Olympic Village has been built with sustainability as a prime consideration. All buildings are designed for maximum energy efficiency, more than 50% have green roofs, rainwater harvesting reduces impact on the municipal water system by more than 40%, and buildings include hookups for electric vehicles. After the games, the village will be transformed into a model residential community—just one more example of the care that's gone into minimizing the Games' environmental impact.

The inukshuk is one of the major symbols of the 2010 Winter Games.

Staying Current

The information provided here was correct when this book went to press, and the general conditions will most likely be as described. You can keep abreast of any changes by checking the official Vancouver 2010 website, **www.vancouver 2010.com**. Once you've arrived in Vancouver or Whistler, head for the **public information booths,** located at all the Olympic venues and around the city and resort, for the most up-to-date information.

Before You Go

The Vancouver Olympic Clock started counting down the time to the start of the Vancouver 2010 Winter Games on February 12, 2007.

Sources of Information

Vancouver 2010's official website, **www.vancouver2010.com**, is the best place to go for information on schedules, venues, and visitor services. Participating nations' Olympic committees generally maintain websites with information specific to their citizens. These sites are excellent resources for everything from insight into how a specific team is training to tips on scoring seats for the events that matter to you most. Bear in mind that for many events, you'll need to buy tickets through your home country (see "Buying Tickets," below).

For information on the U.S. Olympic team, go to www.usoc.org. The Canadian team's website is www.olympic.ca. For information on the team from Great Britain, go to www.olympics.org.uk; for Australia,

www.olympics.com.au; and for New Zealand, www.olympic.org.nz. For links to other countries' Olympic committees, go to www.olympic.org/uk/organisation/noc/index_uk.asp.

Buying Tickets

An astonishing 1.6 million tickets have been made available for the Vancouver 2010 Winter Games, with an additional 250,000 available for the Paralympics. Olympic ticket sales are being conducted in four phases. Following an early-request period in October and November 2008, remaining tickets went on sale in spring 2009 on a first-come, first-served basis. Once venue seating configurations have been finalized, sales will close temporarily (summer 2009) while seats are assigned to those who have already purchased tickets. The remaining tickets will then be available beginning in fall 2009, with seats assigned automatically. During the Games, you can snap up any remaining tickets at www.vancouver2010.com, at the individual venue box offices, and at the Main Ticket Centre in downtown Vancouver.

Prior to the start of the Games, only Canadian residents (you must have a valid Canadian mailing address and sign for the secure courier delivery) can purchase tickets directly through the Vancouver 2010 website (www.vancouver2010.com). Residents of other countries must purchase tickets through their National Olympic Committee or the official ticket agent for their country of residence. These agents generally offer both individual tickets and package deals, which may include accommodations, transportation, and meals in addition to admittance to events.

The agents for the major English-speaking countries are:

- **For Australia:** CoSport Australia Pty Limited (☎ 2/9241-5500; www.cosport.com).

- **For Great Britain and Ireland:** Sportsworld (☎ 1235-555844; www.sportsworld.co.uk/vancouver).

- **For New Zealand:** Premier Events (☎ 9/3070770; www.premiereventsgroup.com).

- **For the United States and Canada:** CoSport (☎ 908/766-2227; www.cosport.com).

If you're interested in attending the Vancouver 2010 Paralympic Winter Games, visit the Ticketing Information section at **www.vancouver 2010.com**. Tickets for those events are available on the website starting May 6, 2009.

Package Deals

Tour packages (available through CoSport and other ticket agents) may provide cost savings, but you'll have to be very careful to match the package with the events you're intent on seeing—curling, for instance, might be a bummer if you're more the figure skating type. If you don't find the sort of package you're looking for, consider booking your event tickets and your other travel arrangements separately. But if that's your plan, work fast: Many hotels have already reserved huge blocks of rooms for package guests, and the remainder of their stock is booking up fast. See "The Best Hotels" and "Whistler" chapters for more information on where to stay.

Ticket Prices

The 2010 Winter Games has divided ticket prices into categories, with the number of price categories offered per sport dependant upon the venue's configuration and seating capacity. Category A tickets get you access to the best (and priciest) seats in the house, Category B is one step down, and so on.

Prices vary widely by sport, with figure skating and men's hockey demanding the loftiest prices. Tickets for figure skating range from C$50 to C$450. Hockey tickets (men only) range from C$50 to C$140 for preliminary games to a big, honkin' C$350 to C$775 for the gold medal game. The cheapest tickets are for the biathlon and cross-country skiing (all tickets C$25–C$70), while those for

The Cultural Olympiad

Complementing Vancouver 2010's athletic events, the Cultural Olympiad is a series of multidisciplinary arts festivals spread out over the 2 years leading up to the Games. Launched in 2008, the Cultural Olympiad features exhibits; literary readings; and theater, music, and dance performances held in venues all over Vancouver and Whistler. The program culminates with the 60-day **Olympic Arts Festival,** which begins on January 22 (3 weeks before the start of the Games) and continues until March 21, coinciding with the end of the Paralympics. Held at 30 venues throughout Vancouver and Whistler, the festival will be a showcase for Canadian and international arts and culture, both contemporary and traditional. Admission to many of the events is free. Information and schedules can be found under the Cultural Olympiad tab at **www.vancouver2010.com**.

the sliding sports—bobsled, luge, and skeleton—go for C$30 to C$85. Tickets for skiing, ski-jumping, and snowboard events range from C$50 to C$210 (with most topping out between C$120–C$150), while tickets for speed skating range from C$50 to C$185.

Tickets for the nightly Victory Ceremonies (medal ceremonies followed by concerts) are C$22.

Tickets to Paralympic events are considerably less expensive, with 85% of individual tickets priced at C$20 or less. Tickets to Paralympic alpine skiing events are C$15, while wheelchair curling tickets go for C$15 to C$30, and ice sledge hockey tickets are C$20 to C$50.

Buying for groups of 20 or more will save an additional $5 per ticket on most Paralympic Winter Games tickets.

Getting Tickets at the Last Minute

Although tickets for the most popular sports are hot commodities, it's likely that some tickets to less high-profile events and preliminary rounds will still be available as the games begin through www.vancouver2010.com, at the individual venue box offices, and at the Main Ticket Centre in downtown Vancouver.

Past history is no real guide as to last-minute availability. At the 2006 Winter Games in Torino, Italy, organizers reported selling almost 80% of available tickets before the Games began, but that still left a couple hundred thousand outstanding. The catch? The bulk of the affordable tickets and the vast majority of those for the most popular sports were long gone. At the 2008 Beijing Summer Olympics, which were reportedly the first Olympic games ever to sell out, empty seats were still common on competition days—possibly due to tickets being purchased but not used.

Many tickets sold in advance to sponsors and national Olympic committees (often as part of package deals) find their way into the hands of ticket brokers and scalpers, who sell them for whatever price they'll bring on the day of the Games. Try your best to avoid having to deal with them.

Note: For the first time in an Olympic Games, ticket holders will have the opportunity to post tickets they can no longer use for resale. Buyers will have the confidence of knowing that they are buying legitimate tickets thanks to an active bar code embedded within each ticket.

The Vancouver 2010 Winter Games will begin on February 12, 2010, with much fanfare.

Getting **Around**

The bobsled will be just one of several competitive events at the Games that will take place in Whistler.

Vancouver by Public Transit

Vancouver's excellent public transportation system (p 190) will be the primary means of getting around for visitors during the Games because it's fastest and because there's no alternative: The Vancouver Olympic Committee chose to ban private-vehicle parking at the venues in order to reduce congestion. Instead, ticket purchases will entail an additional "fulfillment fee" that provides the ticket holder with a public transit pass for Metro Vancouver or Whistler good for the date of the ticketed event. Complimentary parking will be provided for transit-pass holders at designated Olympic park-and-ride locations.

The new **Canada Line** branch of the SkyTrain (www.canadaline.ca or www.translink.bc.ca) will be particularly useful to Olympic visitors, providing fast, affordable transportation from Vancouver Airport into Downtown and also between Downtown and the Olympic Village and the Richmond Olympic Oval.

Ticket holders for events at **Cypress Mountain** in West Vancouver will be required to purchase a 1-day round-trip pass for C$12, which will get you from Downtown to the mountain.

Between Vancouver & Whistler

Spectators attending events in Whistler must travel from Vancouver by official Olympic bus along the Sea to Sky Highway (p 132) and pay a C$25 fulfillment fee on top of their ticket cost. There will be no parking for private vehicles at any of the Whistler venues.

Transportation Within Whistler

During the games, transportation between venues in Whistler will be provided by an enhanced **WAVE** (Whistler and Valley Express; http://bctransit.com/regions/whi) public transit system, with a "fulfillment" fee tacked on to ticket sales to cover transportation.

Getting Transit Info

During the Vancouver 2010 Winter and Paralympic Winter Games, **www.vancouver2010.com** will serve as a hub for information on public transit between venues, with continually updated timetables, maps, travel conditions, and news on traffic flows around the venues.

The **Paralympic Games**

Quatchi, Miga, and Sumi—the three mascots of the Vancouver 2010 Olympic and Paralympic Winter Games.

The Paralympic Games, the world's top competition for athletes with disabilities, got their start in England in 1948, when Sir Ludwig Guttmann organized a sports competition for World War II veterans with spinal cord injuries. The games went international 4 years later, and in 1960 an Olympics-style event was held for the first time, in Rome. Since 1988, the Paralympics have been held in conjunction with the Olympics, utilizing many of the same venues. For Vancouver 2010, the Games will include competitions for alpine skiing, cross-country skiing, biathlon, ice sledge hockey (aka sled hockey), and wheelchair curling. Athletes with six different types of disabilities—spinal cord injuries, missing limbs, cerebral palsy, visual impairment, intellectual disability, and "other"—compete using a complicated classification system that allows them to compete both within their class and against each other.

A Trio of Mascots . . . Plus One

You can't have an Olympic Games nowadays without some cute mascots to set the proper tone (or to serve as admittedly adorable souvenirs of the experience). Vancouver will have a trio of mascots (plus a sidekick!) welcoming visitors and athletes to the 2010 Olympic and Paralympic Winter Games. All three of the endearing mascots can trace their roots back to local and First Nation legends. **Quatchi,** a large and gentle sasquatch, and **Miga,** a young and outgoing sea bear, will preside over the Olympics, while **Sumi,** an environmentally conscious animal spirit guide, will host the Paralympics. Bringing up the rear is the first-ever Olympic sidekick, **Mukmuk,** a rare and endangered Vancouver Island marmot whose name is derived from the Chinook word for "food."

Vancouver Venues A to Z

The Vancouver 2010 Winter and Paralympic Winter Games competitions and ceremonies will be held at five venues in Vancouver, one venue each in nearby Richmond and West Vancouver, and four areas of the Whistler Resort. The Games' opening and closing ceremonies will take place at Vancouver's BC Place Stadium and will be the first such Winter Olympics ceremonies ever held indoors. BC Place will also host the opening ceremony of the Paralympics, while Whistler's Celebration Plaza (pending a final decision) will host the closing ceremony.

BC Place. Home to the opening and closing ceremonies of the Olympics and the opening ceremony for the Paralympics as well as nightly Victory Ceremonies, during which each day's winning athletes receive their medals. A celebration concert follows nightly. This stadium holds up to 60,000 spectators under its enormous domed roof. *777 Pacific Blvd., Downtown.* ☎ *604/669-2300. www.bcplacestadium.com.*

Canada Hockey Place. Olympic hockey will be split between the UBC Thunderbird Arena (see below) and this 19,100-seat venue. Known as General Motors Place in its regular, non-Olympic life, it's both the home of the Vancouver Canucks and a big-time concert venue. *800 Griffiths Way.* ☎ *604/899-7400. www.generalmotorsplace.com.*

Cypress Mountain. Located 31km (19 miles) from Downtown, Cypress Mountain will host men's and women's freestyle skiing and snowboard events. The mountain offers 51 downhill ski and snowboarding runs, although they'll be off-limits to visitors during the Games, and room for 12,000 spectators. *Cypress Bowl Rd. (in Cypress Provincial Park), West Vancouver.* ☎ *604/419-7669. www.cypressmountain.com.*

Olympic and Paralympic Village. Located on the southeast side of False Creek, near the Telus World of Science (p 39, ⑧), the village will be home to curlers, figure and speed skaters, freestyle skiers, hockey players, and snowboarders during the Games. Afterward, it will be transformed into a model sustainable community for 3,000 residents. *1 Athletes Way.*

Pacific Coliseum. Located in East Vancouver on the site of the annual Pacific National Exhibition summer fair, Pacific Coliseum is the venue for 2010 Olympic figure skating and short-track speed skating. It holds 14,200 spectators and is reachable via public transportation. *100 N. Renfrew St., East Vancouver.* ☎ *604/253-2311.*

Richmond Olympic Oval. Located in Richmond, BC, right across the Fraser River's middle arm from Vancouver Airport, this purpose-built, 7,700-seat Olympic venue will be home to the Games' speed-skating events. *6111 River Rd. (btw. the No. 2 Rd. & Dinsmore Bridge), Richmond, 14km (8.5 miles) south of Downtown Vancouver.* ☎ *778/296-1400. http://richmondoval.ca.*

UBC Thunderbird Arena. Olympic hockey will be split between this new, 7,200-seat competition venue and Canada Hockey Place (p 219). Located on the University of British Columbia campus on Vancouver's West Side, the Thunderbird Arena will also host the Paralympic ice sledge hockey (aka sled hockey) events. *6066 Thunderbird Blvd. (West Side).* ☎ *604/822-6121. www.thunderbirdarena.ubc.ca.*

Vancouver Olympic/Paralympic Centre. Located just east of Queen Elizabeth Park, this new, 6,000-seat venue will host the Olympic curling and Paralympic wheelchair curling events. *4575 Clancy Loranger Way.*

Whistler Venues A to Z

Olympic and Paralympic Village Whistler. During the Games, athletes will be housed in a mix of apartments, town houses, and hostels in a purpose-built neighborhood in the Cheakamus Valley, a few miles south of Whistler Village near the resort's southern entrance. All Whistler competition venues are less than a 30-minute drive away. *1090 Legacy Way. 5 Callaghan Valley Rd.*

Whistler Creekside. Whistler's oldest section (now completely updated and improved) has a capacity of up to 7,700 spectators and will host the alpine skiing events. Men's events will be held on the Dave Murray Downhill, while women's events and Paralympic alpine skiing will take place on Franz's Run. *2295 Nordic Dr. Whistler Creekside is located about 3 miles southwest of Whistler Village on the Sea to Sky Hwy. www.whistlerblackcomb.com.*

Whistler Celebration Plaza. This new plaza will be the site of nightly Victory Ceremonies (aka medal ceremonies) during the Olympics and will also host the

closing ceremony of the Paralympic Games. *Located along the Stroll in Village North, just off Blackcomb Way, north of the Whistler Brewhouse.*

Whistler Olympic/Paralympic Park. The Olympic and Paralympic biathlon and cross-country ski events and the Olympic Nordic combined and men's individual and team ski jumping events will be held in a compact, 1-sq.-km area that's home to three separate stadiums and 15km (9 miles) of cross-country and biathlon trails. *Located off the Callaghan Valley access road, 16km (10 miles) southwest of Whistler Village.* ☎ *877/764-2455. www.whistlerolympicpark.com.*

Whistler Sliding Center. Bobsled, luge, and skeleton competitions will take place on Blackcomb Mountain, at a new track featuring the world's highest vertical drop (152m/499 ft.) and a capacity of 12,000 spectators. *4910 Glacier Lane, near the Tube Park, Blackcomb Mountain.* ☎ *888/972-7533. www.whistlerslidingcentre.com.* ●